HOW TO RUN A SUCCESSFUL PUB

Visit our How To website at **www.howto.co.uk**

At **www.howto.co.uk** you can engage in conversation with our authors – all of whom have 'been there and done that' in their specialist fields. You can get access to special offers and additional content but most imporantly you will be able to engage with, and become a part of, a wide and growing community of people just like yourself.

At **www.howto.co.uk** you'll be able to talk and share tips with people who have similar interests and are facing similar challenges in their lives. People who, just like you, have the desire to change their lives for the better – be it through moving to a new country, starting a new business, growing their own vegetables, or writing a novel.

At **www.howto.co.uk** you'll find the support and encouragement you need to help make your aspirations a reality.

You can do direct to **www.how-to-run-a-successful-pub.co.uk** which is part of the main How To site.

How To Books strives to present authentic, inspiring, practical information in their books. Now, when you buy a title from **How To Books**, you get even more than just words on a page.

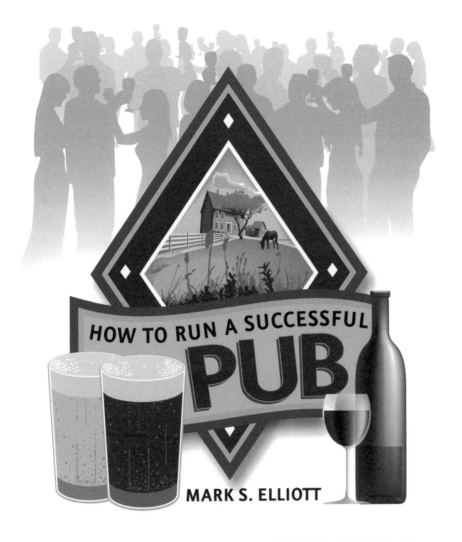

HOW TO RUN A SUCCESSFUL

PUB

MARK S. ELLIOTT

THE COMPREHENSIVE GUIDE
TO FINDING A PUB AND MAKING
IT PROFITABLE —∿— *2nd Edition*

howto**books**

Published by How To Books Ltd
Spring Hill House
Spring Hill Road
Begbroke
Oxford OX5 1RX
Tel: (01865) 375794. Fax: (01865) 379162
email: info@howtobooks.co.uk
www.howtobooks.co.uk

First edition 2006
Reprinted 2007
Second edition 2010

ISBN 978 1 84528 425 1

British Library Cataloguing in Publication Data
A catalogue record for this book is available from the British Library

Produced for How To Books by Deer Park Productions, Tavistock
Typeset by Kestrel Data, Exeter, Devon
Printed and bound by Bell & Bain Ltd, Glasgow

NOTE: The material contained in this book is set out in good
faith for general guidance and no liability can be accepted for
loss or expense incurred as a result of relying in particular
circumstances on statements made in this book. Laws and
regulations may be complex and liable to change, and readers
should check the current position with the relevant
authorities before making personal arrangements.

CONTENTS

ACKNOWLEDGEMENTS

I would like to thank my wife, Michaela, for her assistance with editing this book and her patience and understanding during the many hours that I left her alone while I sat in front of the PC to write another few pages.

Thanks to my family, friends and colleagues who have given me encouragement along the way.

I am also grateful to HM Revenue and Customs, Business Link, The Food Standards Agency, ACAS, The Portman Group, The Performing Right Society, Phonographic Performance Limited, and The Health and Safety Executive, for assistance with my research for this book.

DEDICATION

This book is dedicated to the two 'Mrs Elliotts' in my life – my wife, Michaela and my mother, Norma.

PREFACE

This book is aimed at anyone who is thinking about running their own pub. It has been written to guide would-be publicans through the process of finding a suitable pub, setting up their business and running a successful enterprise. It will also be useful to inexperienced publicans wanting to learn more about making their own pub business a success.

Running a successful pub is not simply about having an outgoing personality and being able to pull a pint. A successful pub must first and foremost be a successful *business*, and publicans must equip themselves with a range of business skills and knowledge with this in mind. Fortunately, these skills and knowledge can be learned through attending training courses, coaching, reading books, by using the internet and through membership of professional organisations.

This book sets out to provide would-be and inexperienced publicans with a broad understanding of all aspects of running a pub, together with numerous ways to maximise sales, control costs, make more profit and, at the same time, abide by legislation that applies to running a pub. It also provides details of where to find more information and develop a greater understanding of the subjects covered.

I hope you will find *How to Run a Successful Pub* a useful and informative guide.

Good luck in your new venture!

Mark S Elliott

1
ALL ABOUT YOU

WHY DO YOU WANT TO RUN A PUB?

So you have decided that you would like to run a pub. What is it that appeals to you? Have you got a burning desire to be your own boss, or work with your partner? Could the thought of socialising with customers and making new friends give you a buzz, or the idea of making money in an environment you enjoy, be what appeals to you?

Whatever your reasons, it is useful to understand what is motivating you. You need to be sure that running a pub is going to satisfy your needs. Ultimately, your motivation is going to play a big part in your success. Motivation will be the difference between driving the business to success or giving up at the first sign of difficulty.

If you have a partner, it is vitally important that you both share the vision. Thinking things through and discussing your plans are a key part of the process. This will ensure that you are well prepared and have a strong foundation on which to build your business. Working towards your dream jointly is also exciting and fun, and will stand you in good stead when working together.

YOUR GOALS, AMBITIONS AND VALUES

What are your personal goals and ambitions, and what do you value in life? Will running a pub be in harmony with these? If your aim in life is to play for Manchester United, then maybe running a pub will get in the way of your ambitions! Similarly, if you value peace and tranquillity above anything else, running a busy pub seven days a week is not the place to find these. It is essential to be clear about what you and your partner feel are the important things in your lives, and what you want to retain as part of your lifestyle.

You may find it helpful to list your personal goals, ambitions and values and prioritise them. What would you be willing to give up or delay until sometime in the future? What could you not live without? Then take some time to look at each of these and see how running a pub will affect them. You may find that running a pub contributes towards many of your ambitions and is in perfect harmony with your values. It may be that you are willing to make sacrifices, and that's OK, as long as you have given these a good deal of consideration before going ahead. It is better to anticipate things, than have them come as a shock to you later.

YOUR SKILLS AND EXPERIENCE

What do you do well? What are you skilled at? What kinds of work have you been involved in? Hopefully, you will find that a number of your skills can be used to run your own pub. These are often called 'transferable skills' – you can transfer them to other types of work. Examples of these would be your customer-service skills gained during your time as a shop assistant or your administration skills gained while working in the office. Both of these can prove useful in running your own pub. Again, it is worth listing your skills for the following reasons:

- It highlights your skills when applying for a pub.
- You can feature them in your business plan.
- It will identify any skills that you lack and need to gain.
- You can use them to plan your pub responsibilities.

To get another point of view of your skills and experience, ask a friend for their opinion.

It is essential that you gain some experience of running a pub before taking the plunge. Fortunately, there are often lots of opportunities to work behind a bar. As well as bar jobs, many licensees welcome showing you the ropes in exchange for a few hours of unpaid assistance. Get as much experience of bar work or running a pub as you can. Practical, hands-on experience is the best way of gaining and improving your skills. It is also the only real way of finding out whether you may be suited to a life in the pub trade.

YOUR PERSONALITY

Are you naturally outgoing and able to talk to anyone? Do you like being in the spotlight? Or are you a shrinking violet who finds communicating with people difficult? Being able to interact with customers is a basic requirement of running a pub. The art of small talk has to be well developed and a genuine interest in people is essential. Being able to smile when you are feeling down, and laugh at the joke that you have heard for the tenth time are all part of the job.

Your personality helps develop the atmosphere of the pub. It is important to remember that your personality and behaviour filters through staff and customers alike. A friendly, upbeat atmosphere attracts many more customers than a depressing or aggressive one. Equally, a licensee who appears uninterested in his customers is unlikely to encourage them to come back.

Running a pub involves dealing with many different types of customer. This takes confidence, which can be developed through bar work and other customer-service roles. The more experience you obtain dealing with different types of people, the more confident you will become.

Like running any business, you need to be able to juggle lots of tasks at the same time. Running a pub is not just about bar work; it's about doing all the behind-the-scenes jobs too: bottling-up; bookwork; cleaning the beer lines etc. You also need to handle the pressures that are associated with running your pub business, for example, paying the bills, managing staff and keeping up to date with legislation.

Your interests

You may find that some of your interests prove useful in running your pub. Being involved in the local darts or football leagues can be advantageous when it comes to running a sports-orientated pub. A passion for food is valuable in operating a food pub. Your interests can also play a part in identifying the kind of pub you would like to run.

Pub teams and clubs can be the cornerstone of a pub's trade. Getting involved with teams or starting clubs can help boost business on the traditionally less busy days of the week.

YOUR HEALTH

Running a pub involves long hours and hard work and you need to be reasonably fit and healthy in order to cope with this. From lifting boxes, moving kegs and standing for several hours behind a bar, a whole range of activities put stresses and strains on your body. If you are not fully fit, or have health problems, taking on a pub can be a recipe for disaster. Many people consider pubs to be unhealthy environments in which to work, particularly due to smoking issues (though this particular concern is to be resolved by Government legislation). It is wise to give some thought to your own health and fitness situation and the impact that running a pub will have on you.

ABILITY TO HOLD A LICENCE

Background

The Licensing Act 2003 states that anyone who authorises the sale of alcohol needs to have a personal licence. In practice, this means that each pub requires a personal licence holder who is designated as the 'Designated Premises Supervisor'. They will be the person who is in day-to-day control of the premises, ie the tenant or lessee. Other members of staff are authorised to sell alcohol by the designated premises supervisor, and therefore are not required to hold a licence themselves.

Requirements

To qualify for a personal licence the applicant must meet criteria set out in the Licensing Act 2003.

These are:

◆ the applicant must be aged 18 or over;
◆ no personal licence held by them has been forfeited in the past 5 years;
◆ they possess an accredited licensing qualification;
◆ they do not have an unspent relevant or foreign offence.

Subject to the applicant paying the necessary fee and providing a Criminal Record Bureau certificate, the licensing authority is legally obliged to grant the application. If any of the first three criteria are not met, the application will be rejected. Where an applicant has an unspent conviction and the police object to the application, refusal of the application is the normal course of action.

What are 'relevant' offences?

Relevant offences that could result in an application for a personal licence being refused include:

◆ those involving serious crime;
◆ those involving serious dishonesty;
◆ those involving controlled drugs;
◆ certain sexual offences;
◆ offences created by the Licensing Act 2003.

Please see Chapter 5, *Licensing Law*, for more details.

YOUR FINANCIAL RESOURCES

Your money

Establishing your current financial situation is an important first step in acquiring your own pub. Don't put this part of the process off until later. To do so may result in a great deal of wasted time and, ultimately, disappointment. The aim of this is to realistically calculate how much money you have to invest in your venture. To do this you need to carefully and honestly look at your assets and liabilities. In other words, what you own (assets) and what you owe (liabilities). When looking at this, it is useful to put the details together in a table, like the example below. You must establish accurate values of your assets and liabilities for this to be meaningful. Note that any liabilities relating to the asset are listed next to it. For example, your house is valued at £100,000 and you have an outstanding mortgage of £60,000. Liabilities are shown in brackets, as this is money that you owe.

◆ EXAMPLE ◆

Asset	£	Liability	£
Cash in bank	£30,000		
Cash ISA	£5,000		
Car	£5,000	Car loan	(£4,000)
House	£100,000	Mortgage	(£60,000)
Shares	£2,000		
		Loan	(£5,000)
Totals	**£142,000**		**(£69,000)**

This example shows that you have assets to the value of £142,000 and liabilities that total £69,000. Your 'net worth' can be established by subtracting your liabilities from your assets: ie £142,000 – £69,000 = £73,000.

So, how does this help you? Well, the example shows that if you sell your assets and added the money raised from these to your bank funds and ISA, you would have £142,000. However, you still owe £69,000, and clearing these debts leaves a balance remaining of £73,000 for you to invest.

This is a simplified example and you should take professional financial advice before making any major decisions of this kind. Selling assets and clearing liabilities may not be the best course of action, and indeed may not be necessary. You will need to take into account any penalties that may be charged, tax implications and the ability to sell assets at a realistic valuation. Your personal circumstances will influence your decisions too. You may not want to take the risk of selling your house, and it may not be practical to sell your car.

However, following the process does give you an overall picture of your financial situation, which will help you to make decisions about funding your business.

Raising additional funds

You may need to borrow money to help set up your business. Careful consideration needs to be given to the following:

♦ Borrowing money adds cost and risk to your business.
♦ Lenders may only fund a small percentage of the total ingoing costs; you will need to find the rest.
♦ Lenders may require a comprehensive business plan.
♦ Use only reputable, established lenders.
♦ Compare interest rates.
♦ Some lenders may not be willing to consider pub finance.
♦ Seek advice from a reputable financial adviser and accountant.

Your bank

The relationship with your own bank is important. If you have dealt with them for some time and have a good reputation, they are likely to be more approachable than a lender who does not know you.

Friends and family

You could have other borrowing options, such as friends or family. These arrangements can provide low interest borrowing and are the only way of securing additional funds for many people. A few words of warning about these options: make sure that you have a written legal agreement drawn up for any arrangements, and be aware that borrowing money from people close to you can put enormous strain on these relationships.

Funding the business is covered in detail in Chapter 4 of this book.

FAMILY FACTORS

The decision to run a pub will affect the whole family. Aside from the risk factor of running your own business, there are practical issues too. In particular, the effect on children, if you have them, needs a great deal of thought. Difficulties vary depending on the ages of children. The issue of childcare can be a problem. Long hours behind the bar make spending time with your children difficult. Expecting children to amuse themselves alone upstairs, or encouraging them to spend time in the bar with you, should be avoided. If you have children, you will need to work out how to balance family life and business commitments.

 Talk to your children about your plans and encourage them to get involved in the preparations.

YOUR SUPPORT NETWORK

Friends and family can provide you with lots of support in your business venture. Whether it be looking after the pub while you take a night off, or giving you encouragement when things haven't gone well, good support can be vital. You may already rely on family or friends now, to help your life go more smoothly. Bear in mind how running a pub might change things. Moving away from your support network means you have to manage things on your own, at least until you have developed new support networks nearby. Alternatively, you may decide that taking a pub close to your support network is a way of maintaining the support, as well as gaining a few extra customers into the bargain!

TRAINING

Running a pub requires a range of skills and these are discussed throughout this book. By comparing these with your own skills, you will identify which of your current skills are transferable and which ones you need to gain.

Bar work, on-the-job training and more formal courses will all help prepare you, and give you the necessary skills. Many breweries, pub companies and other training organisations offer excellent courses and attending these should be viewed as an essential requirement. These range from general courses for new licensees to more specific ones – like handling cask beer or pub marketing. There is a cost for attending these courses but this is more than outweighed by what you will learn.

 Reading as much as you can about the business, and perhaps subscribing to one of the pub-trade papers, will enhance your knowledge and provide you with valuable background

QUALIFICATIONS

Qualifications required to obtain a personal licence

To make a successful application for a personal licence you must hold an accredited licensing qualification. The aim of the qualification is to ensure that licence holders are aware of licensing law and the wider social responsibilities of selling alcohol to the public.

The personal licence syllabus must cover:

◆ personal licences;
◆ licensing authorities;
◆ alcohol;
◆ unauthorised licensable activities;
◆ police powers;
◆ duties of the personal licence holder;

- premises' licences;
- operating schedules;
- permitted temporary activities;
- disorderly conduct;
- protection of children;
- rights of entry;
- prohibitions.

This is normally a one-day course including a short exam. Tuition is provided by means of a training booklet and sessions are led by a qualified trainer.

The Secretary of State has approved the following Personal Licence Qualification courses:

- The BII (British Institute of Innkeeping) Level 2 National Certificate for Personal Licence Holders.
- The GOAL (Global Online Assessment for Learning) Level 2 National Certificate for Personal Licence Holders.
- The GQAL (Graded Qualifications Alliance) Level 2 National Certificate for Personal Licence Holders.

Information on course providers can be found in the Appendix.

Licensed trade qualifications

There is a number of other qualifications available to those interested in a career in the licensed trade. These include HNC and HND courses in Licensed House Management, and degree courses in Licensed Retail. Such courses are not widely available and you will need to check with your local college or university if you are interested in pursuing any of these.

The British Institute of Innkeeping offers a comprehensive range of courses for new and experienced licensees and bar staff. As well as their National Certificate for Personal Licence Holders, they run courses on topics such as cellar management, drug awareness, pub entertainment and conflict management.

Visit the British Institute of Innkeeping for more information: www.bii.org/

Other qualifications

If you do have qualifications in subjects such as business studies, accountancy or marketing, they will be put to good use when running your pub. Knowledge of these subjects can give you an added advantage when it comes to operating the business. Running a pub draws on all your experience and skills and these, plus your business ability, are crucial factors in how successful your pub will be. Gaining knowledge and skills in these specific areas should be a priority.

Brewery and pub company requirements

The majority of pubs are leased and tenanted through breweries and pub companies. Application must be made to them through the Recruitment Department and Business Development Manager/Area Manager dealing with your submission.

With the exception of the requirement for you to hold a recognised licensing qualification, breweries and pub companies will not insist on you having any other qualifications in order to be considered for a lease or tenancy with them. Factors such as your experience, personality, financial situation and a convincing business plan tend to be key areas they would be more interested in. That is not to say that qualifications would be ignored. Relevant qualifications will certainly strengthen your case, and together with your other skills, should be featured on any application.

Buying a freehold pub

If you are proposing to buy a freehold pub, you need to have someone who holds a recognised licensing qualification running the pub. Otherwise there are no legal requirements to hold any other qualifications. However, should you need to raise money to acquire your property, additional relevant qualifications can help inspire a lender's confidence in you.

2

WHAT KIND OF PUB?

WHAT KIND OF PUB DO YOU WANT TO RUN?

Different pubs meet different needs

There is a variety of pubs in the UK, from bustling high-street venues to sleepy, back-street locals, each with its own character and unique attraction to the public. They provide a variety of food, drinks and other facilities such as accommodation, function rooms or business services. The combination of products, service and facilities that a pub offers, influences what type of clientele will use it. Customers will frequent pubs that best meet their needs. The football fanatics, wanting to watch their favourite team on TV, will find a pub with a big-screen TV appealing. The dating couple, on the other hand, are likely to find that a quiet pub with a cosy corner will best suit their needs.

 Visit a cross section of your local pubs and consider which customer needs they are successfully meeting.

Customers' needs change

Customer needs will change with their different roles and activities. The romantic couple could also be football fans: visiting the big-screen pub one day to watch the match and the quiet pub another day, to find a place to chat and gaze into each other's eyes! The same customer will have different roles and be involved in a variety of activities. Their needs will change accordingly, and they will be attracted to pubs that best meet their needs at a particular time.

A PUB CAN MEET DIFFERENT NEEDS

Many successful pubs change their offering to the public over the course of the day, so that different types of customers will be attracted at different times of the day. An example of this would be the pub that opens to serve breakfast to the fishing team, then offers lunches to the shoppers, and in the evening, turns the lights down and the music up to attract younger clientele. The same pub offers different things, to attract different customers, over the course of the day.

Matching a pub to your needs

As we have seen, pubs have to meet customers' needs. Now it is time to think about your own needs: both personal and business. By working through Chapter 1 you will have examined the following:

◆ Why you want a pub.
◆ Your goals and ambitions.
◆ Your skills and experience.
◆ Your values.
◆ Your interests.
◆ Your financial resources.
◆ Family factors and your support network.

Use these to think about what kind of pub you will be happiest running. Look at how running a particular type of pub will affect your goals and ambitions. Will it be in harmony with what you value in life? What will the effect be on your family and support network?

YOUR IDEAL PUB

Using a checklist will help you to focus on what kind of pub you are looking for. You need to think about the kind of clientele that you would be happiest dealing with. Any social issues relating to the locality like crime and disorder must be considered, together with any potential impact on you and your family.

Your own skills and experience will have a major influence on your decisions too. If you cannot even boil an egg, it is unlikely that you will be able to run a high-turnover food pub effectively! Some skills can be gained through training but you also have to be realistic about your abilities too.

Using the 'Ideal Pub' checklist

To use the checklist, tick the boxes that describe your ideal pub. You can add requirements such as number of bedrooms and any important local facilities that you will need. Note which geographical areas you are willing to consider and what capital you have available. Further comments can be added to the end of the checklist.

A copy of this checklist can be found in Appendix (vi).

Ideal Pub Checklist

Capital available: **Geographical area:**
£

Location:	Clientele	Facilities	Catering	Other requirements
town centre	locals	catering kitchen	no food	no. of bedrooms -
suburban	young persons	car park	snacks	garage
estate	executives	beer garden	bar meals	**Local facilities**
neighbourhood	office staff	function room	restaurant	school
rural	families	games room	buffets	hospital
village	couples	live music	outside catering	transport links
main road	manual workers	big-screen sports		
	students	disco		
	gay community			
	shoppers			
	OAPs			

Other things that you require: **Other things that are important to you:**

You can use your checklist to compare different pubs in order to decide which best suit your requirements. It makes the process of finding a pub and reviewing options more efficient, which is useful when sifting through pub vacancy details, often a daunting task. It also enables you to prioritise which pubs to visit as part of your research rather than having a haphazard approach. This certainly saves a great deal of time and effort. Being clear about your requirements also demonstrates to recruiters that you have thought things through and this will give them confidence in your application.

STYLE OF OPERATION

Breweries and pub companies often categorise their pubs into different styles of operation. These categories are used in advertisements and by brewery and pub company recruiters to help their recruitment process and also to target marketing activity. It is helpful to know something about this when looking for a suitable pub.

The procedure involves banding similar pubs together. Breweries and pub companies do use slightly different terminology to describe the same categories. Some of the more regularly used ones are given below, together with their main characteristics:

◆ Young Persons' Venue (YPV) – Main clientele are in the 18–30 age range. Venues are typically located in town or city centres with an emphasis on music, trendy drinks and a modern up-to-date image. They often have high staffing levels as speed of service is important during busy periods. Food is sometimes available, although this may be snack or fast food.

◆ Traditional local – Traditional pubs are located in built-up residential neighbourhoods. They can be male orientated with an emphasis on pub games, sport and traditional drinks. Local customers from the immediate vicinity, travel to the pub on foot. The pub fosters a sense of community. The food offering is often limited.

◆ Destination food pub – This is a 'drive-to' pub with a high proportion of food sales. Customers are drawn from a wide area. There is an emphasis on quality of food and good service. They are often located in rural areas. Wine and soft drinks are popular.

Other categories include: Live Music Venues (LMVs), Student pubs and Sports pubs.

LOCATION, LOCATION, LOCATION

Catchment area and trading style

Location is crucial for a pub's success. A pub's location, together with its style of operation, will determine which customers use it. For example, a traditional local pub mainly attracts customers from its immediate vicinity. Most of these customers will walk to the pub. Its catchment area may only be a radius of a quarter of a mile. A destination food pub, on the other hand, attracts customers travelling by car and from a much wider area. A catchment area of 15 miles radius is not uncommon.

Once you find a pub that may be suitable, ask yourself some questions:

♦ What kind of clientele does the pub attract currently?
♦ What types of people live within its catchment area?
♦ Are there enough potential customers to build trade further?
♦ Could the style of operation be changed to attract more customers?
♦ Which other pubs would you be competing with?
♦ Is anything in the area going to change that might affect trade?

Prominence and visibility

An attractive, prominently positioned pub acts as its own advertisement. Pubs that are visible to the public have a higher profile than those that are hidden. High-street locations, main roads and roundabouts are prominent, sought-after locations. Less prominent pubs need to work harder at communicating with their customers and potential customers. These can be a success and there are many examples of hidden gems.

Footfall and traffic

These are two pieces of jargon used to describe how many potential customers there are in the immediate vicinity of the pub. In other words, how busy the area is. A pub located on the high street may have thousands of potential customers walking by each day. Another pub, located only a hundred metres away, in a side street, may only have several hundred potential customers walking by. Obviously, the pub on the high street will have a greater potential to attract customers than the one situated in a side street. It is worth checking how busy a location is at different times of day and on different days of the week.

Compare the levels of foot traffic at different locations by counting the numbers of passers-by over a set period.

Personal considerations

The location of your pub should be within easy reach of other facilities that are important to you. If you have children, the quality and proximity of the local schools will be of concern, as may leisure facilities and hospitals. Local issues like levels of crime may be significant and should be investigated. Transport links may be a factor for family and other support network contacts. Put simply, would the area be somewhere you would enjoy living and is it practical for your lifestyle?

DECIDING TO BUY OR RENT

Deciding whether to buy or rent your pub is often determined by the capital you have available, plus any amount you can borrow. An average tenancy or new lease will require capital in the region of £15,000–£40,000. Buying an existing lease, on assignment, can cost on average between £75,000–£150,000 and buying a mid-range freehold pub will cost between £300,000 and £500,000.

Other factors that will influence your decision will be your attitude to risk and the level of support you will need. Tenancy and leased pubs often have the backing of a brewery or pub company who will provide training and ongoing support. With a freehold pub there is no such support.

TENANCY

What is a tenancy?

Tenanted pubs are operated under a tenancy agreement. This agreement is offered by the owner of the property, (normally a brewery or pub company) to individuals wishing to become a pub tenant. The pub tenant runs the pub as their own business and is responsible for paying all the bills. They take on the pub by paying for fixtures and fittings, stock and a deposit. A rent is paid to the owners, and tenants have some obligations to decorate and repair their pub. Tenants may be 'tied' to buying certain drinks products direct from the brewery or a brewery nominated by the pub company. Agreements typically run for 3 or 5 years, with some having a guaranteed option to renew the agreement, subject to a rent review. Rents are reviewed on a specified basis; some rents are increased annually in line with inflation.

What's good about a tenancy?

A tenancy allows you to acquire an established business for a relatively small outlay. It is the traditional agreement that has been offered by breweries for the last century and is a well-established way of operating. Many breweries and pub companies now offer excellent training courses that you will be required to attend before you take on your pub. Ongoing support and advice is provided and there will be regular visits from their representatives (known as Business Development Managers or Area Managers).

Agreements have protection under the Landlord & Tenant Act 1954, which means that your position as tenant is legally protected. You cannot be asked to leave the pub during the course of your tenancy unless you are in serious breach of your agreement or have accepted terms to leave for some other reason.

The tie

The agreement may 'tie' you to buying specified drinks directly from the brewery or a brewery nominated by the pub company. Drinks prices are displayed in the price list that should be issued to you at the early stages of any discussions to take on a tenancy. You may find that identical drinks can be purchased from other suppliers more cheaply than you can buy them from your tied supplier. This can be a frustration for many tenants. However, the rent for your pub has been calculated taking into account the prices of the products you are tied to buying. To buy from unauthorised suppliers is regarded as a major breach of your agreement and one that may result in legal action against you. If you want to take on a tenanted pub, the tie is something that you will have to accept and adhere to.

Ties will vary between different tenancies, some being full ties and others, part ties. A full tie is where you are fully tied to buying all drinks products from the agreed supplier. A part tie only ties you to buying certain drinks products, for example, a beer and lager only arrangement, where you are free to purchase wines, spirits and minerals from elsewhere.

Discounts

The brewery or pub company may offer discounts on drinks products purchased from them. Depending on the agreement, these discounts may only be available if you exceed certain targets or may be immediately applicable for certain products. Prior to offering a pub, the brewery or pub company estimates how much discount is likely to be earned from them, and take this into account when calculating rent. This estimate is based on what they expect you to sell. The more you sell, the more discounts you earn. Here are some general tips on discussing discounts with a brewery or pub company:

◆ ask how the discount scheme works;
◆ make sure you understand it;
◆ ask them to explain how any 'anticipated discounts' have been worked out;
◆ be realistic about how much discount you are likely to earn;
◆ seek advice from an accountant if necessary.

Amusement machines

It is normal practice for the brewery or pub company to take a share of income from any amusement machines you have on your premises. The tenancy agreement may also require you to only use machine suppliers that are recommended by the brewery or pub company. For more information, see Chapter 18, *Amusement Machines*.

Trading accounts

Most tenants are not required to disclose their trading accounts to the brewery or pub company. Nor are they obliged to show this information to anyone wanting to take on their pub when they are planning to leave. There is no purpose in disclosing this information as they are not selling on their business. It is the responsibility of the brewery or pub company to find a replacement tenant when an existing tenant decides to leave. This is one of the downsides to taking on a tenancy: a lack of trading accounts. Any decision has an added element of risk. This can be minimised by putting together your own financial forecasts. (See Chapter 3 for details.)

Rents

The setting of rents is generally based on turnover and profitability. In calculating a pub's rent, the brewery or pub company will initially assess the pub's turnover based on 'fair maintainable trade' (FMT), ie their prediction of the turnover that a competent hypothetical tenant or lessee could achieve whilst operating the pub. From this they prepare an estimated profit and loss forecast using industry standards as a guide to the pub's operating costs. The rent is then based on this. It should be noted that the brewery or pub company profit and loss forecast is simply an estimate – although hopefully an accurate and professionally assessed one. However, if in the course of preparing your own financial forecasts, you can demonstrate that the rent appears unfair, then you may be able to renegotiate this. It is worth asking how the rent has been assessed and whether it reflects how the pub is currently trading. The forecasted fair maintainable trade may be higher than the present turnover of the pub. In such cases, you may be able to negotiate a 'stepped rent', ie one that starts low and increases in stages over a period of time, to give you time to build up the business.

How rents are calculated

Typical tenancy rents are based on:

◆ 8–12% of forecasted turnover;
◆ 40–50% of forecast net profit – excluding rent.

Forecasted turnover is a pub's total sales revenue, including food sales, gaming machines and any other income earned, such as letting accommodation. All figures are calculated excluding VAT.

An example of a simplified rent calculation is given here (note all figures exclude VAT):

Total turnover	£200,000
Gross profit (calculated at 45% of turnover)	£90,000
Less: total expenses before rent applied	£50,000
Net profit before rent is applied	£40,000

Rent calculation

1 Rent if calculated as 10% of turnover £20,000
   ie £200,000 x 10% = £20,000
2 Rent if calculated as 50% of net profit before rent £20,000
   ie £40,000 x 50% = £20,000

Either calculation results in an annual rent of £20,000 that leaves a net profit after rent has been applied of £20,000.

Net profit before rent is applied	£40,000
Less: annual rent	£20,000
Leaves: net profit	£20,000

Rent payment and reviews

VAT will be payable on your rent, but only applies to 90% of the total rent, this being assessed by Customs and Excise as the commercial element of your rent. They regard the remaining 10% as being your domestic portion and it will therefore not be subject to VAT.

Using the above example:

£20,000 x 90% (commercial element)	=	£18,000
(£18,000 of your rent will be subject to VAT)		
£20,000 x 10% (domestic element)	=	£2,000
(£2,000 of your rent will not be subject to VAT)		

Based on a rate of 17.5%, VAT of £3,150 will be added, resulting in a total rent payable of £23,150. Rents are normally charged in advance usually on a fortnightly or monthly basis.

Repairs

There is normally an obligation under the terms of your agreement to repair and decorate your pub. The extent of this obligation varies from agreement to agreement, and should be clearly understood prior to signing. Decorating the interior of the premises and undertaking minor repairs are normal tenancy terms, with the brewery or pub company being responsible for painting the exterior and dealing with any major repairs. Sometimes pubs can be left in a poor state of repair and decoration. It is worth inspecting the premises thoroughly prior to signing a tenancy to identify any major areas of concern. These issues should be raised with the brewery or pub company at an early opportunity, and written confirmation should be requested following any verbal promises made to attend to these.

Ingoing payments and expenses

Ingoing payments are made up of fixtures and fittings and stock, which are purchased from the outgoing tenant, and a deposit that is paid to the brewery or pub company. There are also fees relating to the transaction and a requirement for working capital. These are discussed in more detail in Chapter 4, *Funding the Business.*

Compare the details of tenancy and lease agreements from various pub companies and breweries to see how they vary.

LEASE

What is a lease?

Leased pubs are operated under a lease agreement and are similar to tenancies. The lease is offered by the owner of the property to individuals wishing to become a pub lessee and they run the pub as their own business. Rent is paid to the owners on an ongoing basis. Agreements typically run for 10, 15 or 20 years plus.

Similarities with a tenancy

◆ The agreement is offered by the owners of the pub.
◆ You run the pub as your own business.
◆ Rent is paid on an ongoing basis.
◆ Rents are calculated in a similar way, but higher percentages may apply to the calculation, eg 10–15% of turnover or 45–55% of net profit before rent.
◆ Some or all products may be tied.
◆ You are required to pay for fixtures and fittings, stock and a deposit.
◆ There is ongoing support from brewery or pub company.

Differences between a lease and a tenancy

◆ There is a longer period of agreement for a lease.
◆ You are able to sell on (assign) the lease and charge goodwill.
◆ You are likely to be responsible for all repairs and decoration.
◆ You may need a solicitor to act for you when signing the lease.
◆ You may require a property surveyor to prepare a structural survey of the premises.
◆ You may have to wait 2 or 3 years before you can assign.
◆ You will be responsible for finding a buyer and negotiating a price for selling on the lease if you decide to leave.

◆ Ingoing costs tend to be higher to cover legal and professional fees and stamp duty charges.
◆ Running costs are higher to cover additional repair, insurance and decoration expenses.

What's good about a lease?

A lease can be sold on when you decide to vacate your pub. This is called 'assigning' the lease. If you have run a successful pub you may be able to charge 'goodwill' for the business. The value of your lease (also known as the lease premium) should be professionally assessed by a property valuer experienced in pub leases. They will look at how profitable your business is and how many years remain on your lease. They do this to calculate what a buyer would expect to earn if they bought the pub from you. Pubs with good profits are valued more highly than ones with lower profits. Buyers will also demand to see up-to-date, verified financial accounts that support the price of your lease.

Two ways to acquire a lease

There are two ways to buy a lease:

1 Acquiring a new lease from the owners of the pub.
2 Buying an existing lease by assignment.

Acquiring a new lease

Acquiring a new lease involves dealing with a brewery or pub company directly. All discussions and interviews take place with them. Normally the lease will be offered without a premium being charged. Actual financial accounts will not generally be available (as in the case of a tenancy). Your profit and cash-flow forecasts will need to be estimated from sales information provided by them. Main ingoing costs will be:

◆ fixtures and fittings;
◆ stock;
◆ a deposit.

Buying a lease by assignment

Buying a lease by assignment involves dealing with the seller of the lease directly. All negotiations take place with them and the brewery or pub company will only be involved in order to vet your application.

Ingoing costs will be higher than if you bought a new lease because the seller will be charging a premium on the lease, taking into account goodwill. However, the price should be supported by financial accounts for the business. It is advisable to seek advice from your own accountant or property valuer when deciding whether the asking price is a fair one.

Once you have bought the lease on assignment, you are required to abide by its terms and pay rent to the brewery or pub company. Ongoing contact will be with them and there are no further dealings with the seller of the lease.

Repairs

Your obligations to repair the premises under a lease are much greater than a tenancy. You are normally responsible for attending to all repairs under a lease, including any structural problems that may occur. It is therefore essential that you are aware of any repair problems before you take on the pub. A full structural survey is recommended and should be used in any negotiations. You will need to budget for the cost of maintaining your pub and these should form part of your business plan and any financial assessment you make of the pub.

FRANCHISE

You may sometimes see pubs offered under a 'franchise agreement'. In these circumstances, the pub is leased but with some special clauses included in the terms of the agreement. These may include an obligation to use a nominated accountant and stocktaker, and to share trading figures with the brewery or pub company. Additional training, information manuals and consultancy services may also be available to you.

Whether this type of arrangement is right for you will be influenced by your attitude towards disclosing your financial figures and having some additional obligations as part of the agreement. You may welcome the chance to work more closely with the brewery or pub company and take advantage of their expertise.

Other terms, such as repairs, assignment and tie can vary from agreement to agreement and need to be fully understood before you sign up.

FREEHOLD

What is freehold?

Freehold is where you buy the pub outright and become the owner of the premises. The term 'freehouse' is often applied to these pubs, though historically, it tended to refer to the fact that the pub was 'free' from a drinks tie rather than 'freehold', which is property terminology. You own the bricks and mortar and are able to make all decisions about how you run your pub. Buying a freehold pub generally requires you to have much more capital available than for a lease or tenancy, and you tend to have to run the pub with limited support from your suppliers.

What's good about a freehold pub?

You own the pub and so are able to make your own decisions about how you operate it. You do not have brewery or pub company agreements to abide by and you are not accountable to them. You decide which drinks to stock and you can shop around for the best suppliers. Owning the premises means that you can plan for the long term. Any investment decisions you make can be assessed over a longer period. There are no rent reviews or renegotiations of agreements that can disrupt long-term planning.

As you build your business, the value of the pub is likely to increase too. You may be able to sell on your pub for more than you bought it.

Capital requirements

Buying a freehold pub requires more financial resources than a lease or tenancy. An average freehold pub will cost in the region of £300,000 to £500,000 to buy. Pubs with higher turnover and profitability will command a higher price than less successful ones. Obtain professional advice from a public house valuer, chartered surveyor or accountant as to whether an asking price is reasonable.

You may be able to borrow money to fund your purchase, but most lenders will require you to have a minimum of 30% of the asking price. You will also have to budget carefully to ensure that any loan can be repaid, and fees and interest rates need scrutiny too. See Chapter 4, *Funding the Business*, for more information.

Structural survey and repairs

It is important to have a thorough structural survey undertaken prior to making an offer for a freehold pub. Any repair issues need to be identified as they will be your responsibility once you have bought the property. Significant repair issues may provide an opportunity to negotiate on price or may be sufficient to dissuade you from going ahead.

Trading agreements with breweries

As the owner of a freehold pub, you have the ability to choose which drinks to stock and which suppliers to use. Many freehold pubs choose to have trading agreements with breweries. These are agreements under which the pub buys its drinks supplies from the brewery. Terms will cover price and discounts available, delivery, payment terms and beer dispense equipment. They are negotiated through a brewery representative, normally from its Free Trade department. These arrangements may be linked to a brewery loan, which some people use to help purchase their freehold pub. In these circumstances, the brewery agrees to lend you an amount of money to help purchase your freehold pub, eg 60% of the asking price. In return, you agree to stock some of their products on which you get discounts. When you start trading with them, this discount is then deducted from the value of the loan rather than off the price of the products you buy from them. In this way, the loan is reduced each time you purchase products from them.

If you have not used a brewery loan to fund your freehold pub, drinks discounts are deducted from the cost of the products or, in some cases, paid directly to you in the form of a bonus.

Other drinks suppliers

An alternative to purchasing your drinks supplies directly from a brewery is to use a wholesaler. Wholesalers stock a range of products from various breweries and drinks manufacturers. Some operate on a cash-and-carry basis while others provide a full delivery service with credit facilities. They operate by offering drinks supplies at discounted prices. Wholesalers operate in virtually every area of the UK. Most of these are reputable businesses but there are some less respectable operators too. It is advisable to do some research when deciding whether to use them to supply your drinks supplies. Factors like product quality and service need to be considered along with price and credit terms. Dealing with well-established wholesalers and ones with a good reputation is a way of avoiding potential problems.

MANAGED HOUSES

A managed house cannot be regarded as your *own* pub, and is therefore outside the scope of this book. However, for the sake of completeness a brief explanation of this type of pub operation is given below.

What is a managed house?

A managed house is a pub owned and operated by a brewery or pub company. All the staff are employed by them and they retain all profits. Managers are appointed by the brewery or pub company to run the pub on their behalf under strict guidelines and supervision. Managed houses tend to be high turnover, high profit pubs that the brewery or pub company want to maintain direct control over.

What's good about running a managed house?

Running a managed house is an opportunity to operate a high turnover pub without the risk of business failure. You will receive a set wage and earn a bonus if things go well. Major decisions are made by the brewery or pub company and they are responsible for paying the bills. The pub is run to a preset formula which includes staffing levels, choice of suppliers and product range. Managers are recruited by the Managed House department of the brewery or pub company.

Managers undergo comprehensive training prior to appointment and on an ongoing basis. The skills, experience and discipline gained while managing a pub are extremely valuable. These skills can be very successfully applied to running a pub business, like a tenancy, lease or freehold.

Some managers do not want the pressures of being self-employed and are happy in their existing roles. The lack of risk and a guaranteed income are very attractive to them. They would rather manage a pub on someone else's behalf than have one of their own. Professional pub managers are highly sought after and often enjoy long, rewarding careers with breweries and pub companies.

An employee

Running a pub as manager means you are an employee. You are employed and supervised by someone. You will not have the freedom or flexibility to make decisions or gain the rewards from building up or selling on a successful business. Your efforts may well be someone else's rewards. You may also feel that the levels of supervision and rules and regulations are too stifling.

Whether you feel that managing a pub is appropriate for you will depend on your attitude and your circumstances at the time. Managing a pub will be your only option if you do not have sufficient capital to acquire one of your own.

3

FINDING THE RIGHT PUB

THE RIGHT PUB FOR YOU

We looked at identifying your ideal pub in the last chapter, and how to
complete the checklist that was shown, to clarify your requirements. This
checklist can now be used to assess the suitability of different pubs.
This focuses your pub-hunting activities, saving you a great deal of time
and effort.

WHERE TO LOOK

Tenancy, lease and freehold pubs are advertised in a variety of places.
Knowing where to look greatly improves your chances of finding the right
pub for you. You will need to make time to search these different sources
and to visit pubs that match your requirements. This can be a time-
consuming activity. The main places to look for suitable pubs are:

◆ Brewery and pub company websites – (tenancy and lease).
◆ Pub valuer and business transfer agents websites – (freehold and lease
  assignments).
◆ *The Publican* and *Morning Advertiser* licensed trade newspapers – (freehold, lease and lease assignments).
◆ *Daltons Weekly*, a magazine containing businesses for sale – (freehold
  and lease assignments).

A list of useful websites, including major UK tenanted and leased pub operators and business transfer agents, is given in the Appendix.

Many other useful websites can also be found via an internet search. Entering phrases such as 'pub company', 'pub leases' or 'pubs for sale' into the Google search engine will provide good results. To a lesser extent, pubs are also advertised in local newspapers and via 'to let' and 'for sale' boards that are sometimes displayed on the outside of pubs.

Brewery and pub companies

Once you have established which geographical areas you are willing to consider for the location of your pub, it is worth targeting breweries and pub companies that have pubs in these areas. This can be a little difficult as many pubs 'branded' as a particular brewery may now in fact be owned by someone else! The majority of pubs in the UK are owned by a small number of pub companies and breweries. The major pub company and brewery websites give details of the areas in which they have pubs. Many have interactive maps to search for vacancies in a particular region.

If you wish to be considered by a brewery or pub company, you will need to register with them and complete an application form. Once registered, they will send you details of their tenancy and lease vacancies on an ongoing basis. See Chapter 7, *Applying for a Tenancy or New Lease*.

You can find lists of breweries and pub companies under the 'members list' of the British Beer and Pub Association website: www.beerandpub.com

Pub valuer and business transfer agents

These companies operate in a similar way to estate agents. Individuals place their pubs for sale or lease through them and are charged a fee for this service. Some companies specialise in the licensed trade and others offer a broad range of businesses for sale. They generally have detailed websites listing the pubs they have for sale and they often advertise extensively in trade and business newspapers. You can subscribe to their mailing lists in order to receive details of newly advertised pubs. Any initial contact about a particular pub should be made through them. They will then arrange meetings and viewings. Remember that such companies are acting on behalf of the seller and their aim is to find a buyer for the pub that has been placed with them.

The Publican and *Morning Advertiser* newspapers

The Publican and *Morning Advertiser* are two well-respected newspapers for the licensed trade. They are published weekly and have a comprehensive section which displays pubs for sale and lease. Many pub valuers and business transfer agents advertise their pubs in them, and they are also excellent sources of information on all aspects of the licensed trade. Subscribing to each of them is recommended.

Dalton's Weekly

Dalton's Weekly is a newspaper that advertises a whole range of items, services and businesses for sale. It is often used by pub valuers and business transfer agents to promote the pubs they have on offer. Many individuals wishing to sell their lease or freehold use *Dalton's* to advertise their pubs too. It is useful for comparing prices and for obtaining website addresses and telephone numbers of agents and valuers to contact.

SHORTLISTING SUITABLE PUBS

Once you know where to look for pubs that are available, the next step is to focus on finding pubs that match your ideal. Use your checklist to screen out unsuitable pubs and identify ones you think may match your requirements. Draw up a shortlist and focus on these pubs, requesting more details about them and visiting them to assess their potential.

VISITING YOUR SHORTLISTED PUBS

This is often the most time-consuming part of finding your ideal pub. Locating pubs can sometimes be difficult and may involve lots of travelling. A map or directions to the pub will be invaluable.

If you have the postcode of the pub, you can use www.multimap.com to obtain maps and directions on-line.

When visiting a pub it is best to be inconspicuous. You should respect the privacy of the existing licensee and allow them to run their business without interruption. They are likely to have other people interested in their pub too. Many licensees will not have told their customers or staff that they are leaving. Prospective licensees asking questions or obviously assessing the pub will be very unsettling. It is best to be discreet and make all approaches through the proper channels.

You may quickly reject a pub once you have seen it, while you will need to visit others several times before you make a decision. The aim of visiting a pub is to gather more information on which to base a decision. It is helpful to make notes as you visit each pub so that you can refer to them later. You should assess the customer and the location profiles and then prepare a 'SWOT analysis'. (For information on preparing a SWOT analysis, see later in this chapter.) Many people also consider a 'gut feeling' to be crucial in deciding whether a pub is suitable for them. It is worth making a note about your 'gut feeling' on each of the pubs you look at.

CUSTOMER PROFILES

You need to ascertain what kind of clientele uses the pub, and where they come from. You should really visit the pub at different times, and on different days of the week, to get a true picture of this. Even if there are no customers in the pub, you can pick up clues as to what type of clientele uses the pub:

◆ What type of music is on the jukebox?
◆ What type of drinks are being offered?
◆ What kind of promotions are being run?
◆ What facilities are available?

LOCATION PROFILES

A drive around an area can be very illuminating. It can tell you a great deal about the kind of people who live and work there. It is also an opportunity to investigate competitors' pubs. Does the pub you are interested in seem to meet the needs of the area or does it appear out of place? Are the competitors' pubs meeting these needs more successfully? Is there a gap in the market that could be filled?

Is the pub in a prominent position, in a busy area, or is it hidden away? Remember that the catchment area of a pub will vary depending on the type of pub you are looking at. Bear this in mind when assessing the area around your target pub.

You can find some valuable details about a neighbourhood on-line. Based on Census statistics, information on age profiles, employment, crime, housing and education are available. All you require is the pub's post-code in order to request details of the area you are interested in. This information is excellent for assessing an area and also provides useful background material that can be used in a business plan.

Two websites you can use for researching areas:
http://neighbourhood.statistics.gov.uk/dissemination/ and
www.upmystreet.com/

THE PUB ITSELF

Is the pub in a good general state of repair and does it look attractive to customers? If not, could these issues be easily overcome or are the problems more fundamental? What facilities does the pub have and do they correspond with the needs of its customers and the neighbourhood? What is the standard of the fixtures and fittings; do they look in good order, or are they falling to pieces and likely to require replacing?

SWOT ANALYSIS

A SWOT analysis is a useful way of evaluating the pluses and minuses of a particular pub. SWOT stands for Strengths, Weaknesses, Opportunities and Threats. It allows you to weigh up the important facts about a pub and also make comparisons with others. It combines everything that you have learned about the pub from research and personal visits. It is also useful to add comments on your overall impression and 'gut feeling' about the pub.

Here is an example of a SWOT analysis for a fictional pub: The Barking Dog.

SWOT Analysis: The Barking Dog pub

Strengths
Attractive pub, good décor.
Beer garden.
Good-sized games room.

Weaknesses
Poor internal layout.
Small catering kitchen.
Poor range of products.

Opportunities
Demand for quick lunchtime snacks from local office workers.
Opportunities to develop pub darts and pool team trade.
Enhance product range.

Threats
Very strong competitor within 500 metres serving high quality pub food although highly priced.

Overall impression and 'gut feeling'
Likeable traditional pub with opportunities to develop lunchtime snack trade – gap in the market not being met by competitors. Beer good. Popular with locals.

The SWOT analysis summarises the important issues about the pub. You should then look at each factor and decide how important it is and, also, whether you can influence or change these issues.

For example, a poor product range can fairly easily be improved, whereas extending the kitchen would be more difficult.

GATHERING FACTS AND FIGURES

Once you have found a pub that meets your requirements and appears to have more strengths and opportunities than weaknesses and threats, you need to consider its profitability.

EXPECTATIONS AND OBLIGATIONS

You must be sure that you have an opportunity to make a profit and that there will be sufficient income to meet your expectations and obligations.

How much money do you need to meet any personal obligations you may have? Mortgage payments on a house that you wish to keep, children's school fees, credit card payments and maintenance payments are all examples of your personal financial obligations. It is important to have worked out how much you must earn to cover them. On top of these, you may feel your efforts in running a pub require a certain level of income to make the job worthwhile. You will have to be realistic about this as it may take time to build up the business to fulfil both your expectations and obligations, and some pubs may never do this. You have two choices:

◆ Find a pub that will meet your expectations and obligations.

Or

◆ Adjust your expectations and obligations.

PRICE RESEARCH AND COMPETITION

Any research you do in an area must include the pub's competitors. The aim is to ascertain what their strengths and weaknesses are and how best to compete with them. Is there something that they don't do well but you could do successfully? Is there a demand in the area for something that is not being met by anyone? What are their standards like, and how good is their customer service? It is also an opportunity to check what prices they are charging for their products. Keeping up to date with what your competitors are doing is also vital once you have taken on your pub.

ASSESSING A PUB'S PROFITABILITY

As mentioned in Chapter 2, trading accounts can sometimes be difficult to obtain. Publicans wanting to assign their lease or sell their pub will need to provide verified accounts to support their asking price. It is their responsibility to find a buyer and so they will be motivated or compelled to provide whatever information may be necessary to achieve this. Tenants, on the other hand, are not obliged to disclose their trading accounts to the brewery or pub company (who are responsible for finding a replacement tenant or offer a new lease).

Profit forecast

In such situations, you will have to gather whatever information is available to put together your own profit forecast. This information can consist of:

◆ Sales information from the brewery or pub company, ie what products they have purchased in the last 12 months.
◆ Machine income, which can be provided by the brewery, pub company or machine supplier.
◆ Rent details, which will be provided by the brewery or pub company.
◆ Overheads – sometimes outgoing tenants are willing to disclose the main costs such as energy, rates, staffing.
◆ Business rates – see www.voa.gov.uk/business_rates to find the rateable value of any pub (searchable by postcode).
◆ Energy costs – suppliers can provide estimated usage figures.

◆ Profit and loss estimates are calculated by the brewery or pub company and they may be willing to disclose this information to you.

Sales information from the brewery or pub company

Breweries and pub companies maintain large amounts of sales information on each of their pubs. These are provided to their management teams on a weekly or monthly basis. The information usually comprises sales data for broad product categories and is often converted to 'barrels', this being a standard brewery measurement of 36 gallons (288 pints). Sometimes they use the term 'composite barrels' where all products have been converted into an equivalent barrelage.

Ask for the most up-to-date sales information to ensure you know how the pub is trading at present.

ESTIMATING INCOME

Estimating drinks sales

In the absence of more detailed information, you can use ale and lager sales figures provided by the brewery or pub company to give an estimate of annual drinks sales of the pub, also known as 'wet turnover'. It provides a rough guide when you have little else to go on.

To do this, you require two pieces of information:

◆ The quantity of ales and lager purchased from the brewery or pub company over the last 12 months.
◆ The selling price of ales and lager (ie the price a customer pays for a pint in the pub).

◆ EXAMPLE ◆

Sales figures for The Barking Dog:	12 months to October 2006
Product	Sales in barrels
Total ales	100
Total lager	90
Total	190

An average pint of ale sells for £2.00 and an average pint of lager for £2.50.

Step 1 – How many pints of ale and lager have been sold?

We know that there are 288 pints in a barrel, therefore:

Ale sales: 100 barrels x 288 pints = 28,800 pints sold
Lager sales: 90 barrels x 288 pints = 25,920 pints sold

Step 2 – How much revenue do we make from these?

Ale sales: 28,800 x £2.00   = £57,600
Lager sales: 25,920 x £2.50   = £64,800
Total ale and lager sales: = **£122,400**

This tells us that we make £122,400 from selling 100 barrels of ale at £2.00 and 90 barrels of lager at £2.50, over a 12-month period.

Step 3 – How can we use this to estimate wet turnover?

Steps 1 and 2 estimate revenue for ales and lagers only. However, we can use this figure as a guide to total wet turnover that includes cider, stout, wine, spirits, soft drinks and other drinks.

Ale and lager sales account for approximately 65–75% of total wet turnover in an average traditional pub. Food pubs tend to sell a lower proportion of ales and lagers as a percentage of all drinks sold. This is because they sell large quantities of wine and soft drinks. Traditional local pubs tend to sell mainly ales and lagers, so these form a large proportion of their overall drinks sales.

◆ EXAMPLE ◆

If The Barking Dog was a traditional local pub, it may be reasonable to assume that ale and lager sales are 75% of its total wet turnover. From this, we can estimate overall drinks sales.

To calculate this:
Divide £122,400 by 75, then *multiply* the result by 100 = £163,200

Wet turnover is therefore estimated as £163,200, and ale and lager sales account for £122,400 of this (which is 75% of total wet turnover).

Note: These figures all include VAT, which would not normally be included in profit and loss forecasts. See explanation below.

Estimating machine income

Machine income is your earnings from amusement machines, pool table and jukebox. In the case of many tenancy and lease agreements, machine income is split between the brewery or pub company and the licensee. Income varies greatly from pub to pub. Amusement machines are often played by a very small core of a pub's clientele and income fluctuates with their use. An approximate guide would be 1–5% of wet turnover.

Estimating total food sales

Food turnover can be notoriously difficult to estimate. If details of food sales are unavailable, then an estimate is the best you can do.
Some ways to try to do this are as follows:

◆ Speak to local food suppliers for guidance.
◆ Count the number of available covers (place settings) in the pub.
◆ Count the number of customers having food at different times of the week.
◆ Check the menu for average meal prices (don't forget to include starters and sweets).
◆ Estimate the weekly number of customers eating meals.

◆ Multiply the number of customers by the average meal price.

◆ Ask the brewery or pub company for their assessment.

Estimating income from accommodation

Bed and breakfast accommodation is providing a useful additional income source for more and more pubs. If the pub has suitable facilities then it could be worth considering. If the pub you are interested in operates bed and breakfast facilities, you need to take into account income you will earn from these. If accurate information is not provided, it will have to be estimated. Here are some pointers:

◆ Note the total number of rooms.

◆ Note the room rates (room price).

◆ Estimate the occupancy rate (ie what percentage of rooms are occupied).

The total number of rooms and the rates for the rooms can be easily obtained, the occupancy rate can be more difficult to establish. Occupancy varies depending on the type of accommodation, price, location and other environmental factors. As a guide, major hotels generally run at 65–70% occupancy rates. Pub accommodation is more likely to be in the 25–35% range. Some pubs can enjoy higher levels where they have regular weekly stays from contractors or business people, or are located in a tourist area.

◆ EXAMPLE ◆

5 (rooms) x £25 (room rate) x 365 (number of days) x 25% (occupancy rate) = £11,406 (estimated annual income from accommodation).

ESTIMATING RUNNING COSTS

You will require details of running costs in order to assess a pub's profitability. If accounts are not available to you, the following table containing industry estimates of annual running costs of a lease will act as a guide:

Note: The percentage figures are shown as a % of sales turnover (excluding VAT):

◆ Bar staff costs are 8–12% of *wet* turnover.
◆ Food staff costs are 20–25% of *food* turnover.
◆ Accommodation staff costs are 20–25% of *accommodation* income.
◆ Other costs are shown as a percentage of *total* turnover (including drinks, food turnover, machine income and any accommodation income).

Industry estimates of annual running costs

Staff costs – bar	8–12% of *wet* turnover
Staff costs – food	20–25% of *food* turnover
Staff costs – accommodation	20–25% of *accommodation* income
Rent	10–15%
Heat and light	3–6%
Business rates	3–4%
Repairs	2–4%
Marketing	2–3%
Accountant and stocktaker	1–2%
Insurance	1–1.5%
Licences and fees	0.75–1%
Motor expenses	0.75–1%
Water rates	0.75–1%
Bank charges	0.5–1%
Telephone	0.5–0.75%
Equipment rental	0.25–0.5%
Glassware and crockery	0.25–0.5%
Cleaning materials	0.25–0.5%
Waste and refuse	0.25–0.5%
Other miscellaneous costs	2–5%
Entertainment (optional)	based on type of entertainment
Satellite TV (optional)	based on rateable value
Depreciation	based on value of assets

PROFIT AND LOSS

Making a profit

When assessing various pubs you will need to consider whether you can operate the pub at a profit and whether the profit it generates is sufficient to meet your obligations and expectations. To do this you should draw up a profit and loss forecast.

Ask to see the estimated profit and loss forecast drawn up by the brewery or pub company which is normally prepared to calculate rent for a new agreement.

Excluding VAT from calculations

When drawing up a profit forecast we exclude VAT from all figures. This is because we 'collect' VAT on behalf of HM Revenue and Customs and it does not directly affect the profitability of a business. See more details in Chapter 13, *Book-keeping and Accounts*.

In practical terms, this means we have to remove the VAT element from many of the figures we use (if VAT has been charged on the figures in the first place).

◆ EXAMPLE ◆

Using the example of The Barking Dog pub, we have estimated that wet turnover is £163,200. This figure includes VAT, which we need to remove to obtain our 'ex VAT' turnover figure.

An easy way of doing this is to divide the figure by 117.5%. This gives us an ex VAT turnover of £138,894.

To check this, multiply £138,894 by 17.5% (VAT rate) which gives £24,306 (VAT). Adding the two figures together gives £163,200. We use the ex VAT turnover figure in any profit and loss forecasts.

GROSS PROFIT AND NET PROFIT

The terms 'gross profit' and 'net profit' are used in accounts and financial forecasts. Gross profit is often abbreviated as GP and net profit as NP. It is important to understand the difference between the two. In simple terms, gross profit relates to what you sell, and the profit you make after paying for these. Net profit is the profit you have left after deducting all running costs.

GROSS PROFIT

Gross profit is calculated as follows: sales revenue *less* the cost of sales = gross profit.

Calculating gross profit margin (GP£) on specific products

◆ EXAMPLE ◆

You sell a barrel of lager for £720 (sales revenue), which cost you £400 to buy (cost of sales).

Both these figures include VAT, which needs to be removed. This results in ex VAT figures of £612.77 and £340.43 respectively. To work out the gross profit margin, subtract one figure from the other:

Sales revenue (ex VAT)	£612.77
Less: Cost of sales (ex VAT)	£340.43

Calculating gross profit margin (GP£) on turnover

◆ EXAMPLE ◆

Your annual wet turnover is £138,894 (ex VAT), and your drinks purchases for this period are £76,392 (ex VAT).

Wet turnover (ex VAT)	£138,894 (100%)
Less: Cost of sales (ex VAT)	£76,392 (55%)
Equals: Gross profit	**£62,502** (45%)

Gross Profit Percentage (GP%)

Gross profit is often quoted as a percentage of sales revenue/turnover. Using the second example, if we divide the gross profit margin into the wet turnover, the result is 45%. This tells us that 45% of our turnover converts to gross profit. (Cost of sales amount to 55% of turnover.)

Factors affecting GP percentages

The main factors affecting GP percentages on products are:

♦ The price you are able to charge.
♦ What they cost to buy.

Additional factors affecting GP percentages on overall turnover are:

♦ The types and quantities of product you sell: some products can be sold at higher GP percentages than others.
♦ Wastage and theft: if you lose stock items due to wastage or theft, you cannot sell them, so make no profit at all on these.

Industry averages for GP percentages

Typical overall GP percentages on *wet* turnover (based on normal, brewery or pub company list prices, *excluding* any discounts) are as follows:

♦ Low priced local pub   38–40%
♦ Traditional local pub   40–47%
♦ Quality pub   46–52%
♦ YPV (Young Persons Venue)   45–55%

Freehold properties, earning discounts on their drinks purchases, can make over 60%.

Typical overall GP percentages on *food* turnover:

♦ Low-priced/quality food   30–40%
♦ Mid-priced/quality food   40–55%
♦ Higher-priced/quality food   60–70%

Controlling wastage is critical in achieving your food gross profit percentages.

CALCULATING WEEKLY BREAK-EVEN SALES

It is important for you to know the level of sales you require to break even. Break-even is reached when your sales revenue equals your running costs. If your sales revenue is less than your running costs, you are making a loss; if your sales revenue exceeds your running costs you are making profit.

You should work out the value of weekly sales you require in order to break even at your forecasted weekly running costs. The first step in doing this is to estimate your weekly running costs, establish your overall gross profit percentage (GP%), and then follow the steps explained below.

Calculating weekly sales required to break even

Weekly break-even sales are calculated as follows:

Weekly running costs *divided by* GP(%) *multiplied by* 100 = weekly break-even sales (ex VAT).

Then *multiply by* 1.175 (to add VAT) to give weekly sales including VAT required to break even.

◆ EXAMPLE ◆

(using figures from The Barking Dog forecast below)

£875 (weekly running costs) *divided by* 45 (GP%) *multiplied by* 100 = £1944 (weekly sales, excluding VAT, required to break even)

Then, *multiply* £1944 *by* 1.175

NET PROFIT

Net profit (or net loss) is what you have left after deducting all running costs.

Simplified profit and loss forecast for The Barking Dog*	
Annual wet turnover	£138,894
Less: annual cost of sales	£76,392
Equals: annual **Gross Profit margin**	**£62,502** (45%)
Less: Total running costs	£45,502
Equals: annual **Net Profit**	**£17,000**
(*All figures are quoted ex VAT)	

HOW YOU OPERATE THE PUB

Any assessment of a pub's profitability must take into account how you intend to operate the pub. Your vision for the pub may be very different from how it is being run at the moment. You may see opportunities that are currently not being exploited that would have a positive effect on turnover. You may intend to run the pub with different levels of staff, and control costs more tightly than its current occupants do. Your forecasts must also be realistic. It is very easy to overestimate your turnover and underestimate costs. This is easy to do in the excitement of trying to find your pub. A more level-headed approach is to prepare a range of profit forecasts: 'optimistic', 'average' and 'pessimistic'. This helps you look at a range of possible scenarios and assess the consequences of each.

Seek the advice of an accountant with experience of the licensed trade, to help assess the viability of any pub you are interested in.

4

FUNDING THE BUSINESS

HOW MUCH WILL IT COST?

As mentioned in the first two chapters, the amount of money that will be needed to acquire your pub depends on whether you decide to take a tenancy, lease, or buy a freehold property. A new tenancy or lease can be obtained for as little as £15,000, while freehold pubs can cost up to £2 million in some cases. Your options will be largely dependent on the financial resources that you have available. In this chapter, we look at the different ways of obtaining your pub and look at the ingoing costs of each, this being the amount of money you will need to obtain your pub in the first instance, and does not include running costs (as discussed in Chapter 3).

TENANCY

When taking a tenancy, you will be required to purchase the pub's fixtures and fittings, stock and glassware, and pay a deposit to the brewery or pub company. There will also be fees arising from the transaction and a requirement for working capital. If you have any immediate plans to spend money on new items of equipment or to refurbish your pub, then this must be budgeted for too.

Fixtures and fittings

Fixtures and fittings are items of furniture, carpets and equipment used in the business. These items are valued by a valuer, who prepares an inventory of them. Fixtures and fittings account for the main ingoing cost of taking a tenancy. Food pubs tend to have higher fixtures and fittings values due to expensive items of kitchen equipment.

◆ Typical capital required: £10,000–£30,000.

Stock and glassware

Stock is valued by a stocktaker. This includes any items for resale such as drinks products, snacks, crisps, nuts, and supplies of packaged food. Glasses will also be valued together with any bottle or case deposits, and cellar-dispense gas.

◆ Typical capital required: £2,000–£5,000.

Brewery or pub company deposit

A deposit is normally required by the brewery or pub company in order to allow you credit terms on your purchases. A smaller deposit may be accepted for cash with order customers. (Customers who pay for their delivery before they receive their goods.) This deposit gains interest and is paid back to you at the end of the tenancy, plus interest. The brewery or pub company can make deductions from this should you owe them money or leave the premises in a poor state of repair.

◆ Typical capital required: £2,500–£7,000.

Stocktaking and fixtures and fittings valuation fees

You should use a stocktaker and a valuer to act on your behalf.

Expect to pay:

◆ Stocktaker's fees: £75–£100.
◆ Fees for valuation of fixtures and fittings: £400–£1,000 (normally based on a percentage of valuation).

Licence application and associated solicitor's fee

The cost of using a solicitor to make an application for your licence and licence needs to be budgeted.

◆ Solicitor's fee and licence costs: £300–£500.

A solicitor is not normally required in signing a tenancy agreement (except perhaps, to explain the terms of the tenancy to you). In the case of a lease, where the situation is more complex, using a solicitor to deal with the lease transaction on your behalf is advisable.

Training costs

Many breweries and pub companies require you to attend their in-house training courses prior to taking a pub with them. You will also be required to hold an accredited licensing qualification, which can be obtained via local colleges, training organisations or through your brewery or pub company.

◆ Allow: £500–£1,000 to cover training expenses.

Working capital

Though pubs are cash businesses with no delays in customers paying you, it is wise to put aside some working capital to cover day-to-day expenses and any unforeseen eventualities, like equipment breakdown, blocked drains etc.

◆ Allow: £2,000–£5,000 to cover working capital requirements.

LEASE

The cost of acquiring a lease will depend on whether it is a new lease offered by a brewery or pub company, or an assignment of an existing lease.

New lease
Capital required for new leases are essentially the same as for a tenancy:

◆ fixtures and fittings;
◆ stock and glassware;
◆ deposit;
◆ working capital.

You will also need funds to cover fees associated with the transaction:

◆ valuer's fee (fixtures and fittings);
◆ stocktaker's fee;
◆ licence cost and associated solicitor's fee;
◆ training course fees.

Over and above these, further money is required to cover the following fees and expenses that are specific to taking on a leased pub (and are not required for a tenancy):

◆ Legal fees for a solicitor to act on your behalf regarding the completion of the lease: allow £600–£800 to cover these.
◆ Property Surveyor's structural survey of the premises: allow £500–£800 for this.
◆ Some companies require payment of rent in advance: allow 1 month–3 months' rent payment.
◆ Stamp duty land tax (see below).

Buying an existing lease on assignment
The cost of acquiring a pub in this way will require more capital than if a new lease had been issued. This is because the person selling their lease (the assignor), is likely to be asking for a premium for the lease, to account for the goodwill they have built while operating the pub. Successful pubs making good profits will be valued more highly than ones trading less well. The price is determined by a pub valuer, using the pub's profitability and the remaining term of the lease. The price should be supported by verified

trading accounts. Professional advice should always be sought as to whether the asking price is a fair one.

♦ Typical prices range from £50,000–£200,000.

Additional money will be required to cover additional items (as per a new lease, details above), with the exception of fixtures and fittings which are usually included in the asking price. Stamp duty land tax (SDLT) will normally be higher in the case of buying a lease on assignment. This is because SDLT is also calculated on any premium charged.

Stamp duty land tax on leases (lease duty)

Stamp duty land tax (SDLT) is a new tax that was introduced by the Finance Act 2003, replacing the old Stamp Duty system. SDLT is charged on 'land transactions', including leases. Payment of SDLT is the responsibility of the purchaser of the lease. The grant of a lease of more than 7 years generally attracts SDLT. It may also be chargeable on shorter leases that meet particular criteria. The tax payable is based on rent and any premium that is charged, and is quite a complex calculation. There are also circumstances where SDLT may not be chargeable. A solicitor or accountant will advise you on how much SDLT may be payable on your lease.

♦ Allow: £1,500–£4,000 to cover SDLT.

You can use the Inland Revenue SDLT website at: http://www.hmrc.gov.uk/so/new-sdlt-calculators.htm to calculate your Stamp Duty Land Tax.

FREEHOLD

Freehold pub values are based on a combination of the bricks and mortar value and the value of the business, including goodwill. Valuations are calculated by pub valuers and, again, should be supported by verified accounts.

◆ Typical prices range from £250,000–£750,000.

You will also need to have sufficient funds to cover:

◆ stock and glassware;
◆ stocktaker's fee;
◆ licensing costs and associated solicitor's fee;
◆ legal fees relating to the purchase of the property;
◆ structural survey fee;
◆ working capital;
◆ training course fees;
◆ stamp duty (SDLT).

Will VAT be added to the price?

If the seller and purchaser are carrying on the same kind of business, the transaction will be regarded as a going concern, and not be subject to VAT. A pub transferring ownership from a brewery or pub company to an individual may attract VAT. This is because a brewery or pub company carries out a different kind of business to an individual. A transaction between individuals, operating the pub in the same way, is not likely to attract VAT.

It is always worth clarifying whether VAT will be added to the price of a freehold.

Stamp duty land tax on purchase of a freehold

Stamp duty land tax is payable based on the price of the property. Stamp duty land tax rates for transactions as at March 2010 are as follows:

Non-residential property value	SDLT rate
0–£150,000	zero
£150,000–£250,000	1%
£250,000–£500,000	3%
Over £500,000	4%

◆ EXAMPLE ◆

A pub bought for £400,000 would pay 3% SDLT, resulting in a Stamp Duty Land Tax payment of £12,000.

OTHER EXPENSES

Whether you acquire a tenancy, lease or freehold pub, you may also need to budget for the following:

◆ removal expenses;
◆ purchase of any new equipment;
◆ plans to refurbish or redecorate;
◆ any initial marketing or opening costs;
◆ any costs associated with raising additional finance;
◆ professional fees for preparing profit forecast, cash flows or providing advice.

WHERE TO FIND THE MONEY

Options available

The options you have available to fund your pub will depend on what money you have, what you are able to raise by selling some of your assets, and what you can borrow from a lender. Before going ahead, you should seek professional financial advice in order to fully understand the implications.

Using your own money

You need to establish how much money you personally have available to acquire your pub. The exercise in Chapter 1, and discussions with your financial adviser or accountant will clarify what funds you have at your disposal. This may be capital you have readily available, such as bank or building society deposits, or assets that could be sold to raise further money, such as shares etc. A good financial adviser or accountant will discuss the options that you have available, together with their implications. How best to use your cash, and what tax issues may arise, are important questions that need to be answered.

The next step is to decide whether to limit your investment to the capital that you personally have available, or to borrow additional funds to acquire your pub.

Borrowing money

Borrowing money provides you with more capital and therefore widens the choice of pub that is open to you. The downside to this is the added risk and cost to your business. The additional burden of a loan needs very careful consideration. You need to be certain that the business can carry the extra costs involved and to be able to repay the loan.

Lenders have diverse views on the pub business. Dependent on the type of pub operation being considered, some may not be willing to lend you money at all. Those who are willing to lend you money will set limits to the amount of loan, requiring you to make up the balance of any ingoing or purchasing costs.

People with no experience of operating a pub will be considered a greater risk by lenders, than experienced operators. As a consequence, the terms of a loan may be less attractive than for experienced publicans. The performance of the pub is important too, and will be taken into account, together with the applicant's experience. An experienced publican with an excellent track record, who wants to borrow money for a highly profitable business, will give the lender maximum confidence. An inexperienced person with no track record, who wants to purchase a poorly performing pub, will inspire much less confidence.

Choosing a lender

There is a wide range of lenders today. They include the traditional lenders, such as banks, to more specialist lenders who deal with particular types of business.

Your financial adviser or accountant can advise you on which lenders to approach and can help you prepare your case. They will be able to advise you on costs and any specific requirements that a lender will be looking for. A number of specialist, pub finance brokers also provide this type of service. A broker will charge a fee for their work, normally based on a percentage of the loan. If looking at this option, choose a reputable, well-established company.

You can evaluate lenders yourself, using the internet. A good website that compares a wide range of lending deals is: www.moneysupermarket.com

Annual percentage rate (APR)

The Annual Percentage Rate or APR of a loan, takes into account other charges you have to pay, not just the interest on the amount you have borrowed. The APR allows you to compare different loan offers. A lower APR means the loan costs you less than one with a higher APR.

Other things to consider are:

◆ whether there are any penalties for paying the loan back early;
◆ whether the interest rate is fixed or variable;
◆ whether there are any other costs not included in the APR calculation of the loan.

You also need to know how much your monthly payments will be, to ensure that you can afford the payments, and budget for them.

Another useful website, where you can calculate what your monthly payments will be at various APRs and payment periods, can be found in the Tools and Calculators section of the following website: www.moneymadeclear.fsa.gov.uk/home.html

The APR that you are offered on a loan will depend on your credit rating and other lender criteria. Be aware that APRs quoted on advertisements may not necessarily be offered to you. Higher rates may apply to your particular circumstances.

What professional lenders look at

Lenders tend to look at 3 main areas when considering whether to lend money:

◆ the applicant;
◆ the business;
◆ the ability to repay the loan.

They must assess the risk of lending you money. They will take into account your financial track record, including any previous bank dealings, and obtain a credit rating on you. Your financial obligations and your assets and liabilities will be looked at. They will also take into account the impression you make on them since they need to have confidence in you. Lenders need confidence in your business too, and a well put-together business plan is essential in developing this. Lenders need to be sure that you will be able to repay the loan and they will require profit and loss and cash flow forecasts. In some circumstances, they may insist on verified accounts for the pub.

Depending on the size of the loan, the lender may need some form of security before they are willing to go ahead. For example, they may require you (or other people) to sign personal guarantees for the loan, or allow them to put a charge on one of your assets. They also take into account whether you have any secondary income, such as a pension or a partner's wage from other employment.

Their assessment will determine the following:

◆ whether they will lend you any money at all;
◆ how much they are willing to lend you;

- what the interest rate will be;
- what conditions will apply, such as security etc.

Being rejected by one lender does not mean that all lenders will take the same view. It is wise to do your homework and prepare well for any meetings you have with lenders. This will give you a better chance of success.

TYPES OF BORROWING

Overdrafts

An overdraft facility is a service provided by banks whereby they allow you to borrow money up to specified limits. They are useful for covering short-term, cash-flow shortages. As well as the interest rate charged on the overdraft, a fee may be payable too. Interest rates tend to be higher than standard bank loan rates, so borrowing using this method over a long term is likely to cost more. Penalties will be charged if you exceed your overdraft limit, which can be costly.

Loans

Loans are available from banks and a wide range of other lenders. Small loans can be obtained on an 'unsecured' basis. This means that you are not required to provide any form of security for the loan. If you have a good credit rating, small loans can be quick and easy to arrange and many lenders do not require you to confirm what you will be using the money for.

Larger loans, typically over £20,000, may need to be secured against one of your major assets, such as property etc. This means that the lender can sell the asset you have used as security if you fail to repay the loan. Lenders will want to know what the money is to be used for, and require business plans and verified accounts where possible. There will be limits to the amount they are willing to advance you. You may be required to match the amount of their loan with money of your own. Arrangement fees normally apply to setting up your loan.

Many lenders will not be willing to offer loans to fund ingoings for tenancies or new leases, because there is no opportunity of them securing the debt, and there are no verified accounts available.

Commercial mortgages

Commercial mortgages can be used to buy freehold pubs. They are similar to residential mortgages, though tend to carry higher rates of interest to reflect the increased risk to the lender. Like residential mortgages, there is a number of different schemes available and interest rates can be fixed or variable. Mortgages tend to be arranged for a period of between 10 and 25 years and lenders secure the debt with a charge on the property. If you fail to keep up payments, they can use the property to recoup their money.

As well as banks and building societies, a number of brokers can advise you on the options available to you. Set-up fees will be charged on any arrangement and can typically be 0.5–1% of the loan amount. The property will need to be professionally valued and there will be a valuation fee to pay for this. The mortgage may include an early redemption penalty where you would have to pay a fee if you settled the loan earlier than planned.

Lenders will consider loans of up to 70% of the purchase price of the pub, leaving you to cover the balance and other costs connected with the transaction.

Lenders will require 2 years' verified accounts, profit and loss and cash-flow forecasts, and a comprehensive business plan. They also need to have confidence in you personally, and will check your credit rating, assets and liabilities, and track record.

Brewery loans

Brewery loans can be used to purchase freehold pubs. Loans are usually arranged by the Free Trade department of a brewery, and can run for up to 10 years. Interest rates vary according to how much drinks products you buy from them. The brewery agrees to lend you an amount of money in return for you agreeing to sell some of their products. They may require the security of a charge over the property. You pay the full list price for the products you buy from them, and the discounts you earn are used to repay your loan. (As a free trade customer *without* a loan from them, they would normally deduct discounts from the list price or pay them directly to you, periodically.)

There are limits to how much a brewery will be willing to lend you. A normal limit would be based on the 'forced sale' value of the freehold pub. In this case, the brewery may only be willing to advance you up to 80% of the forced sale value of the pub. This being the anticipated selling price of the pub if the brewery had to sell it closed and quickly, to recover their money. Because the loan is repaid through discounts on the products you buy from the brewery, the amount of products you are anticipated to buy also determines how much they will lend you. On average, they will lend £300–£350 per barrel.

◆ EXAMPLE ◆

- For a freehold pub with a price of £400,000, the brewery may calculate that the forced sale value would be £280,000. Based on this they would lend a maximum of 80% of this value, which is £224,000.
- If the pub is trading at 400 barrels per year, based on a rate of £350 per barrel, the maximum advance would be £140,000.

The brewery is mainly motivated by the amount of beer it can sell and the anticipated barrelage will be the primary means of assessing the pub for lending purposes.

Using brewery discounts to add confidence to lenders

Aside from borrowing money from a brewery, their discounts can be used to support loan applications to other lenders. In this case, you would look to borrow money from another source but agree, as part of the terms of the loan, that discounts earned from the brewery would be paid direct to the lender to help repay the loan. This may help to encourage a lender to loan you money where they have some concerns about your application, as it reduces their risk. Similar schemes, where the brewery agrees to pay a contribution towards interest payments from other lenders, have also been used to help raise finance. While such arrangements are not popular practice, it is worth discussing these with your Free Trade representative.

Using equity in your home or other property

Where you have a home or other property that you intend to retain, you can raise money via a residential mortgage arrangement. This will be subject to having sufficient equity in the property on which to secure the loan, and valuation of the property will also be needed to establish this. Decisions to use your home to raise money should not be taken lightly, and professional financial advice should always be sought before going ahead. If you fail to keep up payments, you run the risk of losing your property as well as your business.

There is a number of different ways of mortgaging your home and these are discussed below:

- **First mortgage**: where you own a property outright, a lender (mortgagee) may be willing to lend you up to 95% of the value of the property. They will secure the loan via a 'first charge' over the property. This means they are first in line to recover any outstanding money by repossessing your property, if you default on the mortgage with them.
- **Further advance**: an existing mortgagee may agree to increase the amount of their mortgage in order to advance you more money.
- **Second mortgage**: another lender may lend you money via a second mortgage and take a 'second charge' over your property. They become second in line, behind the first mortgagee, if you default on your mortgage with them. The second mortgage will be dependent on there being sufficient equity in your home. (See section, 'Using your property as collateral', below). The interest rates are likely to be higher than for a first mortgage to reflect the lower security available to the lender. Third and fourth mortgages are possible where there is sufficient equity in the property.
- **Re-mortgage**: this is where a new lender is brought in to clear an

existing mortgage or other borrowings. A new, first mortgage is created over the property and other charges over the property are cleared.

As in the case of commercial mortgages and other forms of loan, there is a bewildering range of mortgage products available and obtaining specialist advice is recommended.

Using your property as collateral

Homes and other property can be used as collateral for other types of borrowing. This is where the property is used as security for a loan. Again, you risk losing the property should you default on payments. To use a property, there must be sufficient equity on which to secure any debt. To calculate the amount of security a property offers, the lender will normally take 80% of the property value, less any outstanding mortgages. An example of this is shown here:

♦ EXAMPLE ♦

Value of property	£200,000
80% of the property value	£160,000
Less: outstanding mortgage	£50,000
Equals: amount of security available	**£110,000**

Loans from family and friends

Family and friends are another potential source of finance and many businesses have been supported in this way. The advantages with these sorts of arrangements are that they know you and (it is hoped) have confidence in you and your business plan. Lending arrangements may be more flexible in terms of interest, repayments and security.

When visiting different lenders to compare deals, ask them initially for an illustration only, as lenders' searches into your credit rating are registered for others to see. Too many credit searches on your records can work against you.

Borrowing money from family and friends can cause difficulties too. Relationships can be damaged if you are unable to repay the loan. You may also find that there is pressure from them to become involved in the business, which you may not want.

When borrowing money in this way, it is best to take a professional and businesslike approach. Put any arrangements in writing, confirming repayment details and rates of interest, plus what is to happen if the loan is not repaid, and whether the lender is to have any involvement in the business. Both parties should sign the document and each hold a copy.

Brewery and pub company support for tenants and new lessees

Breweries and pub companies offer a number of ways to assist people wanting to take a tenancy or new lease with them. Purchasing the fixtures and fittings tends to be the biggest expense when taking on a pub. They often offer fixtures and fittings repayment plans to pay for the cost of these over a period of time, rather than up front. Some are willing to spread the cost of these over a period of several years, but will charge you interest for this facility. Others are happy to defer payment for several months until you have established yourself and started building up the business.

There may be opportunities to build up your deposit with them over several months too. They may well allow you to trade on a 'cash with order' basis with a small deposit, and transfer you to credit terms once they hold a substantial deposit for you.

Many breweries and pub companies have links to lenders where preferential terms are on offer to new tenants and lessees. These can provide an opportunity to help fund the cost of your ingoing.

If you are intending to take a tenancy or new lease, it is worth asking the brewery or pub company what alternative ways to pay for the cost of ingoing are available.

	Tenancy	New lease	Lease by assignment	Freehold
Your own funds	Yes	Yes	Yes	Yes
Re-mortgaging your own property	Yes – subject to available equity	Yes – subject to available equity	Yes – subject to available equity	Yes – subject to available equity
Family & friends	Yes	Yes	Yes	Yes
Loan (unsecured)	Possibly – but normally limited to £20–£25K	Possibly – but normally limited to £20–£25K	Yes – but normally limited to £20–£25K	Yes – but normally limited to £20–£25K
Loan (secured)	Possibly – if using other collateral	Possibly – if using other collateral	Yes – may lend up to 50–60% of lease value	Yes – may lend up to 70% of property value
Overdraft	Yes	Yes	Yes	Yes
Commercial mortgage	No	No	No	Yes – may lend up to 70% of property value
Brewery loan	No	No	Possibly – if free of tie	Yes – may lend up to 80% of forced sale value
Fixtures and fittings repayment plans	Possibly	Possibly	No	No
Deposit build-up	Possibly	Possibly	No	No

5

LICENSING LAW

OVERVIEW

Any business that serves alcohol to customers must be licensed to do so. England and Wales, Scotland, and Northern Ireland, each have their own licensing laws governing this. In England and Wales, there has been radical reform of licensing through the Licensing Act 2003. The new act came into full effect in November 2005.

There has been a recent review of the Scottish licensing system, currently regulated under the Licensing (Scotland) Act 1976. The Nicholson Committee suggests a wide number of changes. These bring Scottish licensing law broadly into line with the situation in England and Wales.

Northern Ireland's licensing regulations are covered by the Licensing (Northern Ireland) Order 1996. However, a consultation paper, *Liquor Licensing – The Way Forward*, was launched on 1 November 2005, setting out the Government's proposals for the reform of liquor licensing in Northern Ireland, and the consultation period lasted until 31 January 2006. Changes to the liquor licensing procedures are earmarked for 2011.

THE SITUATION IN ENGLAND AND WALES

The Licensing Act 2003 has changed the way pubs are licensed in England and Wales. The act amalgamates 6 previous licensing regimes and promotes 4 licensing objectives:

♦ the prevention of crime and disorder;
♦ public safety;
♦ the prevention of public nuisance;
♦ the protection of children from harm.

Key changes to the act are the following requirements:

♦ All premises undertaking licensable activities must have a premises licence.
♦ A designated premises supervisor (DPS) must be named on the premises licence.
♦ Anyone who authorises the sale of alcohol must hold a personal licence.

Along with these changes, a number of others has been brought in relating to:

♦ opening hours;
♦ children in pubs;
♦ entertainment;
♦ processing licensing applications.

PROCESSING APPLICATIONS

Local councils (Licensing Authorities) are responsible for dealing with all licensing applications. The location of the pub dictates which licensing authority will be responsible for processing the licence, or any changes to it. Your local authority will be happy to forward all necessary application forms and guidance notes to you.

Many local councils' websites will give details of their licensing code of practice and may also provide a facility of downloading application forms and any supporting documents.

Although it is quite possible to make licence applications yourself, normal practice is to use a solicitor experienced in such matters. This ensures that the application is correctly submitted. A solicitor will also be able to advise you if any problems arise.

PREMISES LICENCE

Premises where licensable activities take place must be licensed under the act. Such activities include the sale and supply of alcohol, entertainment and late night refreshment. Pubs are therefore required to have a premises licence in order to trade. As part of the application for a new premises licence, an operating schedule must be submitted. This sets out how the premises propose to operate, including opening hours, details of licensable activities, the designated premises supervisor (DPS), and how the licensing objectives are supported by the pub. The premises licence stays in force at the pub and can only be varied by a formal application. In practice, this means that anyone taking on a pub will adopt the operating schedule as per the premises licence. If they want to make changes to the premises licence, they must make an application to the licensing authority and the police. Any changes will be measured against the licensing objectives. Local residents, businesses and other experts will have the right to make representations about the changes. A hearing may result and the decision to adopt, reject or amend the proposals will be made by the licensing authority.

Notice must be given of any changes of ownership or control of the pub to both the licensing authority and chief officer of police. Applicants must be at least 18 years old. In cases where the chief officer of police believes that the transfer may undermine the crime prevention objectives, the police may object to the transfer.

The premises licence must be displayed in a prominent place in the pub.

DESIGNATED PREMISES SUPERVISOR

Each pub must have a designated premises supervisor (DPS) who will be a point of contact for the licensing authorities, the police or fire services if problems occur at the premises. As such, they are named on the premises licence. The designated premises supervisor must hold a personal licence and will generally be the person in day-to-day control of the pub.

The designated premises supervisor is responsible for authorising every supply of alcohol at the pub, but this does not mean they have to be personally present at every transaction. They give authority to other members of staff to make sales. Neither is a designated premises supervisor required to be on the premises at all times. They can leave the premises in the hands of staff as long as they are contactable should problems arise. However, it should be remembered that the designated premises supervisor and the holder of the premises licence may be held responsible where staff are caught committing an offence under the Licensing Act.

PERSONAL LICENCE

A personal licence allows the holder to sell alcohol for consumption on or off any premises covered by a premises licence. The licence is portable and lasts for 10 years, after which it can be renewed for a further 10. To qualify for a personal licence, an applicant must meet certain criteria laid out by the Licensing Act:

◆ The applicant must be over 18 years old.
◆ They must not have had a personal licence forfeited within the previous 5 years.
◆ They must possess an accredited licensing qualification.
◆ They must not have been convicted of any relevant or foreign offence.

Where the applicant fulfils all these criteria, the licensing authority must grant the application. If any of the first 3 requirements are not met, the application must be rejected. Where an applicant has been convicted of any relevant or foreign offence, the licensing authority must notify the chief officer of police, who may object to the application. In the case of a police objection, the normal procedure would be to reject the application, unless there are exceptional and compelling circumstances which justify granting it. If the police do not object, and the application meets the other requirements of the Licensing Act, the application must be granted.

CRIMINAL RECORDS CHECKS

All applicants are required to produce a Criminal Records Bureau Certificate to the licensing authority. All applicants must disclose whether they have been convicted outside England and Wales of a relevant offence or equivalent foreign offence.

 Any UK resident can obtain a criminal record check from the Criminal Records Bureau. They can be contacted by telephoning: 0870 90 90 844. More details are available on their website: www.crb.homeoffice.gov.uk

Under the Data Protection Act, you can also request that the police provide you with details of any information about you, held on the Police National Computer. Contact your local police station for more details about this procedure.

What are 'relevant offences'

Relevant offences include:

◆ Serious crime, including theft, burglary, firearms, violence and handling stolen goods.
◆ Serious dishonesty, including deception, false accounting, fraudulent evasion of duty, forgery and counterfeiting.
◆ Misuse of drugs, including production, supply and possession.
◆ Certain sexual offences.

◆ Offences under the Licensing Act 2003 or previous acts relating to licensing.

◆ Certain offences under the Trades Descriptions Act 1968, relating to alcohol.

◆ Certain offences under the Road Traffic Act 1988, involving drugs or alcohol.

 The above list of offences is not exhaustive and you are advised to discuss what may constitute a relevant offence with your solicitor before making your application for a personal licence.

CONVICTIONS WHILE HOLDING A PERSONAL LICENCE

If you are convicted of a relevant or foreign offence after you have been granted your personal licence, you are required to notify the court that you are a personal licence holder. You must also notify the licensing authority, who will notify the chief officer of police. If the police consider that continuing the licence would undermine the crime prevention objective, they may well insist on a hearing that could lead to the licence being revoked.

THE LAW RELATING TO HOURS OF OPENING

The Licensing Act 2003 allows flexible closing times rather than the fixed times that used to apply. It allows the possibility of the premises remaining open for up to 24 hours (if a publican felt that this was commercially viable). The actual hours of opening that are granted by the licensing authority will take into account the impact on local residents, businesses and the expert opinion of various authorities in relation to the licensing objectives. If no objections are raised, then the hours will be granted. Where there are objections, the licensing authority has discretion to determine what opening hours to allow.

THE LAW RELATING TO THE PROVISION OF ENTERTAINMENT

Under the new licensing system, the premises licence covers the provision of regulated entertainment. This replaces the old procedure of applying for a separate public entertainment licence. A pub providing this type of entertainment must have this incorporated into its operating statement. This would have been submitted with the original premises licence application and can only be varied through a formal application for variation.

Regulated entertainment covers the provision of entertainment or of entertainment facilities. Entertainment includes:

◆ live music;
◆ any playing of recorded music;
◆ performance of dance;
◆ indoor sporting events;
◆ boxing or wrestling events;
◆ showing of films;
◆ any entertainment of a similar description to live music, recorded music or dance.

'Entertainment facilities' are facilities enabling people to take part in entertainment. This includes:

◆ making music;
◆ dancing;
◆ entertainment of a similar description to making music or dancing.

An example of an entertainment facility is a dance floor.

Live broadcast entertainment, for example showing broadcast TV, is exempt from the regulations. Playing recorded music that is incidental to other activities, for example a jukebox, would also be excluded. However, having a jukebox where a dance floor is also provided would fall within the requirements. A disc jockey would be regarded as regulated entertainment too. Pub games like darts and pool would not normally need to be authorised, unless played for the entertainment of an audience. Exhibition darts matches or championships staged for spectators would be considered regulated entertainment.

The consequence of not obtaining a licence to cover regulated entertainment, and being convicted, is a fine of up to £20,000 or imprisonment of up to 6 months.

THE LAW RELATING TO CHILDREN IN PUBLIC HOUSES

The Licensing Act 2003 updates the law relating to children in pubs. The new law aims at closing the loopholes and inadequacies of previous legislation, while allowing under-18s access into licensed premises in a safe, family-friendly way.

The legal drinking age remains 18 years of age. The only exception is that 16- and 17-year-olds can drink beer, wine or cider with a table meal while being accompanied by an adult (a person aged 18 or over).

Under the Licensing Act 2003, it is an offence to:

◆ Allow children under 16 on relevant premises that are used exclusively or primarily for the supply of alcohol, if they are not accompanied by an adult (and the premises are open for the sale of alcohol).
◆ Allow an unaccompanied child under 16 to be on relevant premises between the hours of midnight and 5am, when the premises are open for the supply and consumption of alcohol.

Other offences under the Licensing Act 2003 include:

◆ Purchasing or attempting to purchase alcohol for consumption by a child (with the exception of purchasing beer, wine or cider as part of a table meal).
◆ Buying or attempting to buy alcohol by a child.

The prohibitions on unaccompanied children aged under 16 also extend to beer gardens and outside terraces, and not just the bar area.

Where a publican is found to have committed an offence of selling alcohol to children, they may have a defence if they believed that the purchaser was 18 or over *and* they took all reasonable steps to establish the purchaser's age, or that nobody could reasonably have suspected from the purchaser's appearance that they were under 18. A second defence would be where the purchaser looked exceptionally old for his age.

A reliable proof of age card can make the job of checking a young customer's age easier. The Government supports the PASS (Proof of Age Standards Scheme), which approves and accredits proof of age schemes in the UK. It is backed by major retailers and representatives of the licensed trade and its continued promotion and development is encouraged.

Temporary events notices

Temporary events notices (TENs) can be used for the temporary sale or supply of alcohol, provision of regulated entertainment or the provision of late night refreshment, at premises which are not authorised by a premises licence. The licensing authority and the police must be notified of the event at least 10 working days before the event, and the following conditions apply:

◆ A personal licence holder may use a TEN up to 50 times per year.
◆ The number of times a TEN can be given in respect of particular premises is 12 times per calendar year.
◆ The length of time a TEN may last is 96 hours.
◆ The maximum aggregate duration of the periods covered by TENs at any individual premises is 15 days.
◆ The scale of the event in terms of the maximum number of people attending at any one time is 499.

OTHER OFFENCES UNDER THE LICENSING ACT 2003

It is an offence to carry on, or attempt to carry on, a licensable activity without the authorisation provided by a premises licence. An example of this would be endeavouring to sell alcohol without the required premises licence. Up to six months' imprisonment or a fine of up to £20,000 is the penalty for being convicted of this offence.

An offence also occurs where any person working in licensed premises knowingly allows disorderly conduct on the premises (and they work in a capacity which allows them to prevent the conduct). The holder of the premises licence and the designated premises supervisor may also be held responsible. A fine of up to £1,000 applies to this offence.

It is an offence to sell, or attempt to sell, alcohol to a person who is drunk. It is also an offence to obtain alcohol for a person who is drunk. Fines of up to £1,000 are applicable to anyone convicted of these offences.

ALCOHOL-RELATED DISORDER AND POLICE POWERS

The Licensing Act 2003 expands powers of the courts, on application by the police, to close premises within a specified geographical area where disorder is occurring or is anticipated.

Problem premises can be targeted for a review of their licence, by the licensing authority, on grounds relating to any of the 4 licensing objectives. A range of measures may be imposed, including temporary or permanent reduction in their hours of trading, reduction in licensable activities, removal of designated premises supervisors and the revocation of the licence.

THE SITUATION IN SCOTLAND

The Nicholson Committee was established by the Scottish Executive in 2001 to undertake an independent review of Scotland's licensing law. The committee reported their findings in 2003, making a number of recommendations. These would bring Scottish licensing law broadly into line with that of England and Wales. Key recommendations were:

◆ Abolition of the system of 7 different types of licence and the introduction of a single premises licence.
◆ Creation of a personal licence that remains in force for 10 years.

- Abolition of existing permitted hours of opening.
- Mandatory training for all personal licence holders.
- A ban on irresponsible promotions that encourage excessive alcohol consumption.
- Introduction of a national proof of age card.
- Changes to the law relating to children's access to licensed premises but retaining the 18 age limit for consumption of alcohol.

New Scottish licensing laws will be introduced in the near future. In the meantime, regulations under the Licensing (Scotland) Act 1976 (as amended), remain in force.

THE SITUATION IN NORTHERN IRELAND

Northern Ireland has its own licensing laws made under the Licensing (Northern Ireland) Order 1996. A consultation paper, *Liquor Licensing – The Way Forward*, was launched by David Hanson MP on 1 November 2005, setting out the Government's proposals for the reform of liquor licensing in Northern Ireland and the consultation period lasted until 31 January 2006.

Obtaining a licence
Applications for liquor licences are made via the county court. A licence will be granted if the following criteria are met:

- The applicant must hand in an old licence to obtain a new licence.
- The applicant must prove their fitness to hold a licence (character, reputation, financial standing, qualifications and experience).
- The applicant must prove there is a need for the licensed premises in the area.

Objections to applications
The following may object to the granting of a licence:

- the police;
- the district council;

◆ any person who owns, conducts business or resides in the vicinity of the premises.

Renewal and suspension of licences

Once granted, the liquor licence remains in force until the end of the licensing period, which lasts for 5 years. Where the court considers that a premise is no longer a suitable venue to sell alcohol, they will suspend the licence. An example of this would be where the premises are causing disturbance to the general public.

Opening hours

Standard permitted opening hours are:

Weekdays	11.00am until 11.00pm
Good Friday	5.00pm until 11.00pm
Sunday and Christmas Day	12.30pm until 10.00pm

Drinking-up time of 30 minutes is permitted at the end of these periods.

The court may grant additional hours, where these will not cause undue inconvenience to people living in the vicinity, and the premises provide food or entertainment on a regular basis, which continues during the additional opening hours.

Young people

In general, young people under the age of 18 are not allowed in any area of licensed premises that is used mainly or exclusively for the sale or consumption of alcohol. There are some circumstances where a minor can be present, these are:

◆ If they are with an adult who is responsible for them.
◆ If they are the child of the licensee.
◆ If they are 16 years old and have a written contract of employment to work there or are receiving training under a recognised scheme.

- Where the court has granted a Children's Certificate, allowing children to be present until 9.00pm (or 9.30pm when they or the adult are consuming a meal purchased before 9.30pm).
  And:
- They sit at a table away from the bar.

Offences under Licensing (Northern Ireland) Order 1996

It is an offence for a licence holder to:

- sell or supply alcohol outside the permitted hours;
- allow a person whom they know to be under 18 to be present or consume alcohol in their licensed premises;
- allow any person whom they know to be drunk to be present in, buy or consume alcohol in their premises.

The penalty, if found guilty, is a fine and/or imprisonment of up to 6 months.

6

PLANNING FOR SUCCESS

THE BUSINESS PLAN

A business plan is a written document that formalises your ideas and objectives for the business. It covers the management, marketing and financial aspects of the business. It also sets out your objectives, and how you intend to achieve them, and these are backed up by profit and cash-flow forecasts.

WHY DO YOU NEED A BUSINESS PLAN?

There are several good reasons why you should take the time to prepare a business plan for your pub.

- ◆ The process of putting together a business plan means you must undertake research and consider all aspects of the business. This results in you gaining a greater understanding of the business.
- ◆ A well-prepared business plan is essential for raising some types of finance. A good business plan will give lenders confidence in you and your business.
- ◆ Breweries and pub companies may require a business plan as part of your application for a tenancy or new lease. An impressive business plan will give you an edge over other applicants.

◆ A business plan keeps you on track when you are operating the pub. It will enable you to plot your progress and can be a great motivator.

WHO SHOULD WRITE THE BUSINESS PLAN?

You can employ accountants and other business advisers to write a business plan for you. There can be advantages to this. They may have expertise in preparing business plans and it saves you time to do other things. It may also give the business plan added kudos in the eyes of some lenders if it has been prepared by an 'expert'.

Notwithstanding the above, there is no reason why you cannot prepare an excellent business plan yourself. The benefits of preparing your own business plan are a greater understanding of the business, added confidence and being able to justify your plan as being your own. When it comes to operating your business, you will be better prepared and have a greater belief in your business plan.

Doing your own business plan does not mean that you cannot seek professional assistance for some parts of it. An example of this is the financial forecasting, where it is wise to have an accountant prepare profit and cash-flow forecasts for you.

Whatever you decide about who should write your business plan, the most important thing is that you have one!

RESEARCH AND PREPARATION

A good business plan is well researched, ensuring that the information it contains is based on fact, not guesswork. The SWOT analysis, discussed in Chapter 3, *Finding the Right Pub*, is essential research that should be included in your business plan. Early SWOT analyses can be made more thorough with further research, building up as you gain more knowledge about the pub and its environment.

Your own skills and experience are important and should be included in your business plan. This helps to identify key strengths and how roles will be organised to run the business effectively. Look again at Chapter 1, *All About You*, to help you with this.

WHAT IS INCLUDED IN THE BUSINESS PLAN?

A suggested format for your business plan is as follows:

- summary;
- the pub;
- the environment;
- your plans to develop the business;
- marketing;
- management of the business;
- financial forecasts.

Each section is discussed below.

Summary

A well-written summary ignites the reader's interest. It should be logical, factual and summarise the key factors about your business. It may also present requirements for any additional finance that may be necessary. The summary will include succinct details of the following:

- **The pub**: type of operation, whether tenancy, lease or freehold; description of facilities; clientele; key strengths of the pub.
- **The environment**: location; summary of catchment area; analysis of the market; trends; environmental opportunities.
- **Your plans to develop the business**: how you will increase sales; improve profit margins; cut costs or introduce new income streams, such as food or accommodation etc.
- **Marketing**: who your target customers are; how you will promote the business, such as advertising, word of mouth, public relations etc.
- **Management of the business**: your own skills and experience; qualifications; staff and how you will organise roles.
- **Financial forecasts**: ingoing costs; breakeven; profit forecast; how you

will fund the business and whether you require any additional funds to cover the cost of ingoing, or any development plans.

These sections are covered in more detail in the body of the business plan, with at least a page of information on each. Additional pages will be required for your 12-month profit and cash-flow forecasts.

The pub

The purpose of this section is to give the reader an understanding of the type of pub you are intending to run. You need to describe the pub and the facilities that it has available and whether the pub is tenancy, lease or freehold. You should explain what type of clientele the pub attracts, where it comes from and why it uses the pub. A potted history of the pub's recent past may be useful too. Turnover, barrelage figures and rent, if applicable, can be included in this section. You can often find some of this information in the particulars that breweries, pub companies and business agents send out, for pubs that are to let or for sale.

Take some good quality photographs of the pub and include them in this section.

You must give an honest assessment of the pub's strengths and weaknesses. It is important to demonstrate that you have taken time to look at the pub objectively and considered both its positive and negative aspects. You should show how you can maximise the pub's strengths and manage or overcome its weaknesses.

The environment

This section can include both the micro environment in which the pub operates and the macro environment, ie the wider influences that may affect the business. An example of a pub's micro environment would be its catchment area, including local housing, competitors and other businesses. A pub's macro environment includes the social, economic, political and legal issues that may affect the business. Examples of these would be growing trends to eat out (social) or smoking bans in public places (legal). A good source of macro environmental issues is the trade press, which often covers these and explains how they will impact on the licensed trade.

It is important to understand how changes to both the micro and macro environments may affect your business. These changes can be positive or negative and should have been identified in your SWOT analysis as opportunities and threats. Some areas to monitor are:

◆ competitors;
◆ the building and development of properties;
◆ changes to road systems;
◆ local employment issues;
◆ new businesses;
◆ alternative leisure businesses.

The local press, council offices and the public library are good places to gather this type of information.

Your plans to develop the business

You should have a plan on how you aim to develop the business by building on existing strengths and exploiting any opportunities that are available. The overall objective is to earn more profit, and in simple terms, this is done by increasing turnover and/or cutting costs. Examples of ways to develop the business can include:

◆ food, or further increasing the food trade;
◆ accommodation;
◆ new products;
◆ new facilities;
◆ new income streams;
◆ promoting high-profit margin products;
◆ increasing gross-profit margins;
◆ more efficient purchasing arrangements;
◆ encouraging new customers to use the pub;

◆ encouraging existing clientele to spend more;

◆ better cost control;

◆ reducing wastage.

Your development plan should have clearly set objectives. These should follow the SMART acronym and be:

S	**S**pecific (exactly what you are intending to do)
M	**M**easurable (what you aim to achieve in money terms)
A	**A**chievable (how you are capable of achieving it)
R	**R**ealistic (whether you have the resources to succeed)
T	**T**ime based (exactly when you want to achieve it)

Set a SMART objective for each of your development ideas against which you can track your progress.

 Once you are in your pub, transfer your smart objectives onto a wall chart in your office to make sure you are constantly reminded of them.

Marketing

Marketing is a means of communicating to customers and potential customers. The aim of marketing is to satisfy customers' needs and at the same time make a profit.

This section of the business plan should explain how the pub currently serves the needs of its customers and what opportunities there are for attracting more customers or getting the existing customers to spend more. It also needs to identify who your target customers are and how you can influence them. In order to do this you must have a good understanding of what they want and when they want it. The next step is to make sure that what you are offering is attractive to your target customers. You then have to find ways of communicating this to them. Your plans for marketing the pub should be well researched and have SMART objectives.

See Chapter 14, *Marketing*, for more information on this subject.

Management of the business

The most important parts of a business are its people, and above anything else, it is the people running the pub, that are crucial to its success.

This section should focus on your skills, abilities and experience and include any past examples of your successes, qualifications and areas of expertise. It should demonstrate how you will play a positive part in building the business.

You should also show how you divide the responsibilities in order to best utilise your skills and operate the pub effectively. Staff should also be discussed, including any key staff that may be important to achieving your objectives. (An example of this would be a food pub with a highly prized chef.) It should also cover any contingency plans, when people are unable to fulfil their roles or decide to leave the business.

The aim of this section of your business plan is to give the reader confidence in you and convince them that you are capable of making a success of the pub.

Prepare a short CV that highlights your skills and any relevant experience. This can be added to the appendix of the business plan.

Financial forecasts

This section is where you translate your business into hard cash. It shows how much profit you are likely to generate and your cash-flow forecasts. It is the section that will be scrutinised by lenders when you wish to borrow money. It will also be your budget and a means of measuring your performance. As a result, your financial forecasts should be thorough and well researched. Any errors or omissions could have a major effect on your business.

Profit and cash-flow forecasts should cover a minimum of twelve months and show the position broken down month by month for this period. The profit forecast shows the amount of profit (or loss) you predict to make on a monthly basis and excludes VAT, as this does not directly affect the profitability of the business. Costs are usually apportioned equally over the twelve-month period. For example, an annual rent of £12,000 (excluding VAT) will be divided over the year at £1,000 per month.

An example of a profit and loss statement is given in the Appendix.

A cash-flow forecast shows the business's requirement for cash on a monthly basis, over a twelve-month period. It shows the inflows and outflows of cash of the business. Figures are entered into the month when the money is due to be received or paid out and includes VAT. For example, if your annual insurance payment is due in February, the full amount payable would be entered in the column for the month of February. Any VAT or tax payable would be shown in the months that they are due to be paid.

An example of a cash-flow forecast is given in the Appendix.

 Use an accountant to help prepare your financial forecasts.

Where copies of audited accounts are available, these should be included in this section of your business plan, together with any supporting trading information like barrelage figures etc.

Supplementary information

A small number of photos is a useful addition to your business plan. The pub and its main facilities should be included together with a photo of its position. Other information, like location maps, menus, price lists and CVs can be added in the business plan appendix. This keeps the body of the business plan free of clutter.

PRESENTATION OF YOUR BUSINESS PLAN

The presentation of your business plan is important when you are trying to gain the confidence of lenders or recruiters. A well-typed document, with a small number of photographs, and presented in a folder will give it a professional look. Remember that your personal presentation is just as important as a good business plan. Make sure that how you look and present yourself is equally professional.

7

APPLYING FOR A TENANCY OR NEW LEASE

BREWERIES AND PUB COMPANIES

Over the last 15 years the licensed trade has gone through many changes, mainly as a result of the Monopolies and Mergers Commission investigation into its activities, and subsequent legislation – *The Supply of Beer (Loan Ties, Licensed Premises and Wholesale Prices) Order 1989* and *The Supply of Beer (Tied Estate) Order 1989*. The Monopolies Commission had concluded that the major brewers of the time had a stranglehold over the industry and as a result consumer choice was severely limited, and independent producers and wholesalers were unable to compete. The Government issued the 'beer orders' which required brewers with over 2000 pubs, to release from the tie half of the surplus over 2000 pubs, creating 11,000 more free houses. The national brewers were required to allow their licensees freedom to purchase non-beer drinks from any source and sell at least one cask beer. The result has been a complete shake-up of the industry, with several brewers selling their pubs to focus on other activities, and mergers between brewers. Of the original major brewers, only Scottish and Newcastle currently have a significant pub estate remaining. In response to the new shape of the industry and more appropriate legislation to cover the situation, the beer orders were revoked in 2003.

The changes have led to the growth of pub company businesses, who now dominate the industry. Many own large numbers of pubs. In 2005, the top 3 pub companies owned one third of total UK pubs. These operators have steadily increased their pub estates through acquisition over recent years and this trend is likely to continue.

HOW PUB VACANCIES ARE FILLED

When a tenant hands in their notice or their agreement expires, it is the responsibility of the Business Development Manager/Area Manager to find a new tenant or lessee for the pub. The tenancy and lease recruitment department will be notified of the vacancy, and will prepare 'pub particulars', similar to an estate agent's house sale particulars. These will normally give details of estimated ingoing capital required, trading information, and sometimes, annual rent. Details are sent to enquirers and will also be circulated to people who are registered with the brewery or pub company. This information may be displayed on the brewery or pub company website, under their pub vacancy section.

Applications for the pub will be invited and are compiled by the recruitment department. These will then be passed on to the Business Development Manager/Area Manager. They will know the pub well and have a good understanding of the skills, experience and financial resources that a new licensee for the pub will need. Then, they will arrange interviews for anyone who fits the requirements for the pub.

At the same time, the Business Development Manager/Area Manager, who is likely to have access to a database of suitable applicants (a talent bank) held by the brewery or pub company, will contact directly people who may be suitable, and invite them to apply for the vacancy. The manager may also approach existing tenants who they think may be interested in taking on a new pub.

THE ROLE OF THE BUSINESS DEVELOPMENT MANAGER/AREA MANAGER

The role of a Business Development Manager/Area Manger is to maximise sales, and the profit and return on investment for the brewery or pub company, from the pubs that he is responsible for. They will typically have between 40 and 60 pubs under their control which they would be expected to visit on a 4–8 week cycle. The more pubs they have, the less time they have available to support licensees and deal with issues at the pubs.

Along with their responsibility to recruit new licensees, their other duties include:

◆ setting rents;
◆ forecasting and budgeting;
◆ preparing business plans;
◆ dealing with repair issues;
◆ handling licensing issues;
◆ capital development;
◆ marketing and promotions;
◆ providing business advice;
◆ enforcing the tie;
◆ credit control;
◆ training and coaching;
◆ selling new products.

Because of their wide-ranging responsibilities, there is often a great deal of pressure to fill vacancies quickly. A vacancy is often regarded as a problem that needs to be fixed as soon as possible. Presenting yourself as a means of solving this problem is the key to being successful in the recruitment process.

REGISTERING WITH A BREWERY OR PUB COMPANY

The recommended approach is to register with several breweries or pub companies who have pubs in the area you are interested in. Your initial contact is likely to be with a member of the tenancy and lease recruitment department. Take time to talk with them and obtain details of their name and a direct telephone number if possible (they can be a useful contact for you). They will take some brief details from you and will send you an application form and information pack.

APPLICATION FORMS

Your application form is important as it gives a recruiter a first impression of you. Once you receive the application form, it is worth taking time to read it through and think about any questions you are asked. Complete the form neatly and thoroughly and ensure that you use all the available space on the form to make a good impression. Untidy and incomplete application forms will not impress recruiters. There will be a number of questions about your financial situation, which you will need to complete honestly and completely. Completing this section with phrases like 'sufficient capital available' will not help your application. Before you complete the form, you should have an understanding of how you intend to fund the business. You will be required to provide evidence of your capital at the interview stage. This does not mean that you should rush out and obtain a loan, if you require additional finance. But it does mean that you will need to have investigated your ability to raise the required money and perhaps been given an agreement in principle from a lender.

Add a photograph of yourself (or -selves) to the form and make sure it's a good one, not one that looks like a police mugshot!

INTERVIEWS

Breweries and pub companies normally run two types of interview – a general or preliminary interview, and a pub-specific interview. General interviews are for applicants who have registered with the brewery or pub company, but who have not yet applied for a specific pub vacancy. These interviews may be conducted by the recruitment department or a Business Development Manager/Area Manager, or both. The purpose of this interview is to see if you have the general skills, abilities and personality to operate a pub. It also establishes your financial position.

The outcome of this interview will be either that you are added to the brewery or pub company database of prospective licensees, or be advised that you do not meet the required criteria. Anyone on the database will normally be kept up to date on which pubs are available.

Pub-specific interviews are aimed at filling specific pub vacancies. Applicants applying for individual pubs may have already had a general interview or this interview may be their first. The interview will be carried out by the Business Development Manager/Area Manager who is respons-ible for the pub. They will decide who is offered the pub, based on these interviews. Where there are two candidates who are closely matched, a further meeting may take place, before a final decision is made.

Here are some interview tips:

- Present yourself as the solution to the Business Development Manager/ Area Manager's problem.
- Research the pub and area well.
- Prepare a business plan for the pub.
- Ensure that you are clear about how you will fund the business.
- Bring confirmation of your financial position (bank statements etc), plus any letters from lenders agreeing in principle to provide additional finance.
- Turn up a little early.
- Be smart and well presented.
- Prepare for any questions that you may be asked.
- Ask for confirmation of barrelage and rent figures.
- Ask why the vacancy has occurred.
- Ask whether there are any major issues about the pub that you should be aware of.
- Clarify anything you are unsure about.
- Try to relax – Business Development Managers/Area Managers tend to be easy-going people; the interview should not be too gruelling!

NEGOTIATING TERMS

The interview with the Business Development Manager/Area Manager is an opportunity to discuss the main terms of the agreement, such as repairs and rent. If you feel that the initial rent is too high or there is a number of outstanding repairs, it is worth asking whether the brewery or pub company would consider providing some additional support for a new tenant or lessee, such as reducing the rent for a set period, agreeing to complete any major repairs or spreading the cost of fixtures and fittings etc. The best approach is to seek support and not make demands, which is likely to put you in a negative light.

BEING OFFERED THE PUB

You could be verbally offered the pub at the end of the interview or you may have to wait until other interviews have taken place, and be contacted later. A written offer should follow, which you will need to sign to confirm that you wish to go ahead. This outlines the major terms of the agreement, including annual rent. The letter will be subject to contract, which means that it is not binding until a tenancy or lease has actually been signed. It is good practice to send you a draft copy of the agreement with this letter; if you are not sent a copy, you should ask for one. This gives you the chance to read through the agreement (or seek advice) so that you fully understand it.

VIEWING THE PUB

It is important to view the pub thoroughly, including the domestic accommodation, before signing the tenancy or lease. It is an opportunity to raise any concerns you may have with the Business Development Manager/Area Manager. Make sure that any promises made by them are put in writing to you, prior to you signing. (See the 'Repairs' section below.)

FIXTURES AND FITTINGS AND STOCK

Any figures quoted by the Business Development Manager/Area Manager relating to the value of the fixtures and fittings and stock will be estimates.

The valuation of these items takes place on the day you move into the pub. The actual valuation could be higher or lower than quoted and you need to budget for the possibility of paying more than the estimated figures. This may involve finding additional capital or gaining support from the brewery or pub company to help finance the difference.

REPAIRS AND NEW LEASES

In the case of new leases, repairs need special attention. The lease may well be 'fully repairing', which means that once you sign it, the responsibility for all repairs at the pub will be yours. This may include a requirement for you to repair any faults or damage that you inherit when you take on the pub.

Prior to signing a lease with these terms, you should obtain your own independent assessment of the premises, via a structural survey report and any additional reports (eg electrical tests, etc) that your surveyor may recommend. You need to discuss the findings with the Business Development Manager/Area Manager and make sure that any verbal assurances are put in writing before you sign the lease. Where there are significant repair issues, the following options could apply:

- ◆ **Option 1**: The brewery or pub company agrees to undertake all repairs over an agreed timescale.
- ◆ **Option 2**: You agree to make repairs for a reduction in rent or at the quoted rent.
- ◆ **Option 3**: Your responsibility for these repairs is removed and agreed in writing (and the repairs are not completed).

Option 1 is the best solution for the new lessee, as the cost will be borne by the brewery or pub company. How good option 2 is for a new lessee will depend on the cost of the repairs versus the reduction in rent. There is also the inconvenience factor of having to organise the repairs yourself. (However, you may be told that the rent quoted was set to reflect the current state of the premises, and therefore no rent concession is available.) Option 3, while removing liability for the repairs, leaves them undone, which is likely to cause a problem at a later stage if the issues worsen. It can also cause problems when the new lessee decides to sell their lease, affecting the price and leaving a subsequent lessee responsible for repairs (as the immunity from repairing these may not be applicable to them).

REPAIRS AND TENANCIES

There is a much lower obligation for a tenant to repair their pub, usually restricted to internal and minor repairs. Major repairs and structural problems will normally be the task of the brewery or pub company. However, pubs can sometimes be left in a poor state of repair by previous tenants and this causes problems for new tenants. This is particularly prevalent in the domestic accommodation, which is often neglected. While these are often decorative problems, there can be poor quality carpeting and other damage. As well as a financial burden, these can be a major source of stress and inconvenience. Where there are any problems in these areas they should be discussed with the Business Development Manager/ Area Manager. The ideal solution for the new tenant is that the brewery or pub company agrees to fix these.

OBTAINING PROMOTIONAL SUPPORT

After accepting the offer letter, but before signing the agreement, is a good time to discuss whether any promotional support can be provided to help build trade in the early stages. Business Development Managers/ Area Managers are usually able to send you free products, tee-shirts or promotion kits. They may also be able to assist you with other forms of marketing like press coverage, advertising or mailshots to customers. It is worth obtaining whatever additional support you can, to get you off to a flying start in your new pub.

OTHER FORMS OF SUPPORT

Along with the Business Development Manager/Area Manager, there are other brewery or pub company staff that can be very valuable to you. Property surveyors can advise you on a range of property issues, catering managers can advise you on menu development, and their machine controllers can help you with any amusement machine queries. Your Business Development Manager/Area Manager will advise as to who else in the organisation may be able to help you.

SETTING AN INGOING DATE

During the course of your discussions, you will need to agree an ingoing date. In some circumstances, this may be dictated by the previous tenant insisting on leaving on a particular date. Where you do have some flexibility over choosing a date, you need to bear in mind how many things you will need to organise before you move in. The timescale will also be heavily influenced by whether you are taking a tenancy, new lease, lease assignment or purchasing a freehold.

Taking a tenancy is the simplest and quickest procedure (not requiring a lengthy legal process or property surveys). New leases, assignments and freehold purchases can take between 8–12 weeks to complete. (Some breweries and pub companies allow you take the pub on a form of temporary tenancy beforehand while the lease is being dealt with behind the scenes.) Any requirement for additional finance will also take time to arrange. It is best to be realistic about how much time you need to get yourself prepared to take on your pub. It is a stressful time and being highly organised and calling on your support network for help will make things easier for you.

SIGNING THE AGREEMENT

Signing a tenancy agreement is normally done on the day of ingoing. The document will normally be brought to the pub by the Business Development Manager/Area Manager, who will ask you to sign it. (Make sure that you have previously received a copy and clearly understand the contents.) Check that the rent figures, any targets, and other key terms have been correctly entered into the document before you sign it.

Signing a new lease, or taking on an existing lease by assignment, will involve solicitors. You will be required to attend their office to sign the document and make payment. This can be done several days before the ingoing date. Completion of the lease will need to occur before you move in. This will be handled by your solicitor and the vendor's or brewery's or pub company's solicitor.

8

BUYING A FREEHOLD PROPERTY

BUYING THE FREEHOLD

Buying the freehold means purchasing the property outright, and in many ways the process is similar to buying a house. However, in the case of buying a pub, not only are you buying the bricks and mortar of the property but you are buying the business as well.

BEING PREPARED

Professional support

Before you start looking to buy your freehold property, you should ensure that you have a good accountant, solicitor and property surveyor in place. This saves time and focuses your efforts on looking for and purchasing your pub rather than juggling these tasks at the same time as trying to find good professional support. Having your professionals in place also means that you can respond more quickly once you find a potential purchase (see Chapter 9, *Professional Services*, for more details).

Financing the purchase

You must be clear about what financial resources you have available and whether you will need to raise additional money to fund your purchase (see Chapter 4, *Funding the Business*). There is no point in making an empty offer for a pub that you are unable to back up with sufficient funds. To avoid this, you should obtain an early agreement in principle from your lenders that the funds you require will be available to purchase a pub, subject to certain criteria and conditions being met. By doing this you will know what funds you are likely to have available.

FINDING YOUR FREEHOLD

Who will be selling?

In the majority of cases, the seller of the freehold pub will be a private individual who has decided to leave their business. Sellers normally appoint agents to act on their behalf to find buyers, in the same way that estate agents are employed to find house buyers. Some agents specialise in the licensed trade and most pubs are sold through a small number of well-known agents. An internet search, or a trawl through the licensed trade newspapers or *Dalton's Weekly* will identify who the main pub agents are.

Registering with agents

Once you have identified the main agents, it is useful to register with all of them. Many offer a national service and have pubs available throughout the UK. The agents will take details of the area and the type of pub you are interested in, together with the budget you are working to. Registering ensures that you are sent details of any pubs that match your requirements. It can also help if you telephone the agents from time to time, to keep up to date with developments and get advance warning of any pubs that may be being put up for sale in the near future. Your aim should be to help the agent get to know you as a person and not just as a name and address on their database. Building relationships with agents is an excellent way of finding the freehold property you are looking for.

Specific enquiries

If you see a specific pub that you are interested in, advertised through an agent you have not yet contacted, contact them immediately to register your interest and obtain more details about the pub. Good pubs tend to be sold quickly so time is often of the essence!

Private sales

Some individuals prefer to advertise their pubs for sale themselves rather than go through an agent and thus save the agent's fees. Occasionally you will see these pubs advertised in local newspapers or more frequently in *Dalton's Weekly*. In such cases, there will be no middleman and you will negotiate directly with the seller. This may be advantageous, and personal contact can make the whole process easier and quicker. However, some sellers may be too busy or disorganised for this to work satisfactorily and this could result in problems and delays.

ASSESSING DIFFERENT PUBS

Information you should obtain

When enquiring about any pub that is advertised through an agent or private individual, you should obtain as much information about it as possible. Ask for the following information:

- Copies of trading accounts.
- Whether the pub is still trading at the same levels as shown in the last accounts.
- Why the current owners are selling the pub.
- How long they have operated the pub.
- How quickly the owners wish to sell.
- How many staff are employed and whether any key employees will be leaving.
- What hours the pub currently opens.
- What scope there may be for future development.
- What facilities the pub has.
- Whether any offers have been received for the pub.
- Whether the asking price is negotiable.
- When you can view the pub.
- Whether there is anything else you should know about the pub or the area.

Appointments to view the pub

Viewing the pub involves visiting the pub to look throughout the entire premises. For pubs advertised through an agent, you should make all appointments to officially view the pub through them. Bypassing the agent and speaking direct to the seller is likely to annoy them both and should be avoided. In circumstances where the pub is being sold without using an agent, the only approach is to contact the seller directly.

When making appointments, try to arrange to view the pub as soon as possible; leaving it too long may result in someone having their offer accepted before you get a chance to view it. When arranging a time to view the pub, ask when it would be most convenient for the seller to spend some time with you to answer any questions you may have. Aim for a quiet time of the day, when there will be no distractions with customers or deliveries.

Ad hoc visits

In order to get a feel for a pub and the area in which it is located, you should visit the pub on several occasions. These should be at different times on different days of the week. During these visits, don't make it obvious that you are a potential buyer. Simply behave as a normal customer to gain insight into the clientele and how the pub operates.

Officially viewing the pub

Be aware that selling a pub can be stressful and the seller may feel under pressure while you inspect their business and home. With this in mind, be tactful and discreet when viewing.

Prepare a number of questions in advance that you would like to ask the seller or agent. Take time to look at all parts of the premises thoroughly and make lots of notes about the pub and its location afterwards.

Research and SWOT analysis

Back up your viewing with some detailed research of the area and prepare a SWOT analysis for the pub.

Financial viability

Assess the viability of the pub from the accounts that have been provided. Look at any options for increasing turnover and profitability. Consider any potential difficulties you may be faced with. Prepare profit and cash-flow forecasts and seek a professional opinion from your accountant.

Prepare a draft business plan

Prepare a draft business plan from the information you have been given and your initial ideas for the pub. This helps you evaluate the pub further and decide whether you want to make a formal offer. The draft business plan can later be developed into a detailed business plan if your offer is accepted.

Product range

The range of products that a pub offers is important to its success, and changing the product range can affect trade. This is particularly true in the case of draught beers and lagers where there can be significant loyalty for certain brands in some areas. Removing a popular brand and replacing it with a less popular one can reduce your sales. If you are planning to make these sorts of changes, perhaps to obtain a brewery loan, it is wise to consider the impact this might have on your turnover. Research the area thoroughly to establish which products have strong brand loyalty. Conversely, replacing poor performing brands with strong ones is an excellent way of building trade.

THE BUYING PROCESS

Making an offer

When you decide you would like to purchase a particular pub, you need to make an offer. This offer may be at the asking price or below it if there is room for negotiation. You should follow up any verbal offer in writing. Head your letter 'subject to contract' and include this phrase in any communication you have with the seller or agent. This ensures that you are not contractually bound by your offer or any other statements you make prior to signing the contract.

Acceptance

Once your offer is accepted, ask the seller to put it in writing and ascertain the name of the seller's solicitor who will be dealing with the sale.

Appointing your professionals

Instruct your solicitor to deal with the transaction and provide them with details of the seller's solicitor. Contact your property surveyor and arrange for them to prepare a full structural survey and valuation of the pub. Notify your accountant that your offer has been accepted and ask them for any further assistance you may need in preparing your detailed business plan or making your application for additional finance.

Arranging additional finance

Contact your lenders to arrange any additional finance that you may need and present them with your detailed business plan and a copy of the accounts for the pub. Because you have already obtained an agreement in principle for finance, this should make the process easier. Your lender will want to have the pub valued to ascertain that you are paying a realistic price and that there is sufficient security on which to secure the loan. They will generally appoint a surveyor to prepare the valuation report and charge the cost to you. The report will include several ways of valuing the pub, including its 'bricks and mortar', 'forced sale' and 'going concern' values. If you are using other property as collateral for a loan, this will need to be valued too.

Structural survey report

Your property surveyor will prepare a full structural survey for the pub for you. This is a 'warts and all' account of the state of the premises and can be a little daunting. Details of any major repairs should include an estimate of how much money it will take to remedy the problems. It should also include their assessment of the valuation of the pub.

Where the cost of repairs or the valuation is an issue, there is an opportunity to renegotiate the price you are willing to pay, and put in a revised offer taking these into account.

The initial legal steps

◆ The seller's solicitor draws up the contract and sends a copy to your solicitor.

◆ Your solicitor conducts searches with local government departments in order to establish whether there are any legal restraints, planning applications or other legal issues that might affect ownership.

◆ Your solicitor will request documentation from the seller's solicitor, including:

- proof that the seller owns the property;
- details of rights of way or restrictive covenants;
- planning permissions or building consents;
- electrical and gas safety tests;
- damp and woodwork guarantees;
- list of fixtures and fittings.

◆ Your solicitor also sends pre-contract enquiries to the seller's solicitor. These are in the form of a standard questionnaire about the premises to be answered by the seller.

Exchanging contracts

Once the initial legal steps have been satisfactorily completed, you are in a position to exchange contracts. You and the seller sign your copies of the contract and your solicitors exchange them. You are required to pay a deposit at this stage, which is normally 10% of the purchase price. Exchanging contracts is a very important stage since at this point, the contracts become binding, and if you pull out after this you will lose your deposit. A date is set for completing the sale, which can be the same day, but is more typically a couple of weeks later.

Completion

Completion is the date on which you pay for the pub and the seller hands over the keys. It is vital that you have all your funds available for this date. If you are borrowing additional money, your lender will have to arrange for this to be electronically transferred into your solicitor's 'client account'.

Waiting for the money to be transferred can be a nerve-wracking experience and there can sometimes be delays. Double check your solicitor's bank account details and contact your lender two or three days before, to ensure that they have all the correct details. If you are using any of your own money to make the purchase, you will have to pay it to your solicitor in the form of 'cleared funds', such as a banker's draft or bank transfer.

You will require sufficient funds to pay:

♦ the balance of the purchase price;
♦ Stamp Duty Land Tax on the transaction;
♦ solicitor's fees and disbursements.

Additional funds will be required to cover the cost of stock and glassware that will be valued separately. This is normally paid directly to the seller via your stocktaker.

Your solicitor then arranges for the sale to be registered at the Land Registry and for the seller's mortgage to be removed from the title (if applicable).

PRACTICAL ISSUES

Anticipated timescales

The whole process of raising additional finance and purchasing your pub typically takes between 8–12 weeks. At the outset, this does seem a long time but it passes very quickly. Do not be afraid to chase up your solicitor on a regular basis if necessary, to keep the process moving. Small delays here and there can mount up and put back the completion date if you are not careful. Be actively involved in the whole process and well organised. Make sure that you respond to any requests from your solicitor or lender promptly to prevent any delays on your part.

Contact with the seller

A good relationship with the seller can help the whole process move more smoothly. Any complications that arise are sometimes better resolved over a cup of tea with the seller, than by solicitors exchanging letters with each other. But remember to notify your solicitor of anything that has been discussed, so that they can ensure that you are not legally exposed.

In the days between exchange of contracts and completion, it is useful to spend time with the seller at the pub so that they can show you how the business works. It is a good time to become familiar with the pub and equipment, as well as getting to know the staff and some of the customers. It eases you into the business rather than being dropped in at the deep end on completion day.

A final word on buying a property in Scotland

The process of buying property in Scotland is different from the rest of the UK. If you are considering buying a pub in Scotland, you should take advice from a solicitor experienced in Scottish property transactions.

9

PROFESSIONAL SERVICES

WHY YOU NEED TO EMPLOY PROFESSIONALS

You need to employ a number of professionals to support you with acquiring and running your pub. They will help you with the tasks which you lack the expertise or time to do yourself. Good professional help will make your life easier and protect your interests. It is important to have a support network of professionals that you can rely on. Here are some general pointers when dealing with professionals:

♦ Be clear about what you want them to do for you.
♦ Clarify exactly what it will cost you.
♦ Make sure they fulfil your requirements.
♦ If you are not happy, speak to them.
♦ If you continue to be dissatisfied, use someone else.
♦ If you have any major concerns, speak to their regulatory body or Citizens Advice Bureau.

SOLICITORS

What they can help you with

This will depend on how you are intending to acquire your pub and on your needs while operating the pub. The following are circumstances where you may require their assistance:

106

- **Licensing**: to make applications for your personal licence and making any changes to the premises licence.
- **Tenancy advice**: although you may not need a solicitor to complete the tenancy agreement, you may prefer to ask a solicitor to explain the terms of the agreement to you.
- **New lease**: you are advised to use a solicitor to handle the completion of the lease on your behalf.
- **Assignments**: you should use a solicitor if buying (or selling) a lease by way of assignment.
- **Freehold**: you are advised to use a solicitor to handle the freehold purchase on your behalf.
- **Business structure**: assistance in setting up the business structure.
- **Finance**: advice on legal implications and drawing up loan agreements.
- **Drawing up partnership agreements**.
- **Other advice**: employment issues, regulations and legislation, disputes with the landlord.

Choosing a solicitor

The Law Society is the regulating and representative body for solicitors in England and Wales. The Law Society for Scotland and the Law Society of Northern Ireland are responsible for lawyers in Scotland and Northern Ireland, respectively. Their websites can be found at:

www.lawsociety.org.uk   (Law Society, England and Wales)
www.lawscot.org.uk   (Law Society for Scotland)
www.lawsoc-ni.org   (Law Society of Northern Ireland)

 The Law Society and the Law Society for Scotland websites have a search facility to help you find a solicitor in your area.

Solicitors tend to specialise in certain types of legal activity. Choose a solicitor that is experienced in the type of work you would like them to undertake for you. For example, select a solicitor who is used to handling leases for your new lease or assignment, and one with expertise in pub freehold transactions for purchasing a pub. Failing to use a solicitor with expertise in the area you require may result in delays, problems and increased legal costs.

Solicitors must hold a practising certificate issued by their respective Law Society. This guarantees that the solicitor is qualified and has insurance cover to protect you should things go wrong. Always check these before asking a solicitor to act on your behalf.

Solicitors' charges

Solicitors' charges vary and it is worth shopping around to get quotes from several solicitors. Bills are often calculated on an hourly basis but they should be able to provide you with an estimate of how much the bill is likely to be for the work they are going to be doing for you. You should be aware that any additional work they do for you will result in extra charges. It may be useful to set a budget figure with them and ask them to notify you if they are going to exceed it.

Other factors to consider

The location of the solicitor is important, particularly if you have to visit their offices regularly. Travelling long distances to meet with them takes up a great deal of time that could be better used organising the rest of your business. Other factors that may be important to you are that:

◆ your solicitor is accessible;
◆ they respond promptly to your queries and enquiries from solicitors acting for other parties;
◆ they explain things simply, rather than using legal jargon.

Check whether the firm provides any additional services that may be important to you, such as advice on employment law or taxation.

When dealing with a solicitor it is important to remember that they act on your behalf. So do not be afraid of tackling them about anything you are unhappy with. They are there to advise you of your legal position and will not make decisions for you. Sometimes it may be necessary for you to make a decision on a commercial or practical basis, rather than a strict legal one. The important thing is to listen to their advice and understand all the implications, prior to going ahead.

ACCOUNTANTS

What they can help you with

Accountants provide a range of services that can assist you both before and after you have taken on your pub. These are some of the areas that they can help you with:

◆ raising finance;
◆ preparing profit and cash-flow forecasts;
◆ advising you on taxation issues;
◆ advising you on different business structures;
◆ setting up your business;
◆ registering you for VAT and tax;
◆ VAT and tax returns;
◆ setting up your payroll system;
◆ providing monthly management accounts;
◆ preparing your year-end accounts.

Choosing an accountant

You need to be aware that anyone can call himself or herself an accountant. They may have no formal training or be regulated by a governing body. Professional accountants, on the other hand, are required to sit exams and prove their abilities over several years before qualifying. These are normally 'chartered' or 'certified' accountants and should be your choice when you want a professional adviser backed by a regulatory body.

Chartered accountants

In the England and Wales, chartered accountants qualify by passing exams that are set by the Institute of Chartered Accountants in England and Wales (ICAEW). Chartered accountants can be identified by the letters

ACA or FCA after their names. There are similar prerequisites in Scotland and Ireland where the Institute of Chartered Accountants of Scotland (ICAS) and the Institute of Chartered Accountants in Ireland (ICAI) are the respective regulatory bodies.

You can find chartered accountants via the following websites:

www.icaew.co.uk   (England and Wales)
www.icas.org.uk   (Scotland)
www.icai.ie   (Ireland)

Certified accountants

Certified accountants cover all types of financial work for a variety of organisations. They are identified by the letters ACCA or FCCA after their names. Qualifications are obtained by passing examinations set by the Association of Certified Accountants (ACCA). Though they can qualify without sitting a tax exam paper, many are also qualified as tax advisers. You can find details of certified accountants by visiting the association's website:

www.accaglobal.com   (England, Wales, Scotland and Ireland)

Other accountancy qualifications

Management accountants are usually employed by larger organisations and provide managers with information relating to the performance of the business and help with business planning, strategy and budgetary control. They qualify by passing examinations set by their regulatory body, the Chartered Institute of Management Accountants (CIMA). More information can be found on their website:

www.cimaglobal.com

Accounting technicians are not qualified accountants, but are required to pass examinations to be awarded the AAT qualification. They mainly work in supporting roles and have their own professional body, the Association of Accounting Technicians (AAT). You can find more details at:

www.aat.co.uk

Taxation qualifications

A chartered tax adviser (CTA) is a specialist in tax who has passed the Chartered Institute of Taxation (CIOT) qualification. Members use the letters CTA, FTII and ATII after their names. They provide specialist advice on taxation. For full details of their services and a members' directory visit their website:

www.tax.org.uk

Other factors to consider when choosing an accountant

As in the case of solicitors, it is sensible to choose an accountant who is located conveniently and also has experience in dealing with the licensed trade. Cost will be another aspect to consider and it is worth obtaining quotes from several accountants before finally choosing to appoint one. Your accountant's bill will be determined by how much work they do for you. If you do most of the day-to-day bookwork and maintain organised records, this will reduce your accountant's bill.

Monthly profitability

Many people make the mistake of engaging their accountant only to prepare their VAT returns and handle their year-end accounts and taxation. In this situation, your monthly profitability is not assessed and it can be over 12 months before you know whether you have made a profit or not, by which time it is too late to do anything about it!

A better solution is to ask your accountant to prepare monthly 'management' accounts that show your financial position and enable you to make adjustments on an ongoing basis. Though there will be extra costs for this additional service, it is particularly important for new licensees who are finding their feet. The frequency of these reports may be reduced to a quarterly basis, after the first six months of trading. Alternatively you can prepare these reports yourself if you have the necessary skills. Either way, it is essential to always be up to date with how your business is performing.

PROPERTY SURVEYORS

What they can help you with

You should use the services of a qualified property surveyor when acquiring a lease or purchasing a freehold property. They can help you by:

◆ Inspecting premises and providing you with a property survey.
◆ Preparing freehold and lease valuations.
◆ Assessing rents and dealing with any disputes.
◆ Undertaking rating valuations and appeals.

Chartered surveyors are qualified professionals and their regulatory body is the Royal Institute of Chartered Surveyors (RICS). You can find their website at: www.rics.org

Choosing a property surveyor

Choose a chartered surveyor who has experience in the licensed trade. In the case of obtaining a property survey or valuation, check that your surveyor will prepare the report promptly as any hold-ups may cause difficulties. Ask them to provide approximate costs for any repair works that they feel are necessary.

Other factors to consider

Fees vary, so it is wise to obtain quotes from several surveyors prior to appointing one. You can find contact details for chartered surveyors in your area on the Royal Institute of Chartered Surveyors website.

LICENSED TRADE VALUERS

What they can help you with

As the name suggests, licensed trade valuers specialise in the licensed trade. Their main services are:

◆ the valuation of leased and freehold properties;
◆ valuation of trade fixtures and fittings.

They may also provide other services like stocktaking, rent assessments, rating advice and arranging insurance cover.

Some are members of the Royal Institute of Chartered Surveyors. Others are members of various associations of licensed trade valuers, such as the Association of Valuers of Licensed Property. More information and member details can be found on their website: www.avlp.com

Valuation of fixtures and fittings

In the case of taking a tenancy or new lease, the trade fixtures and fittings will be valued on the day of ingoing by a licensed trade valuer. Both the seller (outgoing licensee) and the buyer (ingoing licensee) of fixtures and fittings are advised to have a valuer to act on their behalf. The brewery or pub company may insist that you use a valuer that they recognise. In the past the buyer and seller would each appoint a separate valuer. However, it is now common practice in many areas to use a single valuer, thereby enabling fees to be shared. Licensed trade valuers can also provide you with valuations of leases and freehold properties for both buyers and sellers.

Choosing a valuer

The brewery or pub company can normally provide details of recommended valuers. The outgoing tenant is likely to have details of who carried out the last valuation of fixtures and fittings, when they took on the pub.

You can search for a valuer in your area by using www.avlp.com

Other factors to consider

Fixtures and fittings valuation fees are based on a percentage of the fixtures and fittings value. Fees vary between valuers. As in the case of other professionals, shopping around will get you the best rates.

LICENSED TRADE STOCKTAKERS

What they can help you with

Stocktakers provide an essential service to the licensed trade. Their role is to value the stock you have in hand, calculate how much you have used, check your stock usage against your records, and calculate gross profit margins. They can spot stock losses including theft and wastage, and suggest how you can resolve these problems. They can assist you with pricing your products as well. You are advised to use them for the following:

◆ Valuing your stock on ingoing day.
◆ Providing you with a monthly stocktaking service and report.

Choosing a stocktaker

The brewery, pub company or other licensees are likely to be able to recommend good stocktakers in your area. The Institute of Licensed Trade Auditors is a body that represents stocktakers in the UK and Republic of Ireland. It has over 400 members and provides training for new stocktakers. Members use the letters FILSA or MILSA after their names to signify that they are qualified members of the Institute. Their website: www.iltsa.co.uk provides more information and lists of stocktakers by region.

Other factors to consider

Most stocktakers these days use laptop or handheld computers to help them take stock and provide a stock report for their clients. It is very useful to have a report prepared on the same day that the stocktaker is on site, rather than it be sent to you later. A good stocktaker will discuss the report with you and make recommendations. The reports can be quite complex and it is worth taking time to ask your stocktaker to explain them to you.

 A stock report has little value if you don't understand it.

Choosing a stocktaker that operates in your geographical area is beneficial. Not only will contact be easier, but they will also know the local market, which is useful when considering what prices to charge and which products sell well in the area.

LICENSED TRADE ORGANISATIONS

Licensed trade organisations provide advice, information, training and support to their members. Two well-respected organisations that you should consider joining are:

◆ The British Institute if Innkeeping (BII) – see www.bii.org
◆ The Federation of Licensed Victuallers Associations (FLVA) – see www.flva.co.uk

10

BUSINESS STRUCTURE

THE LEGAL STRUCTURE OF YOUR BUSINESS

The different types of structure

There are four main types of legal structure that can be used when setting up in business. These are:

◆ sole trader;
◆ partnership;
◆ limited liability partnership;
◆ limited liability company.

Choosing which legal structure to use needs careful consideration and you are recommended to seek professional advice from an accountant or solicitor about this. They will inform you which business structure would best suit your circumstances and can make all necessary arrangements for setting up the business correctly.

How the business structure will affect you

The business structure will affect:

◆ How much tax and National Insurance you pay.
◆ What accounts you have to keep and submit.

- What other records you have to maintain.
- Your financial liability for the business.
- Who you have to register the business with.
- How you can raise money.
- How major decisions are made in the business.
- Which regulations will apply to the business.

It is therefore important to obtain the right advice before deciding on what type of legal structure to adopt for your business. The next section gives a brief overview of the four main types of structure together with the pros and cons of each.

SOLE TRADER

The simplest way of starting a business is to become a sole trader and many licensees use this type of business structure. Being a sole trader doesn't mean you have to run the business single-handedly – you *can* employ staff! In the case of a couple running a pub, one person can be registered as the sole trader (and self-employed) and the other will be considered as staff (employed).

Pros

- Quick and easy to set up.
- Registration fees are not applicable.
- Only simple, unaudited accounts are required.
- You make all the decisions about the business yourself.
- Any profits go to you.

Cons

- You are personally responsible for any business debts.
- You need to raise any money for the business yourself.
- You are entitled to fewer social security benefits than if you were employed.

Tax and National Insurance

As a sole trader, your profits are taxed as income. You will pay fixed rate Class 2 National Insurance contributions and Class 4 contributions on your profits. You have to make an annual self-assessment return to HM Revenue and Customs.

PARTNERSHIP

A partnership is where two or more people run a business and share the decision-making responsibilities, business risks and costs. Each partner is regarded as self-employed. A partnership is another popular way of operating a public house business, especially for husband and wife arrangements.

Pros

◆ Can be set up with few formalities.
◆ Each partner shares any profits.
◆ Decisions are shared.
◆ Expertise can be shared and risks spread.
◆ Money can be raised by introducing new partners – 'sleeping' partners may contribute money without being involved in running the business.

Cons

◆ Each partner is personally liable for the business debts even if incurred by another partner.
◆ Partnerships can be dissolved through disputes or the resignation, death or bankruptcy of a partner.
◆ Problems can occur where partners are incompatible.

PARTNERSHIP AGREEMENTS

Partnerships should have a written agreement drawn up that gives details of how the partnership will work. This is just as important in the case of married couples and family partnerships, as it is with any other form of partnership. The partnership agreement will include:

- how much money is to be invested by each partner;
- how profits will be shared;
- how much time each partner is to contribute;
- what spending limits apply;
- what process needs to be followed if partners want, or need to reduce their involvement in the business.

A solicitor will prepare the agreement for partners to sign.

Tax and National Insurance

Partners are self-employed and will be taxed on their share of any profits. Each pays fixed rate Class 2 National Insurance contributions and Class 4 contributions on their share of the profits.

LIMITED LIABILITY PARTNERSHIP

A limited liability partnership is similar to an ordinary partnership in many ways but a partner's liability is limited to the amount of money they have invested in the business (plus any personal guarantees they have given on loans). Limited liability partnerships are a relatively new form of business structure, only being available over the last few years. As a result, they are not yet as common as ordinary partnership arrangements in the licensed trade.

Pros

- A partner's liability for business debts is limited.
- It has many benefits of an ordinary partnership.

Cons

- Its formation is more complicated and expensive than an ordinary partnership.
- You must register with Companies House.
- There are additional rules and requirements.
- Accounts must be filed with Companies House.
- Your financial information is publicly available.

Separate legal entity

A limited liability partnership is regarded as a separate legal entity from its partners. This means that the limited liability partnership itself is responsible for any debts that it runs up, not the individual partners. This is because when a limited liability partnership enters into a contract, it binds itself and not its members.

Tax and National Insurance

Despite being a separate legal entity, a limited liability partnership is treated as a partnership for tax purposes. The limited liability partnership will not itself be chargeable for tax on its profits, instead each member will be taxed on their share of the profits and also be required to make National Insurance contributions as in the case of a partnership. The limited liability partnership and the individual members must make annual self-assessment returns to HM Revenue and Customs.

LIMITED LIABILITY COMPANY

A limited liability company exists in its own right and is owned by shareholders. Shareholders are not responsible for the company's debts (except where personal guarantees have been issued by them), and their liability is limited to the amount of money they have invested in the business. Private limited companies have one or more shareholders, but shares cannot be offered to the public (eg on the stock exchange). Public limited companies must have at least two shareholdes and can offer shares to the public via the stock exchange. The number of licensees using this form of business structure has grown in recent years due to the tax benefits that some people have enjoyed. In order to ascertain whether there would be advantages for you and your business, you should seek professional advice from an accountant.

Pros

- Shareholder's liability is limited.
- A limited company has credibility.
- There may be tax advantages.

Cons

◆ Its formation is complicated.

◆ There are setting-up costs.

◆ You must register the business with Companies House.

◆ You must submit annual accounts to them.

◆ Your financial information is publicly available.

◆ There are additional rules and regulations that you must follow.

◆ National Insurance contribution payments may be higher.

 You can find more information about registering a company or limited liability partnership at the Companies House website:

www.companieshouse.gov.uk

Running a limited liability company

Limited liability companies must have at least one director and a company secretary. Anyone running a pub using a limited liabilty company will be regarded as employees of the business, and not self-employed. Licensees will normally appoint themselves as company directors and will also own the business through the shares that they own in it. Directors may be paid a salary and any business profits can be distributed to its shareholders in the form of a dividend payment.

Tax and National Insurance

Companies pay corporation tax based on the level of profit they earn. The company also has to pay employer's Class 1 National Insurance contributions for all its employees. Directors will be taxed on their salaries and pay Class 1 National Insurance contributions (PAYE). In their capacities as shareholders they may also be taxed on their dividend earnings.

11

OPENING A BANK ACCOUNT

BUSINESS BANKING

When in business, one of the most important relationships you will have is the one with your bank. A good relationship makes running your business easier and a poor relationship can be very disruptive and costly. It is therefore important to choose your bank with care.

Your needs and the needs of your business will dictate what service and support you will require a bank to provide. Choosing your bank should be based on who can best meet your needs for the lowest cost. You should note that charges are applied to business accounts for services that we take for granted as free for our personal accounts. Bank charges add cost to your business and should be carefully checked when comparing different banks.

Your banking needs will change over time, so it is important to review your banking arrangements every couple of years in order to check that you are getting the service and support you require at the best price.

CHOOSING A BANK

If you have a have a personal account with a bank and you are happy with their service, it is useful to speak to them first. If you already have a good relationship with them this may make things easier for you. However, it should not stop you from shopping around for the best deal. If your existing bank is willing to offer you this, fine. If not, look around and choose the one that will.

The following sections cover the key factors that are important in deciding your choice of bank.

Bank charges

Banks charge their business customers for many types of transaction. The amount they charge and the type of transactions that are chargeable varies from bank to bank. Some typical transactions that attract bank charges are:

◆ Paying cash into the bank;
◆ Writing cheques;
◆ Direct debits and standing orders;
◆ Duplicate statements.

A useful tool for comparing different bank accounts can be found at: www.moneysupermarket.com/currentaccounts/ This compares charges and rates of interest of a wide range of banks, making the job of researching the best deals easier for you.

Free banking for new customers

Free banking is provided by some banks for new customers. In several cases, standard bank charges are not applied for 12–18 months, which is very beneficial. Although this can be a great incentive, it is important to ascertain what your charges will be once the free banking period is over.

Location

You will need to pay cash and cheques into the bank on a regular basis. You may also need to visit the branch to set up your account, talk to business advisers and complete other paperwork. Because of this, it makes sense to use a bank that is located close to your pub. Banks with parking facilities or located close to a place where you can park your car will make the task of paying in cash safer and easier.

Night safe facilities

Night safe facilities can be an advantage. These can be used to deposit cash out of hours and on bank holidays, thereby reducing the amount of cash you hold on the premises. This is important from a safety point of view, and your insurance policy may restrict the amount of cash you are allowed to hold on the premises too.

On-line and telephone banking

Many banks now offer on-line and telephone banking services to their business customers. This allows you to check balances, make payments, set up direct debits and standing orders and provides a range of other services. You can use this facility out of normal bank opening hours and eliminate the need to visit the branch for many transactions. It is a great benefit to licensees who are often bound to their pubs for long periods of time.

Access to support and advice

Having access to support and advice can be important, particularly in the early stages of running your business. It is worth checking whether you have easy access to business advisers and the bank manager. Having a single point of contact who knows you and your business can be very helpful.

Overdraft facilities

Having an overdraft facility helps cover your short-term cash-flow shortages. Overdraft facilities vary from bank to bank; some may not offer such a service to new customers while others will.

Loan facilities

You may need additional capital to fund the acquisition of your pub or require finance in the future to further develop your business. Whether they will help finance your business and what rates of interest they will charge needs to be considered.

Merchant services

Accepting debit and credit cards is essential for pubs serving food. Today's customer expects to be able to pay for meals using their plastic. Not being able to accept debit and credit cards is likely to adversely affect your food sales. In order to accept debit and credit cards you require a merchant account. Choosing a bank for your business account that can also provide you with a merchant account can make the process easier, but you can open a merchant account to be used alongside a business account from another bank. See the section, 'How to accept debit and credit cards'.

Business credit cards

A business credit card is useful for making purchases. Some banks may require you to have banked with them for a period of time before they will issue a credit card to you for your business account. Enquire at different banks about this facility.

 The British Bankers' Association website contains lots of useful information about banks and banking: www.bba.org.uk

OPENING A BUSINESS BANK ACCOUNT

Once you have chosen your bank, you will have to complete an application form and provide details of your business and personal identification. You will need to open your business account prior to trading. This can sometimes cause difficulties where the bank needs to verify details of your new pub, which you haven't yet taken on or even signed for. In this case, you will have to support your application with letters of offer, solicitors' confirmations or correspondence from the brewery or pub company.

When opening your account, banks are likely to want to see the following:

- Letters confirming that you have been offered the tenancy or lease, or that you are buying the freehold of the pub.
- Copies of any tenancy or lease agreements.
- Your business plan.
- Certificate of corporation in the case of limited companies.
- A copy of any partnership agreement.
- Your driving licence or passport.
- Recent utility bills.

You will find it useful to open 2 types of account: a current account to deal with your day-to-day transactions, and an easy access savings account that you can use to set aside money to meet your VAT payments. You may also find it useful to open a second savings account where you can accrue money for longer-term developments or as a contingency fund.

RUNNING YOUR BUSINESS ACCOUNTS

Running your accounts properly will build good relationships with the bank and keep costs down. Here are some tips:

- Abide by the terms of your bank accounts.
- Do not exceed your overdraft limit without prior agreement.
- Keep your bank up to date about your business.
- Notify the bank of any problems you are experiencing with the business.
- Check your bank statements regularly.
- Keep your bank records in an organised manner.
- Review your banking arrangements every couple of years to check that you are getting the best deal.
- Renegotiate terms with your bank as your business needs change.
- Use on-line banking and automatic transactions to keep bank charges down.
- Monitor your cash-flow requirements and plan for any anticipated cash shortages.

SAFETY AND SECURITY

As a licensee, you will be regularly paying cash into your bank. Unfortunately, there are people who may see this as an opportunity to rob you. To reduce the risk of this happening vary the times and days you take cash to the bank. This will make it harder for anyone to work out your routine and prepare to steal from you. Don't make it obvious that you are carrying cash; instead put cash bags inside other, less obvious types of baggage, such as a small rucksack. If you travel to the bank by car, park your car as close to the bank as you can, reducing the distance you have to travel on foot. When you are travelling with money in a vehicle, lock your doors. This prevents anyone opening your doors and stealing from you while you are stationary or at traffic lights.

HOW TO ACCEPT DEBIT AND CREDIT CARDS

Merchant accounts

A prerequisite of accepting debit and credit cards is a merchant account to process payments. Currently, 9 banks offer merchant accounts and these are known as 'acquiring banks'. These are (in alphabetical order):

◆ Alliance and Leicester
◆ American Express
◆ Bank of Scotland
◆ Barclaycard Merchant Services
◆ Diners Club
◆ HSBC
◆ Lloyds TSB Cardnet
◆ Natwest/Royal Bank of Scotland Streamline
◆ Ulster Bank

You can also accept debit and credit cards if your business bank is not an acquiring bank. You will still need to open a merchant account with one of the above acquiring banks, who will process the transactions. They will then transfer payments into your business account, which can be at another bank. This usually takes 3–4 days.

Opening a merchant account

Before setting up your merchant account, the acquiring bank will need information about you and your business. They will also need details on anticipated quantity of card transactions, value of transactions and forecast turnover. These are used to assess your business and calculate the level of charges that you will have to pay for the service. Opening an account can take between 2–4 weeks, but could take longer for those with no track record of running a business.

Merchant accounts allow you to process all major debit and credit cards, including Mastercard, Visa, Switch/Maestro and SOLO. To accept major charge cards including Diners Club and American Express you must apply separately to each charge card company before being able to accept them.

PDQ terminal

Transactions are processed using a piece of equipment called a PDQ terminal. These are rented from your acquiring bank for approximately £20 per month. Your PDQ terminal is linked to the acquiring bank via a separate telephone line. When a card is swiped, using the terminal, a message is sent to the acquiring bank, which then checks that the customer has sufficient funds. Once this is verified, the customer has to enter their card pin number or sign a confirmation receipt to authorise the transaction.

 Since February 2006, most payments must be made by chip and pin enabled cards. See the Chip and Pin website for more details: www.chipandpin.co.uk

PDQ terminals come in a variety of forms from small handheld terminals to larger counter-top types. It is worth thinking about what type of terminal will provide good customer service and also fit with your business operation. It may be more convenient to have a portable device if you want customers to pay for meals at their tables.

Cost of accepting card payments

Some acquiring banks require a fee when setting up your merchant account, others will not. Also, as mentioned above, the PDQ terminal will be rented to you at an approximate cost of £20 per month. You will be charged per transaction too. Debit cards are much cheaper to process than credit cards. Debit card transactions tend to be charged at a flat rate of a few pence per transaction. Credit cards are charged at a percentage of the cost of the transaction, usually in the 2–8% range. Transaction costs for charge cards are calculated in a similar way.

You will need to confirm what transaction costs you will be charged by obtaining quotes from acquiring banks. Again, it is worth shopping around to find the best deal for your merchant account.

Chargebacks

Chargebacks occur when a customer later refuses to pay for a card transaction. They can occur up to 6 months after the transaction has taken place. In these circumstances, the bank can transfer this liability to you. This means that they will reclaim the payment back from you by charging your account. In pub transactions, the only real risk of a chargeback occurs when a card has been used fraudulently. For example, a cardholder has had their card stolen, which is then used fraudulently to purchase a meal. The cardholder can refuse to accept this as a valid transaction and a chargeback is later made.

In order to avoid chargebacks of this sort, it is important to verify the identity of the person making the card payment. If a transaction is authorised via your PDQ terminal and you have received a correct pin number or clear signature, you will not be liable for a chargeback. Fortunately, the introduction of new chip and pin technology has greatly reduced the possibility of this type of fraud occurring.

12

ARRANGING INSURANCE

INSURANCE COVER

For many people the subject of insurance is not a very exciting one. Insurance cover is sometimes left until the last minute and not given a great deal of attention. This can be a costly mistake. Obtaining the correct cover will not only help protect you and your business but will also ensure that you do not break the law. Arranging insurance cover needs a little thought, and you are advised to talk to a specialist broker to discuss your requirements and make sure that you and your business are correctly covered.

Remember that you need to be covered from the day you become responsible for your pub.

INSURANCE BROKERS

The insurance industry is regulated by the Financial Services Authority (FSA), which is an independent organisation responsible for regulating all financial services in the UK. Insurance brokers should be registered with the FSA. Always check a firm is authorised by them, or is the agent of an authorised firm before you do business with them. If they are not authorised and things go wrong you will not have access to complaints procedures and compensation schemes. You can check that a broker is registered via the FSA website: www.fsa.gov.uk/Pages/register or you can telephone them on 020 7066 1000.

Pub insurance is a specialist form of insurance and you should check that your broker has experience of arranging this.

WHAT INSURANCE COVER DO YOU NEED?

The type of cover you need will depend on whether you have acquired your pub on a tenancy, lease, or have bought the freehold of your pub. Insurance cover that you may require can be broadly divided into 4 main types of policies:

1 General pub insurance policies

These can cover:

- public liability;
- employers' liability;
- fixtures and fittings and equipment;
- money;
- loss of licence;
- assault;
- business interruption.

Pub policies are specialist forms of insurance combining a range of insurance cover. This type of insurance is needed for tenancy, lease and freehold pubs.

2 Building insurance cover

This covers:

- The cost of reinstating the building in case of damage or destruction.

This type of cover is usually only required for leased or freehold pubs, as a tenant is not normally responsible for the 'bricks and mortar' of the building. For leases, the brewery or pub company may hold the building insurance policy and you may not need to arrange for this yourself. They may however, pass the cost of the building insurance premium on to you. Claims may also be handled through them. Various tenancy or lease agreements place different obligations on licensees. You should check with the brewery or pub company whether you are responsible for the building insurance and, if so, whether you are required to arrange this cover yourself or be re-charged for the premium.

Where you have bought the freehold of your pub, you will need to arrange building insurance cover yourself. (See below for more details.)

3 Home contents insurance
This is to cover:

♦ your personal possessions.

This is often overlooked when taking on a pub. Your pub policy may well not include cover for your personal items. Separate cover is required to ensure that these are correctly covered.

4 Life insurance
This is to protect:

♦ dependents and the business.

Lenders may insist that you take out life insurance cover to ensure that any outstanding debts can be paid in the event of your death.

Other insurance cover that you may wish to consider includes personal accident and sickness cover and private medical insurance. Please note that the above is not a definitive list and you should discuss your particular requirements with an insurance broker.

SOME IMPORTANT CONSIDERATIONS

Public liability

Public liability insurance covers your legal liability to pay damages to members of the public for injury, death or damage to their property. It also covers legal fees, costs and other expenses. Awards for injury can exceed £1 million. Adequate public liability cover is an essential to safeguard you against such claims.

Employers' liability

The Employers' Liability (Compulsory Insurance) Act 1969 states that you must insure your employees in case of injury, disease or death arising from their employment. You must have insurance cover for a minimum of £5 million. In practice, most insurers offer cover for at least £10 million. You must also display a certificate of employers' liability insurance where your employees can easily read it. You must retain copies of certificates of insurance for up to 40 years.

If you fail to arrange adequate employers' liability insurance you can be fined up to £2,500 for any day you are without cover. You can be fined up to £1,000 if you do not display the certificate of insurance or refuse to make it available to Health and Safety Executive inspectors when they ask to see it.

Fixtures and fittings cover

It is important to have adequate insurance cover for your fixtures and fittings and equipment. Some people fail to insure these items adequately, which can severely limit any claim. (See section, 'Under insured' below, for more information.)

When setting up your policy, the broker will ask how much money you would like your fixtures and fittings to be covered for. You should remember that your policy must cover the cost of replacing these items as new. When your fixtures and fittings are valued on the day of ingoing, they will be valued according to their condition as part of a going concern, not on what it would cost to replace them. Some insurers suggest that you should multiply the value of your fixtures and fittings by 2.5–3 times, for a more realistic estimate of what it would cost to replace them. As a new licensee, you will be setting up the policy before you take over, and the fixtures and fittings may not have been valued at this point. In this case, you can use the estimated value multiplied by 2.5–3 times. (You can adjust this figure once the fixtures and fittings have been actually valued.)

It is important to remember to increase the cover of fixtures and fittings when you have added or replaced any major items. This can be particularly important when you have refurbished or extended your pub.

Redecoration

The cost of redecorating a pub can be very expensive and should be covered within your policy. Make sure you are adequately covered for this.

Stock

You can have a great deal of money tied up in stock and you will need to quote your maximum stock value to the broker, when setting up your cover. You may need to obtain this information from the brewery, pub company or outgoing licensee. Check also with your broker, that cover will take into account any seasonal increases in stock value, such as at Christmas.

Money

Pubs are cash businesses and you will require insurance to cover your money. Insurers will set limits on the amount of money they will allow you to claim. Furthermore, they will limit claims for money located in different places. For example, they will provide more cover for money locked in a safe than left out of the safe. They will also restrict cover for cash in transit and may even exclude money in amusement machines from cover, in some cases.

It is good practice to limit the amount of money you hold on the premises, and ensure that any money that is held is kept in a secure safe. This reduces the risk of theft and keeps you within the limits of your insurance policy.

Building insurance

The premises need to be insured for the full cost of rebuilding, including professional fees and site clearance costs. This figure is likely to vary significantly from the market value of the property and you should obtain professional advice in order to calculate the level of insurance you will need. A chartered surveyor will be able to advise you of this.

In the case of a tenancy or lease, you are unlikely to be required to arrange building insurance yourself, but you should check this and your obligations to repair the property, with your brewery or pub company.

SOME INSURANCE TERMS

Premium

The cost of insurance is known as a premium and is calculated by insurers taking into account their keenness to insure your type of business, level of risk, claims history and your approach to risk management. Many insurers feel that pubs with children's play areas, those running entertainment or located in certain postcodes, are of a higher level of risk and will charge higher premiums for these type of pubs as a result.

Some insurers allow you to spread the cost of your insurance over 12 months by allowing you to pay by direct debit. This can help your cash-flow though you may end up paying more for this option.

Premiums can vary widely between insurers but it is important to check the extent of your insurance cover. A lower premium may mean that cover is not as comprehensive or that you are required to pay a higher excess figure.

Excess

Excess is the first part of any claim that you are responsible for paying yourself. For example, 'a policy excess of £250' means that for a claim of £1,000, you would be paid £750 (if a successful claim were made) as you are responsible for the first £250 of the claim. This also prevents insurers having to pay out on small claims.

All risks

Policies with 'all risk' cover provide more cover than given under a normal insurance policy. 'All risk' covers any loss or damage apart from exclusions stated in the policy. Such policies may attract a higher premium.

Under insured

Being under insured is where you do not adequately cover items to their full value. An example of this would be only insuring your fixtures and fittings and equipment at £15,000, when the true cost of replacing these as new would be £45,000. If you claim to replace all these, your insurer will limit the claim to a maximum of £15,000. For smaller claims, for example to replace part of your fixtures and fittings, a claim may be reduced pro-rata in line with how much you are under insured.

Inspection prior to cover

An insurer may instruct their representative to inspect your pub prior to arranging cover. Their purpose is to inspect the premises in order to assess risk. It is best to organise your insurance cover in good time to take account of this eventuality.

Conditions and exclusions

Insurers may place certain conditions on covering you. They are likely to insist on working burglar alarms and fire alarms. They may ask you to upgrade door and window locks or add extra sensors throughout the pub. You may have to confirm that fabrics are fire retardant and internal doors are up to the required fire resistant standard. In a small number of cases, they may require CCTV to be installed. They may also exclude cover for certain things. It is important to understand any conditions or exclusions that may apply to a policy and attend promptly to any issues that have been raised by your insurers.

13

BOOK-KEEPING AND ACCOUNTS

BOOK-KEEPING

What is book-keeping?

Book-keeping is maintaining records of the financial transactions of a business including details of income and expenditure, bank statements, invoices and other paperwork required for accounting purposes. It allows you to check your performance against your budget, monitor your cash-flow and be properly prepared for VAT and tax payments. It can also help identify theft and unnecessary wastage.

Simple day-to-day book-keeping includes recording your income and expenditure into a cash book (which can be a paper or computer system), checking your cash and keeping your paperwork, like bank statements, invoices, delivery notes and till rolls in an orderly manner.

Who should do it?

Book-keeping is such an important task that it shouldn't be passed on entirely to someone else, simply to be forgotten about by you. It is something that you need to be involved in at some level. This may mean doing all the paperwork yourself or having the routine work done by someone else, but keeping a close eye on the overall situation. The important thing is to know how your business is performing. The more involved in book-keeping you are, the better informed you will be about your business.

Unfortunately, doing the paperwork is often regarded as the least exciting part of running your business, and it is easy for your book-keeping to fall behind as you focus on more interesting tasks. It is vital that you adopt a routine that enables you to keep up to date. It is better to do your book-keeping on a 'little and often' basis, than leaving the paperwork to mount up (making it even more daunting to deal with).

Some people feel intimidated by book-keeping, believing that to do it they have to be proficient at mathematics. This is not the case. Using a calculator to add and subtract is about as difficult as it gets! Being organised and disciplined is more important than having mathematic ability.

Doesn't my accountant do my book-keeping?

A qualified accountant is a highly skilled professional and their fees reflect this. Your accountant's bill will be based on the amount of time they spend dealing with your affairs, so asking your accountant to deal with the routine paperwork for your business is not generally cost effective. Your accountant's time is put to better use on more complex tasks such as VAT, taxation and year-end accounts.

Well-kept books and organised paperwork enable you to present your accountant with clear information, which reduces the amount of time they have to spend preparing your accounts. This should result in lower accountant's fees.

Legal requirements

Not only is keeping proper records beneficial to you, it is also a legal requirement, with penalties of up to £3,000 for failing to do so. Depending on the legal structure of your business, you must keep your business record for between 5 and 6 years.

Book-keeping systems

It is best to talk to your accountant to get their advice on setting up your book-keeping system. They will have a good knowledge of each type of system and can advise you how they would like your records presented. Systems can include simple cash books like *Simplex*, *Everite* and *Collins* or more sophisticated computer software such as *Sage*, *QuickBooks* and *Clearlybookkeeping*. You are advised to keep your system simple, and a basic cash book may be perfectly adequate for your needs, rather than the more intricate accounting software that has many features you may not require. However, if you are more confident in your book-keeping and computing abilities, software packages can save time and can present data in a variety of ways that may be useful to you.

Using a book-keeping service

A popular method used by many people in the licensed trade is to use a book-keeping service. The best of these are backed by qualified accountants. The book-keeper provides the licensee with weekly record sheets onto which they record daily income and expenditure details. Receipts and paid invoices are attached to this document and sent to the book-keeper on a weekly basis. The sheets allow a carbon copy to be retained by the licensee.

Dependent on the level of service that the licensee pays for, the book-keeper will calculate VAT and prepare VAT returns, provide monthly or quarterly management accounts (see below) and offer cost control advice. The basic service costs around £25 per week. Although you are likely to still need an accountant to prepare your year-end accounts and deal with your taxation, a book-keeper provides a useful service. When considering using a book-keeper it is worth checking whether:

◆ The service is something you need.
◆ You really need someone else to do the work.
◆ You will lose touch with an important part of your business.
◆ The benefits outweigh the costs.
◆ The book-keeper is suitably qualified and experienced.

You can find more details about book-keeping and find suitably qualified book-keepers from the Institute of Certified Book-keepers. See their website at: www.bookkeepers.org.uk or telephone: 0845 060 2345.

'Five S' approach

Whichever book-keeping system you use, there are some key principles that should be adhered to. The 'Five S' approach is a helpful way of remembering these:

1 **System**: set up a system and stick to it. Make book-keeping part of your routine.
2 **Simple**: keep your system simple and easy to maintain.
3 **Separate**: keep your business and your personal finances separate.
4 **Secure**: keep the information secure and keep copies of your records where possible.
5 **Storage**: store your paperwork in an organised way and keep records that cannot be copied in a fireproof container.

Other good practice

- If you use any money from your till to pay for anything, always put a receipt in it immediately.
- Always pay money into your till for any drinks or snacks you consume.
- Keep your till rolls as part of your business records.
- Print off Z readings at the end of the day and keep these with your records. (Z readings are a printed summary of sales for the day which your till can print off. Z readings clear the till of this information, while X readings give the same information, but do not clear the till of the data.)
- Check that the cash (and any receipts) in your till at the end of the day reconciles with your till readings. Keep a record of this information.
- Check your bank statements monthly against your paying-in book and cheque book and your list of standing orders and direct debits.

- Set up payments for gas, electricity, rates and telephone on monthly direct debit.
- Don't leave cash lying around your office – always keep it in a locked safe (and restrict who has access to your safe).

YEAR–END ACCOUNTS

What are year-end accounts?

Year-end accounts are a summary of your business transactions that shows what profit (or loss) you have made, and details your assets and liabilities. Your profitability is shown in a 'profit and loss account' and your assets and liabilities are shown in a 'balance sheet'. Your accounts are normally drawn up by a qualified accountant who will also be dealing with your tax matters.

As a sole trader or partnership you are not required by law to have a formal profit and loss or balance sheet drawn up, but it is still good practice to do so as the information will be required for your self-assessment tax returns. Well-presented accounts are also important if you want to raise money or sell the lease or freehold of your pub. They also provide you with a clear indication of how the business is performing.

Who needs to see them?

In the case of a sole trader or partnership, no one needs to see your accounts legally, but you will have to submit tax returns which amounts to supplying the same information that is displayed in your accounts.

In the case of a limited company or a limited liability partnership, you are required to have formal accounts drawn up, which must be submitted to HM Revenue and Customs, and Companies House. Small companies and limited liability partnerships can submit unaudited, abbreviated accounts to Companies House if they meet certain criteria (which pubs operating in these ways are likely to meet). There are strict deadlines when accounts must be submitted to HM Revenue and Customs and Companies House, and failure to adhere to these can result in substantial fines and other penalties.

When are they drawn up?

Accounts are drawn up at the end of your financial year, which is normally a 12-month period; however, they can be shorter or longer than 12 months in some circumstances. The choice of your financial year should be discussed with your accountant, taking into account taxation and operational issues.

Presenting your business records to your accountant promptly and in a well-organised way will help prevent any delays in preparing your accounts. If your accountant has to chase lost invoices or bank statements this will hinder the process and possibly cost you more money in the long run.

Understanding your accounts

It is important to understand the information presented in your accounts. Rather than simply having your accounts posted to you, ask your accountant to go through them with you and explain what the figures mean and how things can be improved for the future. Learning a little about accounting is very useful. You do not have to become an expert, but it will give you a greater understanding of your business as well as the confidence to ask your accountant or book-keeper questions about your financial performance.

When finding out is too late!

The time between starting to run your pub and receiving your first year-end accounts can be up to sixteen months. Your results can come as a shock. If your accounts state that you have lost money or have not made as much as you anticipated, it's too late to change the situation. This is why it is important to have some way of monitoring your performance on a regular basis, allowing you to try to improve things, if necessary, by making adjustments to the way you run your business.

At the start, drawing up a profit and loss report and monitoring your cash-flow on a monthly basis is essential. As you become more established, you may feel that a quarterly profit and loss report is adequate. (Cash-flow should continue to be monitored monthly.) Your accountant or qualified book-keeper can prepare this information for you if it is not something you are able to do yourself.

VAT

What is VAT?

VAT, or Value Added Tax, is a tax on sales of goods and services. VAT registered businesses collect VAT on the Government's behalf, by making payments to HM Revenue and Customs.

'Input tax' is the VAT a business pays on its purchases and 'output tax' is the VAT it charges on its sales. If a registered business receives more output tax from its sales than input tax from its purchases, it has to pay the difference to HM Revenue and Customs. This is the normal trading situation for a pub business.

Sometimes a business may have paid more input tax than output tax, and in this situation HM Revenue and Customs will issue a refund for the difference. An example of this would be where the business has purchased expensive items of equipment on which VAT is charged. The business may have paid out more VAT to the supplier of the equipment than the VAT collected from its own customers.

 For more information on VAT and tax payments, visit HM Revenue and Customs website: www.hmrc.gov.uk/index.html

Rates of VAT

Goods and services that are VAT-rated are called 'taxable supplies' and the value of these supplies is called your 'taxable turnover'. There are three rates of VAT in the UK:

◆ 17.5%   (known as standard rate);
◆ 5%   (known as reduced rate);
◆ 0%   (known as zero-rate).

There are also other goods and services on which VAT is not charged, these are known as 'exempt supplies'.

Examples of reduced rate items:

◆ fuel and power used in the home;
◆ women's sanitary products.

Examples of zero-rated goods are:

◆ most food (except meals in pubs, restaurants, cafes and hot take-away food and drink);
◆ books;
◆ newspapers;
◆ children's clothing and shoes.

Examples of exempt items are:

◆ insurance;
◆ betting, gambling and lotteries (but not takings from fruit machines);
◆ certain types of education and training.

When do you need to register for VAT?

Registering for VAT is compulsory for businesses with an annual turnover above the VAT threshold. (In February 2010, this figure was £68,000, but this figure is regularly revised.) Businesses with a turnover of less than the VAT threshold can register for VAT voluntarily, which can be advantageous in some cases. For example, a business with higher than average input tax payments and lower than average output tax, may find it beneficial. Businesses under the VAT threshold may also consider that VAT registra- tion gives them more credibility in the eyes of customers and suppliers.

How do you register for VAT?

You register for VAT by completing form 'VAT 1', plus:

◆ VAT 2 – if your business is a partnership.

◆ VAT 68 – if you are taking over an existing business and wish to keep the previous owner's VAT number.

From 1 April 2010 you will have to submit your VAT Returns online and pay any VAT due electronically if either of the following applies:

◆ you have an annual turnover of £100,000 or more (exclusive of VAT)

◆ you register or should have registered for VAT on or after 1 April 2010 (regardless of your turnover).

Contact the VAT helpline for assistance with registering for VAT, tel: 0845 010 8500 8am to 8pm Monday to Friday, excluding Bank Holidays.

Forms must be sent to the HM Revenue and Customs office that is responsible for businesses in your postcode area. You can also register on line via the HM Revenue and Customs website: www.hmrc.gov.uk

You should be sent your VAT registration number within 3 weeks of registering.

Failing to register

It is important that you register at the correct time as you may receive a financial penalty if you fail to do so. The amount of the penalty will depend on how late you are. You will be registered from the date you were liable to be registered, and you will have to pay VAT to HM Revenue and Customs even if you did not charge it to your customers.

What must you do once registered?

Once you have registered for VAT, you must charge VAT to your customers, keep proper records and accounts for VAT, and send in VAT returns regularly.

You must ensure that any invoices you receive from your VAT-registered suppliers display their VAT number and you must do the same for any invoices you issue.

VAT returns

The VAT return (form VAT 100 or Welsh equivalent VAT 100W) is the form you use to notify HM Revenue and Customs of the amount of VAT you are submitting for payment or are claiming back. You will normally receive these every 3 months, for the period known as your 'tax period'. You can arrange for VAT returns to be issued on a monthly basis, if you wish.

You will be required to complete the return with details of the value of goods you have bought and sold and the respective VAT due, or being claimed. You can also now send in VAT returns via the HM Revenue and Customs website.

Different VAT schemes

Accounting for VAT in the standard way can be time-consuming. However, there are alternative VAT accounting schemes that may suit your business better. These include:

◆ Annual Accounting scheme (you must have been registered for 12 months or more to apply).
◆ Flat Rate scheme (your total turnover must not exceed £187,500 – as at February 2010).
◆ Retail schemes (a range of schemes is available to different retailers).

Your accountant will advise you on which scheme will be most suitable for you to operate.

Putting money aside to pay your VAT

If you have set up to pay VAT on a quarterly basis, it is good practice to set some money aside each week to cover your anticipated VAT payment, rather than having to find the money at the end of the quarter. To do this, open a savings account and pay into it between 6% and 7% of your weekly takings, which will approximately cover your quarterly VAT payment.

Using the services of an accountant or book-keeper

The majority of licensees use the services of their accountant or qualified book-keeper to register them for VAT and ensure that VAT is correctly calculated for their VAT returns. Unless you are confident that you have the time and the ability to do these, you are advised to leave this aspect of your business to the professionals.

INCOME TAX

What is income tax?

Income tax is a direct tax which is levied on the income of private individuals. Taxable income includes wages, salaries, investments, interest, dividends, benefits and any income from self-employment.

How will you be taxed?

The way you will be taxed will depend on the legal form of your business and the way you run your business. You will be taxed differently if you define your employment status as 'self-employed' or 'employed'. For example, in the case of a couple, if the husband had set up as a sole trader, he would be regarded as self-employed while his wife may be regarded as employed. If the same couple set up their business as a limited company, they would both be regarded as being employed by the business.

Income tax for employees

Employees will be taxed at the prevailing rates, normally through the PAYE (Pay As You Earn) system, where the employer deducts tax and National Insurance payments from wages or salary payments. Everyone must keep a record of their income for a minimum of 22 months after the end of the tax year.

The company is also required to provide an employee with the following:

◆ itemised wage slips;
◆ an annual P60 (showing total earnings);
◆ an annual P11D (summarising any taxable benefits).

Income tax for directors

Directors must also complete a self-assessment tax return, giving details of salary, fees, divided payments and any other taxable benefits like a company car.

Registering as self-employed

If you are self-employed, you must register with HM Revenue and Customs within 3 months of starting up. This includes sole traders and standard partnerships. They will register you as self-employed and arrange for you to pay the correct National Insurance contributions (see below).

Income tax for the self-employed

If you are self-employed, you should automatically receive a tax return at the end of the tax year (5 April). If you are not sent one, it is your responsibility to obtain one. There are penalties for missing the deadline for returning the form, or not paying tax that you owe.

If you are self-employed, which includes sole traders and partners in a standard partnership, you pay tax on your business profits or your share of the profits and not on the amount of money you pay yourself (ie your 'drawings'). You will also be taxed on any other income you earn, for example, salary or wages from any other work, interest on savings and dividends from shares. You may also be taxed on the disposal of certain assets. You will be able to claim allowances that reduce the amount of tax you pay dependent on your circumstances. These tend to be reviewed annually and can be found on the HM Revenue and Customs website.

You are required to keep accurate records of all your business transactions including any amounts you have paid into or taken from the business. Purchases and expenses need to be supported by invoices, unless they are for small amounts. By law, you are required to keep your business records for at least 5 years and 10 months after the end of the tax year.

Income tax for partnerships

Business partners in a standard partnership are normally regarded as self-employed, but income tax is applied in a slightly different way than in the case of a sole trader. As a partner, you pay tax and National Insurance on your share of the partnership's profits. The arrangement for sharing profits should be clearly stated in your partnership agreement; it is not necessarily the case that profits are split equally between partners. Profit sharing may be based on factors like levels of investment or time spent running the business.

CAPITAL GAINS TAX

What is capital gains tax?

Capital gains tax (CGT) is a tax charged to individuals on gains made from selling or disposing of assets. (Limited companies are charged corporation tax in these circumstances.) Capital gains tax is normally paid as part of your self-assessment tax return. Assets include property, shares and the goodwill of a business. It is particularly important to understand the tax implications when you are considering selling on your lease or the freehold of your pub.

A capital gain occurs when there has been an increase in value of an asset when you come to sell or dispose of it compared with what you paid for it. There are various allowances and reliefs that you can use to offset against any capital gains. You are advised to seek professional guidance from your accountant about the tax implications of selling any major assets and what allowances and reliefs you may be able to claim.

CAPITAL ALLOWANCES

What are capital allowances?

Capital allowances are tax allowances that enable you to deduct a proportion of these costs from your taxable profits, thereby reducing your tax bill. You can claim capital allowance on certain types of purchases and investments. Examples of these are:

- vans or cars;
- equipment;
- furniture;
- computers.

The amount of allowance depends on what you are claiming for and when you claim it. The allowance will be based on a percentage of the purchase cost, which excludes VAT if you are VAT registered. Use your income or corporation tax return to claim your allowances. Your accountant will advise you.

SELF-ASSESSMENT

Self-assessment tax returns for individuals
Your tax payment is calculated from your self-assessment tax return which is issued in April each year and covers the period from the previous 6th April to 5th April (the tax year). For example, the 2005–06 tax year covers the period 6th April 2005 to 5th April 2006.

Your core tax return is known as an SA100 and you will also have to complete additional pages:

- Employment (SA101) – if you are an employee or company director.
- Self-employment (SA103) – if you are a sole trader.
- Partnership (SA104) – if you are self-employed in a partnership.

Returns can be completed on line or sent by post to HM Revenue and Customs.

Partnership tax returns
If you operate a standard partnership, you will also be sent a partnership tax return (SA800), which a nominated partner will be required to complete on behalf of the partnership.

Deadlines for self assessment tax returns
Some key dates for the return of your self-assessment tax returns are as follows:

- 30th September – if you want the HM Revenue and Customs to work out how much tax and National Insurance contributions you owe. HM Revenue and Customs cannot guarantee to tell you what to pay in time for the deadline if returns are received after this date.

- 31st January – is the absolute deadline for returns to be received by HM Revenue and Customs. If you miss this deadline, you will be automatically liable for a penalty of £100.

PAYING YOUR TAX

As a self-employed person, your tax is normally payable in 3 stages:

1   On account by 31st January during the next tax year (normally half your previous year's tax bill).
2   On account by 31st July after the end of the tax year (normally the same as your first payment).
3   A balancing payment or repayment by the next 31st January (calculated on the actual income returned less the payments you have made).

There are automatic penalties if you fail to pay your tax on time. Interest can also be charged on any tax that is overdue.

Take advice

Taxation can be a complicated subject and you should seek the advice of your accountant in order to minimise your tax liability and ensure that you are not penalised for failing to meet your legal obligations.

NATIONAL INSURANCE

What is National Insurance?

National Insurance contributions (NICs) are deductions from an individual's income that fund social security benefits such as incapacity benefit, contribution-based jobseeker's allowance, retirement pension and bereavement benefits.

National Insurance numbers

A National Insurance number is a person's unique reference which enables the HM Revenue and Customs and the Department for Work and Pensions to identify an individual's National Insurance contribution record. This ensures that the correct amount can be paid when a claim for benefit is made. Employees are required by law to give employers their National Insurance number.

National Insurance contributions

You make different contributions depending on your employment status. Employees have to pay Class 1 National Insurance contributions, which are normally collected by the employer via PAYE system deductions from their wage or salary. For the tax year 2010–11, Class 1 contributions were 11% of weekly earnings between £97 and £844 with an additional 1% on earnings above £844. (Lower rates can apply if the employee belongs to a contracted-out occupational pension scheme.)

The self-employed pay Class 2 contributions at a flat rate of £2.40 per week (2010–11) and Class 4 contributions based on their annual profit. For profits between £5,715 and £43,875, Class 4 contributions of 8% of profits apply, with an additional 1% on profits above £43,875 (2010–11).

Your obligations as an employer

If you employ staff, you are required to set up a payroll system in order to:

◆ Work out accurately and deduct PAYE tax and National Insurance contributions from each employee, each pay day.
◆ Record details of deductions and payments.
◆ Pay the money you deduct to HM Revenue and Customs each month or quarter.
◆ Notify HM Revenue and Customs when an employee joins or leaves you.
◆ Report details at the end of the tax year.
◆ Provide your employees with a record of pay and deductions for the tax year using a P60.

You may also need to:

◆ Deduct student loan deductions and stakeholder pension contributions.
◆ Make payments to your employees for tax credits, statutory sick pay and other statutory payments.

Limited companies – additional obligations

Limited companies are also required to pay Employer's Class 1 National Insurance contributions for all employees. For the 2010–11 tax year, this was 12.8% of the employee's weekly earnings above £110 a week.

Paying employee's tax and National Insurance

As an employer, you must pay tax and National Insurance payments to HM Revenue and Customs every month. Payments must reach them by the 19th of each month. However, if you collect less than £1,500 per month in tax and National Insurance contributions, you can apply to pay quarterly. In this case, payments must reach HM Revenue and Customs by the following dates:

◆ 5th July;
◆ 5th October;
◆ 5th January;
◆ 5th April.

To apply for the quarterly payment scheme you should complete a form P31 and forward it to your HM Revenue and Customs office.

National Insurance contributions for directors

For National Insurance purposes, a company director is classified as an 'office holder' and since 1999, alternative arrangements have operated for the assessment and payment of National Insurance for directors. Now, the earnings period for the assessment of directors' National Insurance contributions is an annual one, though payment can be made on account throughout the tax year.

National Insurance forms

Some of the main forms used for National Insurance are:

◆ P11 – Deductions Working Sheet, used to record the National Insurance contributions and tax deducted from employees' pay.

◆ P11D – Reports the cash equivalent of any benefits provided to relevant employees.

◆ P45 – A 4-part form completed to show an individual's pay and tax details up to the date of them leaving their employment.

◆ P46 – PAYE – Notice of new employee, used to inform HM Revenue and Customs about an employee who does not have a P45 to give you.

◆ P30BC – A book of payslips to be filled in and sent to HM Revenue and Customs with tax and National Insurance deductions.

◆ P32 – Employer's Payment Record, used to work out total monthly payments.

Setting up your payroll system

HM Revenue and Customs provide some very useful information on setting up and running your payroll system, including an Employer's CD-ROM, which provides very good guidance.

If you feel that you do not have the time or the means to set up and run your own payroll, there is a number of companies that provide payroll services to other businesses. Your accountant may also provide this facility. If you choose this option, once the system has been set up for your employees, you will telephone the payroll service with the hours your employees have worked. They will then calculate tax and national insurance and prepare wage slips on your behalf.

You can also buy payroll software packages that make the job of running your payroll system easier. Many packages are compatible with HM Revenue and Customs requirements. Look for the Payroll Standard Logo – this informs you that it has been tested by HM Revenue and Customs and meets their specifications.

CORPORATION TAX FOR LIMITED COMPANIES

What is corporation tax?

Corporation tax is a tax paid by limited companies, based on their profits.

It is not payable by the self-employed, but where licensees set up their businesses as limited companies, their company is required to pay corporation tax on its profits.

Notifying HM Revenue and Customs

If your company has any taxable income or profits, you must notify HM Revenue and Customs that your company exists and is liable for tax. You must do this within 12 months of the end of your accounting period (the period for which your accounts are drawn up). Companies House inform HM Revenue and Customs when a company has been registered with them, but it is also your responsibility to notify them yourself.

When HM Revenue and Customs are informed of a new company, they create a computer record for the company and send out a form CT41G to the company's registered address. This form should be completed and returned to HM Revenue and Customs.

Company records

Your company has to keep 'sufficient' records to enable it to make a correct and complete tax return. 'Sufficient' records include:

◆ Details of all receipts and expenses incurred in the course of your company's activities.
◆ Details of all sales and purchases made in the course of trade.
◆ Any other supporting documentation.

For tax purposes, companies must keep their records for at least 6 years from the end of the accounting period.

When is corporation tax chargeable?

A company is generally chargeable for corporation tax on its total profits. Total profits are determined by adding together the profits from its activities and any chargeable gains. Chargeable gains are the profit made when an asset owned by the business is sold for more than the value it was bought for. (This only applies to assets which are not bought and sold as part of the normal trade of the company.)

Capital allowances can be claimed for certain assets and can be offset against your corporation tax liability. (See section, 'Capital Allowances', earlier in this chapter.)

Corporation tax is charged as a percentage of taxable profits: in 2010–11, the rates were:

◆ 21% on profits   £0–£300,000 (small companies' rate)
◆ 28% on profits   £1.5 million and above (main rate)

Marginal relief eases the transition for companies with profits falling between rates.

Self-assessment tax returns

HM Revenue and Customs will send the company a notice to deliver its Company Tax Return (form CT603), 3 to 7 weeks after the end of its accounting period. They will also send a Company Tax Return (form CT600) which you must complete and return to them by no later than the 'statutory filing date'. (You can also use approved software or other authorised version of it.) The 'statutory filing date' is normally the later of:

◆ 12 months after the end of a company's accounting period,

or

◆ 3 months after your company receives the notice to deliver.

There are penalties of up to £1,000 for late filing of company tax returns.

Paying corporation tax

Corporation tax must be paid by the 'normal due date' which is 9 months and 1 day after the end of the company's accounting period. Payment can be made electronically through the BACS or CHAPS systems, by GIRO or by cheque to the company's usual Accounts Office (at Cumbernauld or Shipley). Payment should be sent together with a payment slip, which is issued with the notice to deliver a company tax return.

14

MARKETING

WHAT IS MARKETING?

The word 'marketing' conjures up images of dynamic advertising agencies and million-pound budgets, but the reality is that even the smallest pubs use some form of marketing.

So what is marketing? Well, marketing can be defined as: 'The process of identifying, anticipating and satisfying customer requirements, profitably' (*Chartered Institute of Marketing*).

Marketing is a crucial part of running a business, and though most pubs use some form of marketing, not all of them do it well. Good marketing and focusing on customer satisfaction help businesses be more successful. Marketing is an ongoing process and not something you do once then forget about for a while. It is not just about spending money on advertising, it is about really understanding customer requirements and shaping your business to meet their needs.

The benefits of marketing

The ultimate aim of marketing is to make more profit. Marketing clarifies who your target customers are and helps you to understand their needs. It focuses your business on providing customers with what they want, and satisfied customers stay longer, return more often and spend more money. Satisfied customers can help to promote your business by word of mouth to other potential customers too. Dissatisfied customers, on the other hand, spend little, don't come back, and will let lots of people know about their poor experience. Marketing focuses your business on 'customer satisfaction' and, when done well, can give you a big advantage over your competitors.

IDENTIFYING WHAT CUSTOMERS WANT

Before you can decide how best to give customers what they want, you have to understand them. Some licensees fall into the trap of merely offering what they *think* their customers want, without actually trying to understand their customers at all. Even worse, is where licensees totally ignore what their customers want. For example, deciding to stock a particular product because they themselves like to drink it, and not because it might be enjoyed by their customers!

The best pubs meet the needs of their customers by first knowing what their customers want. This comes from knowing and understanding the pub's catchment area and the people who live and work within it, as well as the competitors who operate there. It also comes from keeping up to date with trends and changes in the industry.

Researching the pub's catchment area through 'desk research' (for example gathering information using the internet) and regularly visiting the area prior to taking on your pub should provide you with a wealth of information. This information can be used to put together a 'marketing plan' of how you intend to promote your business to its customers. (See below for details on putting together a marketing plan.)

While you are running your pub, it is very important to keep up to date with what is going on in your area and update your marketing plan when necessary. This prevents you from being left behind and thus enabling your competitors to take advantage of the situation.

Customers' wants and needs

Customers' basic wants and needs include the following:

- interacting with people;
- meeting people;
- being comfortable;
- feeling safe;
- eating and drinking;
- being entertained;
- having fun;
- relaxing;
- belonging.

When a customer chooses which pubs to visit, they consciously, or subconsciously, choose the ones that satisfy some of their basic needs. Customers' needs are not static and vary with time and circumstances. As different needs become a priority, the customer looks for ways of satisfying these. This results in the customer making new choices according to their needs at the time. For example: 'Customer A', who has not eaten for 8 hours, primarily motivated to satisfy his need for food, may be willing to use a 'shabby' pub because it happens to serve food and is closest to him! Later, looking to satisfy his needs for interaction, belonging and fun, he is willing to travel 2 miles to another pub where his friends will be. This is an example of the same customer having different needs at different times, motivating him to use different pubs.

SATISFYING CUSTOMER NEEDS

The important thing to remember is that customers visit pubs for more reasons than just to drink. Simply selling the best pint around is not enough. In order for your business to flourish, your pub has to satisfy a whole range of wants and needs. Customer satisfaction is directly influenced by the following key areas:

Premises

- convenience of location;

- what facilities are available;
- the quality of the facilities;
- quality of décor;
- quality of fixtures and fittings;
- layout;
- temperature and lighting;
- opening hours;
- parking and ease of access.

Drinks products

- product range and choice;
- product quality;
- presentation;
- temperature;
- prices.

Food

- choice;
- quality;
- presentation;
- value for money;
- methods of payment (eg debit and credit cards).

Licensee and staff

- speed and efficiency of service;
- attentiveness;
- friendliness and approachability;
- product knowledge;
- personal presentation;
- control of premises.

People

- types of existing customers;

- similarity to themselves;
- behaviour;
- friendliness of atmosphere;
- acceptance from existing clientele.

Entertainment

- type;
- frequency;
- quality;
- suitability.

 Research shows that women put the quality of a pub's toilets as the most important factor in deciding which pubs to use!

TARGETING YOUR CUSTOMERS

Target customers

Different types of customer use different types of pubs. It is very difficult to present your pub as the solution for every type of customer's needs. What attracts one type of customer will discourage another. Rather than trying to be all things to all people, you should concentrate on attracting and retaining a few key customer-types by shaping your business to meet their needs. Focusing on a few key customer-types and doing it well is preferable to trying a 'catch all' approach and doing it badly. The customers you want to retain and attract are your 'target customers' and your marketing efforts should be aimed at them.

Existing customers

There are many sorts of customers living and working within a pub's catchment area, each with different needs. Fortunately, you are not starting a business from scratch. Your pub has the benefit of existing customers who feel that your pub satisfies some of their needs.

As a new licensee, your aim is to find ways of building your business by attracting new customers and encouraging your existing customers to spend more.

Getting your existing customers to spend more is the easier of the two ways of building your business. They already use your pub, you know who they are, and something about them. It is relatively easy to find out their preferences and communicate with them. Sales turnover from your existing customers can be increased by encouraging them to visit your pub more regularly and/or spending more on each visit. Your marketing activity for existing customers should concentrate on ways to achieve this.

New customers
New customers can be broadly divided into two kinds:

♦ customers of the same 'types' as your existing clientele;
♦ new 'customer-types'.

Customers who behave in a similar way and have similar needs can be banded together as 'customer-types'. Examples of these are OAPs (Old Age Pensioners), students, executives and married couples etc. Splitting customers down into categories is known as 'market segmentation' and there are some extremely sophisticated ways of doing this. Customers can be segmented by age, occupation, social class, marital status and lifestyle. For our purposes, a simple means of categorising our customers is all that is needed.

 Look again at the 'Ideal Pub' checklist (Appendix vi), which shows some ways of segmenting clientele into customer types.

Attracting similar customer-types to your existing clientele is less difficult than attracting completely new customer-types. The argument here is that customers of the same type as your existing clientele will find your pub meets their needs in the same way it does for your existing clientele. New customer-types are more difficult to attract because you have to speculate more about their needs and find ways of making them aware and interested in your pub. There may also be fundamental reasons why they are not using your pub at present and changes may have to be made in order to accommodate them.

Attracting customers of similar types

You must first assess whether there are sufficient numbers of these customer-types, with sufficient disposable income, within your catchment area to be worthwhile pursuing. Assuming this is the case, and your pub is successfully satisfying the needs of your existing clientele, attracting them is often down to making them aware of your pub and encouraging them to try it. Your marketing efforts should focus on doing this. Once inside your pub, these customers should feel 'at home' with similar types of people around them and the service and facilities that they want.

Find ways of encouraging your existing customers' friends and families to start using the pub.

Attracting new customer-types

You may decide that to be successful you must attract new types of customers to your pub. This may be because your existing customer-types alone are not sufficient to generate the level of profits you are aiming for, or that new types of customer may provide you with an opportunity of building your business that is too good to miss.

But how do you decide which new types of customer to attract? Here are a few questions to help you decide:

♦ What other customer-types live and work within the pub's catchment area?
♦ What other customer-types have high disposable income?
♦ Are they in sufficient numbers to be beneficial to your business?

◆ Can you meet their needs?

◆ Will you be comfortable dealing with this type of customer?

◆ What types of customer are not being catered for by any of your competitors?

◆ What are the implications of attracting these new customers on your existing clientele?

◆ Are there any other implications?

Attracting completely new types of customer is a more difficult way of building your business. Fundamental changes to the way you operate your business may have to be made. (For example, aiming to attract diners to a pub where there are no facilities for serving food at present.) This can be costly and can affect your existing clientele. Communicating with new customer-types is more complicated as you have to find ways of reaching them. There is also no guarantee that you will attract sufficient numbers of new customer-types to make the changes viable. Any plans to make any fundamental changes to your business need to be supported by extensive research, prior to going ahead.

It is possible to make temporary changes to the way your pub operates at different times of the day, or different days of the week, in order to target different types of customer. The aim of these temporary changes is to make your pub more appealing to different types of customers. Different times of the day or week can provide you with an opportunity to attract customers who are not normally around at other times, for example, targeting shoppers with a special lunchtime menu. Traditionally quiet periods can also be filled by making changes that will appeal to new types of customer, such as running Monday quiz nights.

Habit breaking

People are creatures of habit; they do the same things, go to the same shops and use the same pubs year after year. They will even sometimes do so when the service or facilities are less than good. This can be because 'dissatisfaction' in one area may be offset by benefits gained in another. For example, a couple may use a particular pub, despite the fact that the place is not very welcoming, because their friends have always done so.

Sometimes it takes a very bad experience to unsettle customers and make them look elsewhere. However, people's expectations have risen over the last decade and they are less likely to accept poor service or standards than they once were. People are also generally more experimental and mobile than they once were, and are therefore willing and able to try new places and experiences. People's personal circumstances can alter too, which changes their habits. The result of all these changes is a constant flow of 'floating customers' who are not settled and are looking for new pubs to satisfy their needs.

 Ensuring your pub is 'customer focused', with excellent service and standards and backed up with good marketing, puts you in the strongest position to capture 'floating customers'.

COMMUNICATING WITH CUSTOMERS

In this case, 'communicating' means doing so in a marketing context, not just chatting about the weather to your customers!

Why do you need to communicate?

Communication is a two-way process that achieves the following:

♦ Helps you understand customer requirements.
♦ Helps you convey how you can satisfy a customer's needs.

In order to understand customer requirements you have to listen to them. Running a pub has the advantage over many other kinds of businesses in that you are in direct contact with your customers. Feedback is a constant process, enabling you to gauge customer response instantly; however, a thick skin is occasionally needed! Be aware that you cannot satisfy all of the people all of the time. There can be a danger of listening to only a small number of very vocal customers who are not representative of your clientele. Take time to assess any feedback and ensure you take into account the opinions of a representative sample of your customers. Good quality feedback is essential for keeping in touch with customer needs and sounding out potential changes you may be planning. Regard it as free market research.

 Start a suggestion scheme for customers and staff with a suggestions box on the bar. Award a prize for any suggestions you use.

You must also convey to customers and potential customers how your pub will satisfy their needs. This 'marketing message' needs to be communicated regularly and in a variety of ways to your target customers. This reinforces the loyalty of existing customers and attracts new customers who may not have previously been aware of you.

Purpose of your marketing message

Marketing messages are used to promote your pub, its products and services. Messages can focus on different things and have different specific objectives. For example, to make the public aware that you have refurbished your pub, promote a theme night or launch a new menu.

To be effective, your marketing message should adhere to the AIDA acronym:

A   Awareness   (to build awareness)
I   Interest   (to create interest)
D   Desire   (to create desire)
A   Action   (to encourage action)

Your message should make customers aware of what you are offering and stimulate their interest. The message needs to be appealing enough to motivate them to take action and try whatever you are promoting. Whatever you are planning to promote to your customers, make sure your message contains the AIDA elements and with your target customers in mind, ask yourself the following questions:

◆ What is your objective?
◆ Will the message catch their attention?
◆ Will it build awareness of your pub, and what you offer?
◆ Will it appeal to their needs?
◆ Will it motivate them to do something?
◆ Will they be clear about what they have to do?
◆ Will the message be memorable?
◆ Will it be consistent with your marketing plan?

Communicating your marketing message

Marketing messages can be communicated in a variety of ways from word of mouth to expensive advertising campaigns. The key to deciding how your messages are to be communicated depends on:

◆ What you are trying to communicate.
◆ Who your 'target audience' is.
◆ What your budget is.

Customers respond best to messages that are simple, distinctive, consistent and repeated. Messages that are too complicated, unclear and inconsistent fail to be effective.

Your 'target audience' is the particular type of customers you are trying to get a response from. They will dictate the method you will use to communicate your message. Research may be required to ascertain how best to reach this audience: finding out where they live, where they go, what they read and listen to, will help you find ways of communicating with them.

Marketing activity costs money and you should set aside a budget to cover this. Costs vary depending on the method used to communicate your message. Some very effective methods of communicating are inexpensive, though you may need to spend time putting them together; and more expensive methods do not necessarily provide better results. You should aim for the most cost-effective methods that are within your budget.

How much you set aside for your marketing budget will depend on your circumstances and your objectives for the business (ie the position you start from and where you want to get to). The larger the gap between these 2 points, the more marketing activity you will need to do. Pubs typically spend an average of 2%–3% of their sales turnover (ex VAT) on marketing activity, most of which is on newspaper advertising. Many other types of marketing activity are more effective but sadly are often ignored in favour of easy to arrange advertising.

EVALUATING YOUR MARKETING ACTIVITY

Blindly spending money on a particular way of communicating month by month, without evaluating whether it is working is akin to throwing money down the drain. Unfortunately, many pubs do just that. They unthinkingly commit to 12 months' paid advertising in the local newspaper because it seems to be a good idea or because their competitors are doing it too. They make no attempt to assess whether their advertising is working. Then they repeat the process again the following year, simply because they did it before!

Evaluating your marketing activity is by no means an exact science; it can sometimes be difficult to work out what impact it has had on your business. However, making an attempt to find a correlation between your sales figures and your marketing activity is better than not doing so and simply hoping for the best. Checking your weekly sales before, during and after any marketing activity is useful, so too is obtaining feedback from your customers. As you build up your sales information over several months, you will become aware of trends and seasonal fluctuations.

Keeping a diary of your marketing activity, together with your weekly sales figures, helps highlight any changes that may be attributable to your marketing activities.

Evaluation is made much easier if your marketing activity incorporates a voucher to be redeemed by the customer. For example, 'claim a free glass of wine with each meal' etc. This allows you to quantify the response you get and also capture useful customer information that can be used for future marketing activity.

Evaluating your marketing activity helps you to ascertain what works and what does not. Spend time and money on what works and drop what does not. Doing so will stop you from wasting money and improve the effectiveness of your marketing.

IMAGE AND STANDARDS

Your image and standards also send a message to customers and potential customers. The way you present yourself, your pub, your staff, your standards and your levels of service send out a strong message to the public. These must be consistent with your objectives for the business and your marketing plan. If your objective is to promote your pub as a high quality food establishment, a dirty pub or dishevelled staff will work against you, even if your food is first-rate. Make sure that your overall image and standards are compatible with achieving your objectives and not sending mixed messages to your customers.

 A customer's first impression of a pub is formed by how clean and attractive the outside of the pub, its gardens and car park appear. If they do not like what they see, they are unlikely to venture inside (no matter how superb its interior, its products or customer service).

SPECIFIC METHODS OF COMMUNICATING

'A' boards

'A' boards are a simple but effective way of promoting your business. An 'A' board is a free-standing, double-sided chalkboard that can be put outside your pub to advertise products, events, offers etc. It can be positioned to help pedestrians and motorists find you, as well as to advertise offers and events. There are restrictions on where you can locate them and your council may object if your 'A' board infringes any regulations.

Flags

Not normally thought of as a method of communicating, flags are very good for attracting attention as they flutter in the breeze, and are therefore good for building awareness. Rural pubs on busy roads can make good use of flags to catch the eye of passing motorists and distinguish themselves from their competitors.

Banners

Banners are frequently used by pubs to promote satellite TV, special events and food. They can be made in a variety of sizes by local suppliers and can be effective at communicating to customers and potential customers. Unfortunately, banners can suffer the ravages of the weather and quickly become discoloured or damaged. Banners also lose impact when they have been displayed for a while. Tired and tatty banners make the outside of the pub look untidy. Use them occasionally for specific periods of time then take them down, to make the best use of them.

Road signs

Rural pubs and pubs in tourist destinations are sometimes able to have road signs made and positioned to direct the public to them. If this is something you are interested in, you should approach your local council. Planning permission may have to be applied for, together with an arrangement fee and the cost of the sign itself. They are permanent fixtures and can be very effective in helping the public to find you.

Chalkboards

Chalkboards can be used for menus, promoting 'beer or wine of the month' and forthcoming events. Simple white chalk on the black background can look very effective, as can displays that are more colourful. Whichever style you decide to use, it must look professional. Make sure that the writing is neat and legible and preferably use someone with artistic talent for any illustrations. Strategically place your chalkboards where they can be seen and don't overdo it; too many can spoil the effectiveness.

 Your local art college is a good place to find a chalkboard artist.

Menus

Menus should be clean, professionally presented, and have mouth-watering descriptions of the food you are offering. Many food suppliers offer free design and printing of menus for their customers and are worth considering. Menus can also be used to promote drinks by recommending wines and beers that compliment the dishes. (See Chapter 17, *Pub Food*, for more information.)

Wine lists

Wine lists are excellent tools for promoting your wines. They too, should be professionally presented with a brief, enticing description of the wines you have available. Wine suppliers, breweries and pub companies are often able to help you put together a wine list and suggest a range of wines that may be suitable for your pub. Some companies also have a facility to print wine lists for you.

Staff shirts

Staff should always be smartly presented and staff uniforms are a means of doing this. Staff shirts can also be a way of promoting products and events to your customers. Messages can be displayed on the shirts: an unusual but effective way of communicating with your customers. This works best if the shirts are used for only a short period of time, rather than the staff wearing the same shirts, week-in, week-out. You can have different 'campaigns' over the course of the year, with different messages promoting different things. Badges are another way of doing this, though being smaller can be difficult to see.

Bar displays

Your bar servery should be regarded as your 'shop window' and is therefore your primary place for promoting your products. Your back bar area is the perfect place for product displays. These can be used to launch new drinks and ones with high profit margins. Try to make your display a little more interesting than simply stacking up a few bottles together. This will add enormously to the impact of the display. For example, displays can be enhanced by adding the following:

◆ dried hops;
◆ good quality imitation vines;
◆ imitation ice;
◆ photographic backgrounds;
◆ humorous props and images;
◆ lights;
◆ movement;
◆ colour.

You can also tie in displays with seasonal changes and major events. Being creative with your displays will increase their success significantly. Displays should be changed monthly, as they will not be noticed by your customers after that. It is also advisable to limit the number of products you are promoting in this way to no more than one or two at any one time, otherwise your back bar can look too cluttered. You need to invest time to keep your displays fresh and creative. You can ease the burden by enlisting the support of some of your bar staff to help you with these. Make it fun by running competitions for the best displays created by them.

Point of sale material (POS)

Point of sale material (POS) are items like drip mats, bar towels, ice buckets, posters, tent cards and glassware. Most of these items are provided by breweries, pub companies or other suppliers, and tend to promote their big brands. These provide another means of communicating with, and influencing customers. Linking in point of sale material with back bar displays adds to the overall impact.

Be aware that point of sale material quickly becomes tatty and needs to be discarded. Displaying poor quality point of sale material has a negative impact on your image. Try to make sure you have sufficient supplies by regularly asking your brewery, pub company and other suppliers for new stocks.

 Supermarkets have superb displays that they use for all the major celebrations throughout the year. They throw out this display material after each event. Make contact with your local store manager and ask if you can have it. You can make use of it the following year for your own displays.

Newsletters

Newsletters are a much underrated method of communicating with your customers and potential customers. They can be used to keep your customers up to date with activities at your pub. You can include news of new offers, entertainment, promotions and competitions. They are best written in a friendly, light-hearted style and produced on a monthly or quarterly basis. You can also include photographs. They can be easily put together using inexpensive computer software.

Newsletters can be distributed in the following ways:

◆ From central points within the pub – for example, 'The Barking Dog News-stand'.
◆ Posted to addresses of subscribers.
◆ Posted generally to homes in your catchment area.
◆ By email to the email addresses of subscribers.
◆ In other places by agreement – for example, hairdressers, shops, libraries etc (make sure they are places used by your target customers).

Direct mail

Direct mail is using leaflets or letters posted speculatively to homes in your catchment area. You can buy lists of addresses from marketing companies that can target particular types of people. They will provide the entire service from putting together your leaflet/letter to addressing and posting them. The cost of this service can be expensive and a 3% response from this form of marketing is regarded as very good. Newsletters, as described earlier, tend to be better received by their recipients, as they seem less like junk mail. They can also be sent in this way. Rather than using the professional approach, you can put together your own leaflets and pay someone to deliver them. You can also arrange for leaflets to be inserted into newspapers by your local newsagent for a fee.

Websites

The dramatic increase in internet users over the last few years is set to continue. Having your own website constructed is relatively inexpensive and can be an excellent way of promoting certain kinds of pubs. Your target customers will dictate whether a website would be useful. Having a website can attract new customers and be a means of your existing customers keeping up to date with activities at your pub.

If your target customers are internet users (and this figure is growing every month) they may use the internet to look for the products, services and activities that you offer, thus your website may be effective in attracting new customers. The key is to think about what your target customers may use the internet to search for. If your pub offers what they are looking for, then having your own website will help them be directed to you. Having a website is particularly useful for pubs:

◆ providing accommodation;
◆ offering regular entertainment;
◆ serving meals;
◆ located in a tourist area;
◆ offering specialist activities;
◆ with historical connections.

These are the types of subjects that are likely to be searched for by internet users and therefore these types of pubs may benefit from having a website. A word of caution: websites are ranked by 'search engines' (Google, Yahoo, Alta Vista etc) based on how relevant the content of your site is to search terms used. A good web designer will help optimise your website, but there can be no guarantees where your site will be ranked.

You can also promote your website address via any of the other methods in this chapter. This enables your target customers to find your website directly without searching for specific subjects. To maximise the number of visitors your website gets, you should display your website address in every available place.

Once people have found your website you can encourage them to interact with you by collecting feedback, obtaining email addresses and entering competitions. This can provide you with information which enables you to contact your target customers directly by email and electronic newsletters etc.

Set up a system that enables local office workers to email you their lunchtime food orders in advance. Their lunchtime break is often limited and this service will be regarded as extremely beneficial to them.

Internet advertising

Coupled with having your own website is internet advertising. This is where you pay for your pub website to be advertised on other parts of the internet, such as other websites and search engine results pages. This can be an excellent way of attracting visitors to your website. The two main providers of this type of service (with their website addresses) are:

◆ Google Adwords   https://adwords.google.com
◆ Yahoo   http://searchmarketing.yahoo.com

These work by displaying the advert for your website when particular search terms are entered into a search engine by an internet user. This system differs from normal search engine results that are displayed for free. Your advert will be displayed at the top or side of the normal search results. They are also displayed on other relevant websites. You pay only when a user clicks on your advert and is directed to your website. Advertisers bid for their position: the more you bid, the higher the position of your advert.

Social Networking sites and Blogging

Social networking sites provide an excellent opportunity to market your pub free of charge. Social networking sites like Facebook, Twitter and blogs can be used to promote your business and inform customers and potential customers about events, promotions, new products and other launches. YouTube can be used to show off your pub's facilities.

Setting up an account with any of these sites is easy, but remember to keep a regular flow of news and activity flowing through your pages to ensure you keep visitors/followers interested and up-to-date.

Here are some useful website addresses:

- www.facebook.com
- www.twitter.com
- www.blogger.com
- www.youtube.com

Directories and guides

Directories and guides provide another means of promoting your pub. Examples include *Good Beer Guides*, accommodation and food guides, tourist guides and pub directories. These are produced by a range of individuals and companies. Some will include your details free of charge, while for others there will be a fee payable. To decide whether to pay for this form of marketing, you should check whether there is any potential for your target customers to read it and how many copies of the guide or directory will be produced and circulated.

Club and society newsletters

Often local clubs and societies have their own newsletters in which you can place inexpensive (or free) adverts. This may enable you to reach potential new customers in a low cost way. A trip to your local library will often uncover a large number of these groups. Supporting clubs and societies is also a good way of attracting new customers, especially where you allow them the free use of your function room, or provide them with a few sandwiches for their meetings.

Public relations to obtain media coverage

Public relations, or PR as it is known, is a superb way of marketing (though little used by licensees). It should be at the top of your list of ways to promote your pub. It is little used by licensees only because most of them think it is more complicated than it actually is. PR done well can generate media coverage free of charge, which would cost you an equivalent of hundreds or thousands of pounds in paid advertising. Two ways of obtaining free media coverage are:

◆ issuing press releases;
◆ building relationships with journalists.

Newspapers, magazines and radio stations are always looking for stories. By contacting them and providing them with details of something of interest about your pub, you can often get free coverage. To do this, send a press release to the editor or telephone their news desk. To stand a chance of getting coverage you will have to inform them of something that will be of interest to their readers or listeners. You will stand a better chance of publication if your news item is:

◆ weird;
◆ unusual;
◆ funny;
◆ frightening;
◆ linked to local issues;
◆ linked to local history;
◆ very important;
◆ about awards you have received;
◆ about famous people or celebrities;
◆ about animals.

When planning any events for your pub, try to add a twist to them in order to get them publicised. Run-of-the-mill happenings and events will be of little interest to journalists. For example, a worm-charming competition is much more newsworthy than a karaoke competition!

You have the option of notifying the press and local radio *before* the event is due to take place, in the hope that they will come along, or you can notify them afterwards. In which case you should include some good quality photographs for the press so that they can use them in any article they publish.

It is quite possible to 'manufacture' your own news stories, but you will have to be very convincing. Make sure you are not seen *making* the crop circles in your beer garden!

If you run a quality food pub, a good review from a food critic is a sought-after endorsement. A good review will have a positive impact on your business. Find out who your local food critic is and invite them to your pub for a complimentary meal.

Sponsorship

Licensees frequently sponsor sports teams that use their pubs; providing shirts for the football team or sponsoring the annual fishing match are typical examples. As a licensee, you will regularly be approached for sponsorship, which can be expensive. If sponsorship is something you wish to consider, set an annual budget and stick to it. (You can fend off any unwanted enquiries by telling them that your budget is already allocated.) Think whether the type of sponsorship you are considering is the best use of your money. There may be other kinds of sponsorship that are more appropriate to your target market or that you can gain some useful media coverage from. For example, the local media are likely to be interested in you sponsoring the children's ward of the local hospital, but not interested in you paying for your domino team's tee-shirts.

It is good practice to review your sponsorship each year to ascertain if it has been of value to your business. For example: paying for an expensive football strip for a team whose members rarely use your pub may be of limited benefit to you.

'What's on' guides

Most local newspapers and radio stations feature a guide to 'what's on' in your area. Events and activities are normally listed free of charge. It is worth finding out the name of the person who compiles these and keeping them regularly updated of anything that may be of interest to them. It pays to plan your events and activities well in advance in order to give you time to properly advertise them.

Newspaper and magazine advertising

Paid advertising is often the first choice for licensees wishing to advertise their pubs, mainly because it takes little thought or preparation. However, the results of paid advertising are often disappointing. Your advert can be buried amongst several similar adverts and may not even be noticed by your target customers. If you are considering this form of marketing, here are some pointers:

◆ Follow the AIDA principles and clarify your purpose (see the earlier section, 'Purpose of your marketing message').
◆ Check whether the publication will be read by your target customers (the advertising staff can provide you with their readership information).
◆ Ask for the publication's circulation figures.
◆ Negotiate the price of the advert (don't pay what is initially quoted).
◆ Don't commit to a run of adverts before evaluating the impact of advertising in the publication.
◆ Have an eye-catching headline (not your pub's address).
◆ Make the advert simple and distinctive.
◆ Ask for it to be positioned on a right hand page or the right hand side of a page (the human eye notices adverts more effectively if they are positioned in this way).

If you are considering paying for advertising make it a small percentage of your overall marketing budget. There are many other effective ways of communicating with your target customers.

Radio and television advertising

The cost of advertising on radio or television prevents many small businesses from promoting themselves in this way, and pubs are no exception. There are less expensive ways of advertising on radio and television such as running adverts at off-peak times: (advertising at 3am will cost you much less than at 3pm). Smaller local radio and cable television stations also provide a less expensive means of advertising. In each case though, the prices will be lower because audience numbers are smaller.

Unless you have a pub with a very high turnover that justifies advertising in this way, you will need to use other marketing methods to reach your target customers. Rather than paying to advertise, try to obtain free coverage through the PR methods mentioned earlier. Interesting or very humorous news items about pubs are occasionally broadcast on national television and much more frequently on regional television. Don't be afraid of contacting the big radio and television stations if you have a great story. It can lead to some excellent publicity for your pub.

OTHER MARKETING ACTIVITY

Other forms of marketing activity help you communicate with and interact with your customers. Fun events and activities can attract people who do not normally use your pub, and if they enjoy themselves, they can become regular customers. These events generate interest and build the loyalty of your existing clientele. Running them on less busy days of the week also helps to boost your sales.

Tasting nights

Tasting nights are used to promote specific drinks. They are a good way to launch new products and promote products with high profit margins. The aim of these nights is to persuade people to try the product and encourage them to purchase the drink in the future.

Events like wine tastings are increasing in popularity, and are best run by someone with a reasonable knowledge of the subject. These are a good way of 'educating' customers about wine and introducing them to better quality wines.

These nights are often supported by your brewery, pub company or other supplier, who may provide free stock, and promotion kits and point of sale material for the event.

Samples

Aside from organised tasting nights, providing a small free sample to a customer who has asked what a particular drink is like is preferable to trying to describe the product to them. This 'try before you buy' approach allows the customer to try the drink and ensure they like it before purchasing it. It is particularly good for draught beers and lagers and wine. You can obtain very small plastic 'shot glasses' from licensed trade suppliers to use for this.

Party nights

Party nights provide fun and entertainment for customers who will often talk about the night for weeks afterwards. They can be themed around annual events, for example, St Patrick's Day and Hallowe'en or other themes like beach parties, hog roasts, and fancy dress. Party nights should be appropriate for the type of pub and clientele. Try to be creative and look for unusual events, people or places on which to base your party nights.

 You can find lots of ideas on the BBC 'on this day in history' website: http://news.bbc.co.uk/onthisday/

Festivals

Beer and food festivals can be run on a small scale, very successfully in your pub. These can be run over a day, or several days. For a beer festival, you will need to obtain a range of cask, and/or bottled beers. As a tenant or lessee, this will be dependent on the product range that you have available, or whether your brewery or pub company will make a special allowance for you to purchase products not normally supplied by them. If you are intending to run a cask beer festival, it is likely that you will need to have additional beer pumps fitted (on a temporary basis) and you should speak to your brewery or pub company representative well in advance to see if this can be arranged. Some companies hire temporary bars and beer dispense equipment, which can be used for setting up a bar area in an annex to the pub or marquee. (Make sure that you obtain any necessary permission from your licensing authority.)

Food festivals are a good way of promoting your pub as a food venue and building good relationships with local suppliers, if you involve them in the event. They can feature particular types of food for example: 'curry festivals' or 'sausage festivals', or can be used to generally showcase local produce. Food festivals can include free samples, cookery demonstrations, free recipes or cut-price meals, and can be linked to drinks that may compliment the food that is on offer. Try to make your festival a little bit different so your event stands out, and perhaps make it an annual event.

RESPONSIBLE PROMOTIONS

There has been a great deal of publicity lately about binge drinking and alcohol-related antisocial behaviour. The Government has called for the licensed trade to help stamp out this type of behaviour through responsible drinks retailing schemes, and the police have added their weight by clamping down on drunkenness and antisocial behaviour by members of the public. In response, the British Beer and Pub Association (the leading organisation representing the brewing and pub sector whose members account for 98% of beer brewed in the UK and own more than half of Britain's pubs) have issued guidelines on how drinks promotions should be run. They have stated that an irresponsible promotion is one that encourages or incites individuals to drink to excess, or behave in an antisocial manner, or that fuels drunkenness. They have identified the kinds of promotions that should *not* be operated because of the disproportionate risk they will lead directly to alcohol misuse and antisocial behaviour. These are:

♦ Reward schemes that are only redeemable over short periods, thereby encouraging the purchase and consumption of large quantities of alcohol over a short period of time.

- Drinking games, as these tend to encourage either speed drinking or the drinking of large quantities of alcohol.
- Promotions that involve large quantities of free drinks, eg women drink for free.
- Entry fees that are linked with unlimited amounts of drinks, eg '£x.99 on the door and all your drinks are free' or 'All you can drink for £x.99'.
- Promotions that are an incentive to speed drinking or encouraging people to 'down their drinks in one', eg 'If you finish your first bottle of wine by 9.00 pm, the next one is on us'.
- Promotions linked to unpredictable events, eg 'Free drinks for 5 minutes after every goal'.
- Promotions that encourage or reward the purchase or drinking of large quantities of alcohol in a single session.
- Promotional material that is linked to sexual imagery implying sexual success or prowess.
- Promotions that encourage either an excessive drinking session or a pub crawl.
- Promotions that involve driving in any way.
- Promotions that refer to consuming alcohol to recover from previous over-indulgence, or glamorise excessive or irresponsible drinking (effects of intoxication should not be referred to in any favourable manner).
- Promotions that are not respectful of contemporary, prevailing standards of taste and decency and are degrading or gratuitously offensive through images, symbols, figures and innuendo.
- Promotional material which is demeaning to any gender, race, religion, age, or minority group.
- Use of images/symbols/characters or persons in promotional material that appeal primarily to those under the legal purchase age: characters should be used only if it is clearly established that their primary appeal is to adults (use of any cartoon character popular with children is unacceptable).
- Direct or indirect references to drug culture or illegal drugs in promotional material.
- Association with violence or antisocial behaviour in promotional material.

You can find more information about promoting drinks responsibly, on the following websites: www.beerandpub.com, www.portman-group.org.uk, www.responsibledrinksretailing.co.uk

YOUR MARKETING PLAN

Like any other business activity, marketing is more successful when it is planned. Your 'marketing plan' focuses your marketing activity on your target customers. Your plan does not have to be overly detailed but it does need some thought and time to prepare. It forms part of your overall business plan for the pub. It should be used as a working document to monitor your progress and not simply completed then filed in a desk drawer. Marketing is too important to be left to chance or be done in an ad hoc way. Planning your marketing and displaying your intended activities on an annual year planner is a good way of making sure you keep on track.

Your marketing plan should include the following:

- Your overall aims for the business.
- Your image of how your successful pub will operate.
- Your overall marketing objectives.
- Your target customers and their needs:
   — existing clientele;
   — similar types of customer;
   — new types of customer.

- How you will ensure their needs are met:
   — premises;
   — drinks products;
   — food;
   — licensee and staff;
   — people;
   — entertainment.

- Other marketing activities:
  - events and activities;
  - calendar of planned activities and events.

- Changes that need to be made:
  - purpose and objectives;
  - timescales;
  - cost;
  - who will make them?

- Communicating with your target customers:
  - objectives;
  - methods of communicating;
  - frequency;
  - budget.

- Your main competitors:
  - what types of customer they attract;
  - what they offer;
  - what they charge;
  - what recent changes they have made;
  - what they do better than you;
  - what you do better than them.

- Feedback and review:
  - what has been achieved?
  - what has worked?
  - what can be done more effectively?
  - what still needs to be done?
  - what changes still need to be made?

Your marketing plan draws together all your planned marketing, helping you coordinate and clearly target your activities as well as evaluating their effectiveness. When putting together your annual marketing plan, you may benefit from taking a day away from your business, which may help you to think more creatively about it. It is better to invest time planning your marketing than to throw money away on methods that require little effort but are ineffective. Good marketing is one of the keys to success.

15

STAFF

BENEFITS OF HAVING GREAT STAFF

On average, 70% of a pub's turnover goes through the hands of its staff and only 30% is taken via the licensee and their partner. This means that your staff have a big impact on your success, whether it is through the quality of their interaction with customers or their trustworthiness. Inattentive, impolite or uncaring staff will damage customer relations and dishonest staff can prove very costly to you. Great staff on the other hand, will generate goodwill, build customer loyalty and take on some of the burden of running your pub.

STAFF THAT COME WITH THE BUSINESS

Employee rights

When a business is transferred, employees' rights are protected under the Transfer of Undertakings (Protection of Employment) Regulations 1981 (TUPE). This means that their terms and conditions must remain the same as they were prior to the transfer and their continuous employment period is preserved.

When you acquire your pub, its staff transfer with the business and you become legally responsible for them. Their employment with you does not count as new employment. Dismissing staff or changing their terms and conditions risk legal consequences. For example, if, because of the transfer, you dismiss an employee who has one year's employment or more, they can automatically claim to have been unfairly dismissed. If you change an employee's terms and conditions because of the transfer, and the employee is compelled to resign as a consequence, they may have a right to claim that they were constructively dismissed.

Your right to make changes

As an employer, you have a right to dismiss staff if there is an economic, technical or organisational (ETO) reason which necessitates changes to the workforce. Then you may be able to dismiss fairly, provided you have followed the correct procedure. In practice, ETO reasons are narrow and you should seek legal advice before dismissing staff on these grounds. If you do dismiss staff for such reasons you will be required to make them redundant and follow the correct redundancy procedures.

Employee morale

Employee morale is often affected when a business is transferred. When you acquire your pub, its staff may be anxious and uncertain about their future. It is good practice to meet with staff as soon as possible after you have taken over, or even prior to taking over, with the permission of the outgoing licensee. Either way, it is essential to make sure that staff are reassured and understand your plans for the business. Good morale is important and communication plays a vital part in developing and maintaining it.

Be prepared for staff leaving

Sometimes you will find that members of staff decide to leave when you take over, despite your reassurances and positive plans for the future. Speaking to staff prior to taking over may help you identify employees that are not planning to stay with you long-term, but occasionally employees leave even though they have said they will not. This is more of a problem when the employee is a key member of staff such as a cook, chef or senior bar staff. You need to be prepared for this eventuality and have thought about how you will replace them at short notice if necessary.

STAFF TURNOVER

Staff turnover is the rate at which employees leave you. Every time an employee leaves you, there is a cost to you for replacing them. Advertising, interviewing, induction and training takes time and costs you money. When staff turnover increases, this puts pressure on your resources and may indicate that there are problems with morale. Low staff turnover means that you have a stable team of employees.

Due to the nature of the business, there tends to be a reasonably high staff turnover in the licensed trade. Many bar staff do not view their work as a long-term career. Jobs tend to be low paid and attract people who are looking for temporary or seasonal work. However, reasonable rates of pay, a good working environment and opportunities for staff to gain additional training and experience are ways to build employee loyalty and keep staff turnover at a minimum.

Monitor your staff turnover every 6 months by working out how many employees leave as a percentage of your total staff.

TAKING ON NEW STAFF

Recruitment

When an employee leaves or your business expands, you need to recruit new staff. Because of the importance of having good staff, it is essential to spend time trying to recruit the best people you can. Think about the type of person who will fit into your business and be able to interact with your customers in a positive way. Consider what skills and experience they will need to fulfil their role. Do you want someone who has had experience of doing the job before, or will you be happy to train them your way?

Job descriptions and person specifications

To help clarify your ideas, draft a simple job description, which lists all the major tasks involved in doing the job. From this, you can prepare a person specification for the role that identifies essential and desirable attributes. This helps you concentrate on the attributes required to do the job and makes the task of comparing candidates easier. An example of an abbreviated person specification is shown below:

Job Title: Bar staff		**Wage:** £5.80 per hour
Summary of job: General bar duties including serving drinks and meals to customers. Required to work 26 hours per week including Saturday and Sunday evenings.		
Attributes Experience:	**Essential** Minimum of 6 months' experience in a similar role.	**Desirable**
Personality:	Pleasant, outgoing personality.	
Physical:	Able to work behind a bar for extended periods.	
Specialist knowledge:		Knowledge of wines.
Training:		Hold British Institute of Innkeeping Barperson's National Certificate.
Qualifications:		Hold recognised licensing qualification.
Other requirements:		

Advertising your vacancies

Once you have prepared your person specification, you can use this to put together a brief job advertisement, which highlights the kind of person you are looking for. Fortunately, most vacancies will be filled without the need to place expensive newspaper or magazine advertisements. (Occasionally, more specialist roles, such as chefs may need advertising in this way.) Here are some low-cost ways to fill your vacancies:

◆ Ask your existing staff if they know anyone who may be suitable.
◆ Advertise in your pub window.
◆ Advertise at the bar or in the pub toilets.
◆ Advertise in your local jobcentre.

Interviews

Interviewing potential staff should be done in an area away from the day-to-day distractions of running your pub. Plan to see applicants at a quiet part of the day when you can devote time to interviewing them properly. This can be difficult when you are approached by someone interested in your vacancy while you are in the middle of a busy period. In these circumstances, rather than having a rushed conversation, explain to them that it is not convenient and arrange to see them again at a more suitable time. If you have advertised your vacancy in the job centre, you can specify on the advert when candidates should telephone you or visit you to discuss the position.

Interviews can be kept informal over a cup of coffee, but make sure that you are prepared and are clear about the kind of skills, personality and experience you require. Have details of the job description and person specification with you, together with rates of pay. Keep notes on each applicant that you can refer to after the interview. Explain the role and what you expect of them. Work through the person specification to gauge whether their skills and experience match your requirements. If they have been employed in the licensed trade before, ask if you can contact their previous employer for a reference if necessary. Answer any questions the applicant may have and explain to them what will happen next. (If you have a number of applicants to interview, you should let them know when you will notify them if they have been successful. Alternatively, you may be in a position to offer a person the job at the end of the interview.) Follow up any verbal offer of employment in writing, confirming the summary of the job, rates of pay, hours and start date.

Discrimination

Anyone who considers that they have been discriminated against during the process of recruitment and selection can make a claim to an employment tribunal, who may award them compensation. The law penalises anyone discriminating on the following grounds:

◆ gender;
◆ race;
◆ disability;
◆ religion or belief;
◆ sexual orientation;
◆ trade union membership;
◆ age.

To avoid potential discrimination claims, make sure you base your staff selection on the requirements of the job and treat all applicants fairly and consistently.

Eligibility to work in the UK

Anyone you employ must be eligible to live and work in the UK. It is a criminal offence to employ anyone, aged 16 or over, who doesn't have permission to work in the UK. The maximum penalty is currently £5,000 per illegal employee. Prior to taking on a new employee, you should check and keep a record of documents confirming an individual's eligibility to work in the UK. If requesting documents at an earlier stage of the recruitment process, you must ensure that you ask all applicants for the same information to avoid claims of discrimination.

By law, there are two lists of documents that are acceptable as confirmation of an individual's right to work in the UK. You can find details of these and more information on this subject at: www.workingintheuk.gov.uk

Induction procedure and training

It is good practice to have a planned induction procedure for new employees. This does not have to be detailed or complicated but it should help introduce the individual to the pub, their colleagues and your customers. You should also ensure that they are clear about what you expect of them: their tasks and the standards you require. It helps to induct new employees during less busy periods where you can devote time to them and allow them to become familiar with their new environment. A typical induction procedure for bar staff will include:

- Introductions to other members of staff.
- Familiarisation with the pub layout.
- Familiarisation with beer dispense equipment and glassware.
- Use of tills.
- Location of products, bar layout and stores.
- Characteristics of main products.
- Location of first aid and fire fighting equipment.
- Safe use of equipment.
- Health and safety issues.
- How you like customers to be addressed.
- How you like the telephone answered.
- General standards of service and cleanliness.
- Details of any special offers and sales promotions.
- Who they should speak to in case of queries or difficulties.

Make time at the end of your new employee's first session to check that they are happy with things and follow this up again at the end of their first week. It is a good opportunity to clarify any areas of their job that they are unsure about and a good time for you to 'correct' anything that you are not happy with.

The level of training new applicants will require depends on how experienced they are at doing the job. Inexperienced staff will need to be coached by you or other capable members of staff. Even new staff with years of experience may have picked up bad habits or do things differently from how you want them to be done. It is worth running through their main tasks to ensure that they understand what is expected of them. Ongoing training keeps staff up to date and motivated. Try to incorporate some regular training for all staff into your business routine. Training sessions do not have to take up a great deal of time; short sessions can be just as effective. Make use of suppliers, local colleges and any information you pick up yourself from the licensed trade press (which features many excellent training tips). Keep a record of the training you have given to your staff.

CONTRACTS OF EMPLOYMENT

Contracts of employment are legally binding agreements between an employer and employee. The contract is made up of both oral and written agreements and is formed when an employee agrees to work for you for pay. Contracts include:

◆ Express terms – those terms which are explicitly agreed.
◆ Implied terms – terms which are implied, such as those that are common practice in the industry and terms which are too obvious to mention like not stealing from an employer.
◆ Incorporated terms – terms incorporated from other documents, such as company handbooks.
◆ Statutory terms – terms imposed by law such as not to discriminate, maternity pay etc.

As an employer, you are required by law to provide a new employee with written details of their main terms and conditions within 2 months of employing them. This written statement must cover:

◆ The names of the employer and the employee.
◆ Job title or a brief job description.

- The date when the employment (or period of continuous employment) began.
- Remuneration and the intervals at which it is to be paid.
- Hours of work.
- Holiday entitlement.
- Entitlement to sick leave, including any entitlement to sick pay.
- Pensions and pension schemes that may be applicable.
- Entitlement of employer and employee to notice of termination.
- Where the position is not permanent, the period for which the employment is expected to continue or, if it is for a fixed term, the date when it is to end.
- The place of work.
- Disciplinary and grievance procedures.

You can vary an existing contract only with the agreement of your employee. Any agreed changes should be put in writing at the earliest opportunity. However, some contracts may contain express terms which allow you to make reasonable changes to your employee's working conditions such as varying their duties etc.

If you impose changes to the contract that are not agreed by your employee, they have the right to take action for breach of contract. (If your employee continues to work under the amended contract without objection, they may be regarded as having agreed to the changes.) Your employee can take the following action for breach of contract:

- Where there is a fundamental breach of contract, they could regard this as bringing the contract to an end and leave their position. They have the opportunity of making a claim through an industrial tribunal for constructive dismissal (subject to them having the necessary qualifying service period).
- They may continue to work under the varied contract under protest, not accepting the new terms and treating the changes as a breach of contract and dismissal from the original contract. They may be able to make a claim for unfair dismissal before a tribunal (subject to qualifying service).

COMMUNICATING WITH STAFF

With a small number of staff, it is relatively easy to keep in touch with them on a one-to-one basis. However, if you have a large number of staff you may need to consider other ways of communicating with your employees. Short team meetings can be useful ways of improving communication between you and your staff. They are a chance for you to bring staff up to date with issues, discuss changes and equally importantly, obtain feedback from your staff. Staff meetings are also an opportunity to provide your employees with additional training in the following areas: product knowledge, sales techniques, using new equipment, legislation etc.

Ask your brewery, pub company or other supplier to come along to your team meeting to conduct a short training session for your staff.

A staff noticeboard is another way of communicating with your employees. Industry news and information from the licensed trade press can be displayed on it, as well as your forthcoming events and marketing activity. Staff will soon ignore noticeboards that have not been updated recently or have dog-eared displays. Keeping your staff noticeboard fresh and clutter-free will encourage staff to use it.

Communication is a two-way process and you should aim to foster an environment that encourages your staff to give you suggestions and feedback. This can be done in a variety of ways: informally directly to you, or via team meetings or through suggestion schemes. Encouraging staff to give you feedback helps reduce problems and makes them feel more involved in the business.

STAFF INCENTIVES

Recognition and reward are great motivators, and incentivising your staff is an excellent way of motivating them and improving your sales. These schemes work by firstly deciding what you want your staff to promote, then running the incentive for a period of time and rewarding the highest achieving staff for their efforts. Incentives are best run over a short period, such as a month. Incentive schemes can be used to promote a variety of things. For example, sales of coffees or desserts in food pubs. They can also be used to reward the best promotional displays, money-saving suggestions or marketing idea. Staff rewards can include bottles of wine, trophies, tickets to events and gift vouchers. Running staff incentives does involve a little administration and some cost, but the effect on your staff, and the positive impact on your sales, makes the money and effort worthwhile. Try to run a staff incentive every month or second month if you can.

MINIMUM WAGE

The minimum wage is a legal right which covers almost all workers above compulsory school-leaving age. There are different minimum wage rates for different groups of workers as follows (rates effective 2010):

◆ The main rate for workers aged 22 and over: £5.80 an hour.
◆ The development rate for 18–21 year olds: £4.83 an hour.
◆ The development rate for those no longer of compulsory school age: £3.57 an hour.

Refusing to pay the minimum wage is a criminal offence, with fines of up to £5,000. Dismissing an employee when they become eligible for the minimum wage or a higher rate of minimum wage is regarded as unfair dismissal. (Workers do not have to work for a qualifying period for this to be enforceable.)

OTHER RIGHTS ON PAY

Equal pay

As an employer, you must treat men and women equally as far as their terms and conditions are concerned; this includes their pay. Men and women doing the same, or broadly similar types of work must be treated uniformly. Individuals who feel that they have been unfairly treated have a right to complain to an employment tribunal under the Equal Pay Act 1970. They are able to make a claim up to 6 months after leaving the employment to which their claim relates. Claims can include pay arrears including sick pay, holiday pay, bonuses and overtime payments. This can be claimed for a period of up to 6 years (5 years in Scotland).

Statutory Maternity Pay

Women are entitled to Statutory Maternity Pay (SMP) if they have been employed by their employer for a continuous period of 26 weeks or more, ending with the 15th week before the expected week of childbirth. (To qualify, she must have average weekly earnings at least equal to the lower earnings limit for National Insurance contributions.) As an employer, you are responsible for making SMP payments, which are then reimbursed by the state. Payment levels and duration (as at 5 April 2009) are as follows:

◆ Paid for a maximum of 39 weeks.
◆ Six weeks at 90% of her average weekly earnings (with no upper limit).
◆ 33 weeks at a flat rate of £124.88 or 90% of her average weekly earnings if that is less than the flat rate.

Small employers (those whose total NI liability is £45,000 or less in the previous tax year) may recover 104.5% (from April 2010) of the SMP they pay. This money can be claimed in advance to help with your cash flow.

Women who do not qualify for SMP may qualify for Maternity Allowance (MA). This is paid by JobCentre Plus and is based on the woman's recent employment and earnings record.

Maternity leave

Pregnant employees are entitled to 26 weeks ordinary maternity leave, regardless of how long they have worked for you. Women who have completed 26 weeks' continuous service with you by the beginning of the 14th week before the expected week of childbirth can take 'additional' maternity leave. Additional maternity leave starts immediately after ordinary maternity leave and continues for up to a further 26 weeks. Additional maternity leave is usually unpaid unless a woman has contractual rights to pay during her period of additional maternity leave.

A pregnant employee must notify you of her intention to take maternity leave by the end of the 15th week before the expected week of childbirth, unless this is not reasonably practicable. She must tell you:

◆ that she is pregnant;
◆ the week her baby is expected to be born;
◆ when she wants her maternity leave to start.

A woman can change the date when she wants to start her leave providing she tells you at least 28 days in advance (unless this is not reasonably practicable). You must respond to a woman's notification of her leave plans within 28 days unless the woman has varied that date. You should write to your employee, setting out the date on which you expect her to return to work if she takes her full entitlement to maternity leave. The earliest date a woman is able to start her maternity leave is the beginning of the 11th week before her baby is due.

Statutory Paternity Pay

To qualify for Statutory Paternity Pay (SPP), male employees must:

◆ Have, or expect to have, responsibility for the child's upbringing.
◆ Be the biological father of the child or the mother's husband or partner.
◆ Have worked continuously for their employer for 26 weeks ending with the 15th week before the baby is due.

Statutory Paternity Pay is paid by you for either 1 or 2 consecutive weeks that the employee has chosen. SPP (at 2010), is the same as the standard rate of Statutory Maternity Pay – £124.88 a week or 90% of average weekly earnings if less than £124.88. Employees who have average weekly earnings below the Lower Earnings Limit for National Insurance purposes (£95 a week from April 2010) do not qualify for SPP. Employees who do not qualify for SPP, or who are normally low paid, may be able to claim Income Support and other benefits while on paternity leave.

Paternity leave

Employees who are eligible can choose to take either 1 week or 2 consecutive weeks paternity leave (not odd days), which normally needs to be taken within 56 days of the child's birth. Employees must inform you of their intention to take paternity leave by the end of the 15th week before the baby is expected, unless this is not reasonably practicable. They must tell you:

- the week the baby is due;
- whether they wish to take one or two weeks' leave;
- when they want their leave to start.

Paternity leave and maternity leave have the same procedures for varying leave dates and required responses from employers.

Statutory Adoption Pay and leave

Employees who adopt have rights to Statutory Adoption Pay (SAP) and adoption leave that are broadly similar to Statutory Maternity Pay and leave. Paternity Pay and leave is also available to adopters in the same way as it is for birth parents.

Holiday pay

Under the Working Time Regulations 1998, employees have the right to 4 weeks paid leave each year and payment for any untaken leave upon termination of their employment. An employee's holiday entitlement should be stated in their contract of employment. Part-time workers are entitled to the same holidays as full-time employees, calculated on a pro-rata basis. For example, an employee working 2 days per week is entitled to 8 days' paid holiday (their normal working week multiplied by 4).

There is no statutory requirement to allow employees to take paid leave on public holidays. Any right to take time off at these times will depend on the terms of the employee's contract of employment or may have built up through custom and practice. Paid time off during public holidays can be counted as part of the statutory 4 weeks holiday entitlement. You can control when employees take leave by expressly stating this in their contract of employment. For example, restricting the amount of time the staff can take off during busy trading periods.

Your employees are required to give you sufficient notice of their intention to take a holiday. This notice should be twice as long as the period of leave. For example, an employee wanting to take 1 week's holiday must give at least 2 weeks' notice. You are able to refuse holiday requests providing you give your employee prior notice of your refusal, equivalent to the period of leave they requested.

Statutory Sick Pay

Statutory Sick Pay (SSP) is payable to employees who are unable to work due to sickness. It is payable by you for up to a maximum of 28 weeks. To qualify for SSP, employees must satisfy the following conditions:

◆ Have been sick for at least 4 or more days in a row (known as a period of Incapacity for Work).
◆ Earn, before tax and National Insurance, an average of £95 a week (earnings are averaged over an 8-week period before the sickness began).

SSP is payable daily for days that employees would normally work. These are known as Qualifying Days (QDs). SSP is not paid for the first three QDs in any period of sickness. As at April 2009, the standard rate of SSP was £79.15 per week. Payments are made by you in the same way, and at the same time, as you would normally pay your employee. You may be able to recover some of the SSP you have paid from the income tax and National Insurance contributions you pay to HM Revenue and Customs.

Employees are required to inform you as soon as possible that they are sick. Individual employment contracts may specify how employees are to notify you that they are sick. However, you must not impose unreasonable requirements on sick employees, such as making them report their sickness in person, or more than once a week during their period of sickness. You can ask for evidence that your employee is sick. This will usually be in the form of a 'sick note' issued by their GP. However, employees can be asked to fill in your own self-certification form or complete a form SC2 which is available from their GP's surgery.

Employees unable to claim SSP, or if their SSP has ended, must ask you for a form SSP1. You are required to complete this form prior to passing it on to your employee. They will then use this form to claim Incapacity Benefit via their local jobcentre.

See HMRC website for more information about SSP:
www.hmrc.gov.uk/employers/ssp-faq.htm

STAKEHOLDER PENSIONS

If you have 5 or more employees, you may need to offer them access to a stakeholder pension scheme which is registered with the Pensions Regulator. Stakeholder pension schemes are designed to offer low charges, no transfer costs and low minimum contributions of £20 or less. You do not have to make contributions to this pension but you will have to make deductions from an employee's pay if asked. You may be exempt from having to provide access to a stakeholder pension scheme if you:

◆ Employ fewer than 5 people.
◆ Offer all employees aged 18 or over a personal pension scheme through which you contribute an amount equal to at least 3% of your employees' basic pay.
◆ Offer an occupational pension scheme that all your staff can join within a year of starting work with you.

You do not have to provide access to a stakeholder pension for any employee:

◆ Who has worked for you for less than three months.
◆ Who is a member of your occupational pension scheme.
◆ Who cannot join your occupational pension scheme because they are under 18 or within 5 years of the scheme's pension age.
◆ Whose earnings fell below the National Insurance lower earnings limit for 1 or more weeks within the last 3 months.
◆ Who has refused to join your occupational pension scheme.

 You can find more information and a register of approved stakeholder pension providers on-line at: www.thepensionservice.gov.uk

GRIEVANCE PROCEDURES

Occasionally, your employees may have concerns about their work, employment terms, working conditions, colleagues or other matters. Ignoring grievances or handling them badly can lead to many problems including:

◆ disciplinary issues;
◆ poor performance;
◆ resignations;
◆ complaints to employment tribunals.

By law, you must specify in your employees' written terms and conditions, your procedure for handling grievances (which must comply with the statutory grievance procedure). It should contain:

◆ Who your employee should raise the issue with.
◆ How the issue should be raised.
◆ What to do if not satisfied with the initial outcome.
◆ Timescales for each stage.
◆ The right to be represented.

Developing good relationships with your employees, and encouraging them to bring any concerns they have to you at an early stage, will prevent issues from growing and causing more problems. The vast majority of concerns are likely to be resolved in this way.

Statutory grievance procedure

If your employee feels that the matter has not been resolved through informal discussions, they have a right to follow the statutory grievance procedure. Employees wishing to use the grievance as a basis of a complaint to an employment tribunal must first follow step 1 of this procedure. (Employment tribunals can adjust any compensation by between 10 and 50%, if either party does not follow the correct statutory procedure.) The procedure involves 3 steps:

- **Step 1**: Your employee must inform you of the grievance in writing.
- **Step 2**: You must meet to discuss the grievance.
- **Step 3**: You must hold an appeal if necessary.

Your employee has the right to be accompanied by a person of their choice, who could be a work colleague or union representative (where applicable).

After Step 2, and within a reasonable timescale, you must inform your employee what you have decided. If they are not satisfied with the outcome, they have a right to request an appeal meeting with you. If, after this stage, they are still not satisfied and they believe that their employment rights have been infringed, they can make a complaint to an employment tribunal.

Employees who have left your employment can also follow up outstanding grievances with you by following the 'modified grievance procedure'. Using the modified procedure is subject to:

- You both agreeing in writing to follow this procedure.
- You not being aware of the grievance previously.

or

◆ The standard procedure was not started, or was started but not completed.

The modified procedure is a 2-step process, which involves the following:

◆ **Step 1**: Your ex-employee writes to you stating the grievance.
◆ **Step 2**: You write back to them, answering the points they have raised.

However, ex-employees are not legally bound to follow this procedure where there are justifiable reasons, such as if it is not reasonably practicable for them to do so, or they are concerned that notifying you in this way may result in threats or harassment. In such circumstances, they may complain directly to an employment tribunal.

 You can find out more about employment tribunals at the Employment Tribunals website: www.employmenttribunals.gov.uk

It should be stressed that most employee grievances are handled on an informal basis, without the need to follow more formal procedures. Ensuring that employees notify you of their concerns at an early stage and dealing with any issues promptly and fairly, will maintain good working relationships and prevent matters from deteriorating.

DISCIPLINARY PROCEDURES

There may be times when you consider that an employee's performance, conduct or other actions are unsatisfactory. In these circumstances, you should take immediate steps to deal with the situation. But before launching into disciplinary procedure, it is best to investigate the situation as thoroughly as possible first. Speak to everyone concerned to gather the facts and then take steps to respond to the situation appropriately.

Standards of conduct

You need to consider what standards your disciplinary procedure will be used to uphold. From these you should draw up rules which set the standard of conduct you expect from your employees. These should be reasonable, non-discriminatory and reflect the needs of your business. It is helpful to consult with your employees prior to imposing any changes.

Your business rules should be clearly communicated to all your employees in a way that they understand. Rules can cover the following:

◆ standards of work;
◆ personal appearance;
◆ conduct;
◆ timekeeping;
◆ absence;
◆ holidays;
◆ smoking;
◆ health and safety;
◆ non-discrimination;
◆ use of facilities.

You should also set out behaviour that will be treated as 'gross misconduct', which is serious enough to lead to dismissal without notice. Examples of gross misconduct may include:

◆ theft;
◆ fraud;
◆ drunkenness or drug abuse;
◆ bullying;
◆ gross negligence;
◆ gross insubordination;
◆ serious breaches of health and safety;
◆ wilful damage to property.

Informal procedures

Minor disciplinary offences should be dealt with informally initially, through discussion with the employee concerned. As in the case of grievance procedures, dealing with the situation informally will, in the majority of cases, resolve the situation without further problems. Where you have given an employee an informal verbal warning, let them know that it is not part of the formal disciplinary procedure, but this will be instigated if there is no improvement in the situation. You may decide that your employee needs additional training or coaching to help improve their performance. Keep brief notes about the informal action for future reference and arrange to review the employee's progress over a period of time.

Series of warnings

Normally a series of warnings should be given prior to dismissal or other form of discipline:

◆ Informal verbal warning.
◆ Formal verbal warning (confirm in writing that you have given them a verbal warning).
◆ Written warning, and possibly a second written warning.
◆ Final written warning.

If the warning has had no effect on your employee and their misconduct continues, you should move on to the next stage. If your employee's conduct has improved, you should agree to 'wipe the slate clean' of any written warnings after a period of, say, 6 months. If the employee's conduct has not improved after the final written warning, then you can consider dismissal. Gross misconduct allows you to dismiss your employee (without notice), with no requirement to follow the above process. However, if you are contemplating dismissing an employee after a series of warnings or after gross misconduct, you must follow the statutory procedure described below.

Statutory disciplinary and dismissal procedure

Your disciplinary procedures must satisfy the requirements of the Employment Act 2002 and be explained in your employees' terms and conditions of employment. If you are contemplating dismissal of an employee or action such as loss of seniority or pay, you must follow the statutory disciplinary procedure. Failing to do so may result in an employment tribunal judging that a dismissal is automatically unfair and can also increase any compensation by between 10–50%. This procedure has 3 steps:

◆ **Step 1**: Set out in writing the reasons for dismissal or other disciplinary action and invite your employee to a meeting to discuss the matter (the employee has the right to be accompanied).
◆ **Step 2**: Hold the meeting, (having given your employee reasonable opportunity to consider their response) informing your employee of any decision you have made, and notifying them that they have a right to appeal.
◆ **Step 3**: Hold a second meeting to discuss any appeal that the employee may have made and notify them of your final decision.

The appeal meeting need not take place before the dismissal or other disciplinary procedure takes place and it is also possible to suspend employees for serious misconduct prior to Step 2.

 You can obtain useful information on handling workplace disciplinary issues from ACAS: www.acas.org.uk or telephone 08457 47 47 47

Handling disciplinary procedures

Depending on your own background and personality, you may find the prospect of disciplining staff a daunting prospect. If you do feel this way, bear in mind that the situation could become much worse if you do not tackle the issues immediately. Ignoring poor performance or misconduct is likely to cause greater problems in the long run for you, your staff and your business. When you do have to discipline an employee:

◆ Stay calm.
◆ Deal with the situation speedily.
◆ Gather the facts.
◆ Let the employee have their say.
◆ Don't discriminate.
◆ Be consistent.
◆ Consider any individual extenuating circumstances.
◆ Be firm and fair.
◆ Keep a written record.

Minimising disciplinary problems

Fortunately, disciplinary problems are relatively infrequent occurrences and they can be further minimised by:

◆ Recruiting the right staff.
◆ Having a good induction procedure.
◆ Training staff properly.
◆ Clearly communicating your expected standards.
◆ Tackling any issues while they are still minor ones.
◆ Leading by example.

Staff are an integral part of your business, and good procedures and working practices help ensure that they make a positive contribution.

16

DRINKS

YOUR PRODUCT RANGE

Your target customers

The range of products you offer should be clearly focused on the types of customers you want to retain and attract. Once you are clear about who your target customers are, you then need to offer them the kind of drinks that they want. Different types of clientele demand different types of products. For example, a Young Person's Venue (YPV) must stock a wide range of Premium Packaged Spirits (PPS) to meet the demands of the target customers it is aiming to reach. A destination food pub must stock a range of wines and soft drinks to meet the needs of its customers.

Regional demands

There are often regional variations in the demand for certain products. Different areas have localised tastes and demands. For example, customers in your area may prefer ale that is dry in flavour, while people in other areas may prefer sweeter ale.

Fashionable drinks

Different drinks come in and out of fashion. This is particularly true of drinks aimed at the 18–24 age group where some drinks are only popular for a few months. If this is the age group you are aiming to attract you will need to keep up to date with changes in demand and with new products that are being launched that may appeal to your target customers. Unfortunately, some breweries and pub companies are slow to respond to changes in demand for these fashionable drinks, or decide not to stock them because they foresee only limited demand for them. This can be frustrating if you are tied to purchasing these types of drinks from them.

The power of big brands

Big brands are often well-established products that have a great deal of promotion and advertising behind them. Introducing big brand drinks into your product range is a good way of developing your sales.

Making changes to your product range

Your pub will have an established product range when you first take it over and you must decide whether it meets the needs of the customers you are targeting. Reviewing your product range should be a regular activity. Here are some recommendations:

◆ Seek advice from your brewery, pub company or other supplier on the types of drinks that will appeal to your target customers.
◆ Find out which brands are the biggest sellers in your region.
◆ Seek advice from your stocktaker on which products make you the most money.
◆ Check your stock reports to find slow-moving products and consider removing them from your product range. Slow-moving products tie up your money and put pressure on your cash flow.
◆ Keep up to date with new products and industry trends by reading the trade press.
◆ Keep up to date with the type of drinks your competitors are stocking.
◆ Obtain promotional support for the introduction of any new products.
◆ Make changes a step at a time, giving your customers the opportunity to accept them.
◆ Train your staff so that they are knowledgeable about any new products.
◆ Review the changes to see if they have been beneficial to your business.

BEER STYLES

Beer is a general description for 4 different styles of beer: ales, lagers, stouts and porters. These styles are produced by different brewing methods, and result in beers with unique qualities and characteristics. Changing consumer tastes and heavyweight advertising campaigns have affected the popularity of these beers over the years, but beer still remains the biggest selling drink in public houses, typically accounting for three-quarters of total drinks sales.

Comparing beers

There are some universal means of comparing beers, which can help establish a drink's characteristics, these are:

◆ Alcohol by volume (ABV) – the strength of an alcoholic drink measured as the percentage of pure alcohol contained in the liquid.
◆ Original gravity (OG) – is a measure of beer's density in relation to the density of water, as measured in the brewing process. The specific gravity of water is 1.000°. This can also be used to indicate the strength of a beer (the higher the gravity the higher the strength).
◆ International Bitterness Units (IBU) – provides a measure of the bitterness of beer: the higher number, the greater the bitterness.
◆ European Brewing Convention (EBC units) – is a means of measuring the colour of beer, where the lowest rating is the palest colour.

 You can find useful information on beer styles at www.craftbeer.com/pages/style-finder

The typical characteristics of the main styles of beer (and 'sub-styles' of each) are given here:

Ales

Ales include 'bitter' and 'mild', as well as 'pale ale', 'brown ale', 'India pale ale' (IPA) and Scottish 'heavy' and 'export' ales. Until relatively recently, ales have been the dominant drink in public houses. Their typical characteristics are described below:

- Standard bitter: medium-bodied beer with medium bitterness. Gold to copper in colour.
  - ABV – 4.1–4.8%
  - OG – 1038–1045°
  - IBU – 28–46
  - EBC – 16–28

- Premium bitter: medium to strong hop aroma, flavour and bitterness. Amber to copper in colour.
  - ABV – 4.8–5.8%
  - OG – 1046–1060°
  - IBU – 30–55
  - EBC – 16–28

- Pale mild: malt flavoured with little hop bitterness. Golden to amber in colour. Relatively low alcohol content.
  - ABV – 3.2–4%
  - OG – 1030–1036°
  - IBU – 10–24
  - EBC – 16–34

- Dark mild: malt and caramel flavoured, little hop flavour or aroma. Deep copper to dark brown (often with red tint) colour. Relatively low alcohol content.
  - ABV – 3.2–4%
  - OG – 1030–1036°
  - IBU – 10–24
  - EBC – 34–68

◆ Pale ale: medium to high hop bitterness with low to medium malt flavour. Golden to copper coloured.
  — ABV – 4.5–5.5%
  — OG – 1044–1056°
  — IBU – 20–40
  — EBC – 10–28

◆ Brown ale: medium body with dry to sweet maltiness. Very little hop flavour or aroma. Deep copper to brown in colour.
  — ABV – 4–5.5%
  — OG – 1040–1050°
  — IBU – 15–25
  — EBC – 30–44

◆ India pale ale (IPA): medium to high hop bitterness and medium maltiness and body. Pale gold to deep copper coloured.
  — ABV – 5–7%
  — OG – 1050–1064°
  — IBU – 35–55
  — EBC – 12–28

◆ Scottish 'heavy' ale: moderate in strength, sweet maltiness and low hop bitterness. Golden amber to deep brown in colour.
  — ABV – 3.5–4%
  — OG – 1035–1040°
  — IBU – 12–20
  — EBC – 20–38

◆ Scottish 'export' ale: sweet, caramel flavoured and malty. Medium-bodied. Golden amber to deep brown in colour.
  — ABV – 4–5.3%
  — OG – 1040–1050°
  — IBU – 15–25
  — EBC – 20–38

Lagers

Lager sales have grown from 1% of the UK beer market in 1960 to almost 50% today. Research into the UK lager market in 2009 by Mintel found the following:

◆ Since 2004, lager value sales fell by 11% to reach £11.4bn in 2009. Nevertheless, it remains the largest selling alcohol drink.

◆ Standard lager (usually an ABV of around 4%) has become increasingly popular compared to premium, and now accounts for three out of five pints drunk.

◆ The two biggest selling brands (Carling and Foster's) are both standard lagers and have benefited from the popularity of their extra cold draught among younger drinkers. Stella Artois is the third largest brand, despite being maket leader in the off-trade*.

◆ Whether lager is served extra cold is the greatest motivator when choosing between brands, influencing 4m regular lager drinkers/ potential drinkers. Second is provenance, with 3m being influenced by whether a lager brand is from a traditional beer making country.

The characteristics of some of the more popular styles of lager are explained below:

◆ German style pilsner: well-hopped and very light straw or golden in colour. High hop bitterness but with a malty residual sweetness.
  — ABV – 4–5%
  — OG – 1044–1050°
  — IBU – 30–40
  — EBC – 6–8

*On-trade includes pubs, clubs, and bars (ie where drink is consumed on the premises) as opposed to off-trade which includes off-licences and super-markets.

♦ European style pilsner: medium-bodied with low to medium hop bitter-
ness. Low residual malty sweetness. Straw to golden in colour.
— ABV – 4–5%
— OG – 1044–1050°
— IBU – 17–30
— EBC – 6–8

♦ American lager: hop bitterness and aroma are light. Malt sweetness light
to mild. Clean and crisp and well carbonated. Light in body and colour.
— ABV – 3.8–5%
— OG – 1040–1046°
— IBU – 5–14
— EBC – 4–8

♦ Australasian or Latin American lagers: light-bodied with low hop bitter-
ness. Very light in colour.
— ABV – 2.9–5.6%
— OG – 1032–1046°
— IBU – 9–25
— EBC – 4–8

Porters

Porter originated in London around 1730 and by the end of the 18th
century had become the most popular beer in England. The fashion for
pale ales eroded the popularity of porter and it is only recently that this
beer has made a small comeback.

♦ Robust Porter: medium to full-bodied beer with hoppy bitterness and
slight malty sweetness. Black in colour.
— ABV – 5–6.5%
— OG – 1045–1060°
— IBU – 25–40
— EBC – 60+

Stouts

A classic ale especially popular in Ireland. Also has a strong following from
dedicated stout drinkers worldwide. Two of the most popular types of
stout are:

◆ Irish-style dry stout: medium-bodied beer with a distinctive dry-roasted bitterness. Black in colour.
  — ABV – 3.8–5%
  — OG – 1038–1048°
  — IBU – 30–40
  — EBC – 80+

◆ Oatmeal stout: medium to full-bodied beer. Full caramel/chocolate like flavour with a smooth profile and less bitterness.
  — ABV – 3.8–6%
  — OG – 1038–1056°
  — IBU – 20–40
  — EBC – 40+

PACKAGING OF BEER

At the end of the brewing process, beer is treated and packaged in different ways to suit the needs of the market. 'Conditioning' is the final process that makes the beer ready to serve. Beer can be either brewery-conditioned, or cask-conditioned. When beer is conditioned by the brewery, prior to dispatching it to its customers, it is known as brewery-conditioned beer, and when beer is dispatched 'unfinished' and allowed to be conditioned in the cask, this is known as cask-conditioned beer.

Brewery-conditioned beers

Brewery-conditioned beers are ready to drink as soon as they leave the brewery. The brewery conditions the beer by chilling and filtering it to remove all the yeast, then pasteurising it to make a sterile product. If the brewery-conditioned beer is to be packaged as draught beer (ie beer that is served via a tap on the bar), it will be placed into containers known as kegs. (Kegs are sealed containers that are pressurised with gas. They are connected to the beer dispense system by a coupling device.) Alternatively, it can be put into bottles or cans. Lagers and many types of ale are treated and packaged in this way.

Cask-conditioned beers

Cask-conditioned beers (also known as 'traditional beers' or 'real ales') are not ready to drink immediately; they need time to condition in the cask. (Casks are special containers that allow you to hammer in a tap and vent the cask.) The brewery fills casks with beer direct from the fermenting vessels and adds a substance called finings to the beer, which ensures that all yeast and proteins are drawn to the bottom of the cask once it is left undisturbed in the pub's cellar. This clarifies the beer and gives it its bright appearance. During this time, a secondary fermentation of the beer takes place in the cask. Cask beer typically takes around 48–72 hours before it is ready to serve via a hand pump.

Learn more about the brewing process from the Beer and Pub Association website:
www.beerandpub.com/beer_brewing.aspx

CIDER

Cider sales have made a recent revival after a number of years of decline in the on-trade. Innovative new products like 'ice filtered' ciders and the promotion of bottled cider to be served with ice, have added to the sales of traditional dry, sweet and premium strength ciders. In the case of draught products, dry ciders tend to be more popular than sweet ones. Two or three big brands tend to dominate the cider market at the moment, but some smaller 'niche' brands are popular in some geographical areas.

DRAUGHT DISPENSE

There are three basic ways of serving draught beer: the handpull, freeflow tap and metered dispense. Each of these is described below:

Handpulls

Handpulls (also known as hand pumps) are the traditional way of serving cask-conditioned beer. Handpulls draw beer from the cask, and dispense it into the glass, when the handpull is pumped manually. It is a simple but effective way of dispensing beer. Note: they are used only with cask beers and not those packaged in kegs.

Freeflow taps

Freeflow taps raise from the cellar keg beer that is under pressure from gas. CO_2, or a mixture of CO_2 and nitrogen, is used to pressurise the beer. The tap is manually held open to dispense beer into a glass. Some taps have a creamer that can be used to add a creamy head to the beer at the end of dispense.

Metered dispense

Metered dispense is also used to dispense keg beers. Metered units automatically dispense a measured half a pint of beer each time a switch is pressed. Metered units must be calibrated when they are installed (and regularly checked) to ensure that they accurately dispense beer in the required amounts. Metered units should be Government stamped with the Crown Stamp to confirm that they have been checked and approved by Trading Standards.

Gas and electric pumps

Where the pub's cellar is located a long distance (horizontally or vertically) from its bar, a gas or electric pump can be used to assist with dispensing keg beer. These pumps are located in the cellar and push the beer through the lines. They can be powered by gas or electricity.

Gas and gas systems

Both CO_2 and a mixture of CO_2 and nitrogen are used to dispense a range of keg beers today. These gases are also absorbed by the beer giving it special characteristics. These characteristics can include the CO_2 'bite', which is typical of many lagers or the smoothness produced by using nitrogen with CO_2 to dispense 'smoothflow' and 'smoothpour' ales.

Gas systems can be rented or more frequently, are loaned to you free of charge from your brewery or gas supplier. The brewery or gas supplier is responsible for maintaining the equipment and can be called out to deal with any faults. CO_2 and mixed gases (CO_2/nitrogen mixes) can be purchased together with your beer supplies or from other local gas suppliers. The mixed gases come in different percentage mixes, for example: 60/40 or 70/30 mixtures (ie 60% CO_2 to 40% nitrogen mix, or 70% CO_2 to 30% nitrogen mix). Each keg beer product must be dispensed using its recommended gas or mixed gas, otherwise faults can occur, and the beer will not be served at its best. Your brewery or pub company will advise you on this.

Beer cooling systems

Due to changing customer demands, many beers are served at a much lower temperature than they used to be. Though lager has traditionally been served at a lower temperature than other beers, the introduction of 'extra-cold' and 'super-chilled' lagers has reduced these temperatures further. Other products have followed suit.

In days gone by, the temperature of the beer was dictated by the temperature of the pub's cellar. Nowadays, technology in the form of cooling systems is used to cool products. These consist of:

◆ Cellar cooling: a cooling unit that cools the whole of the beer cellar.
◆ Remote coolers and 'python systems': these cool the beer lines by circulating chilled liquid through a snake-like sheath that surrounds the beer lines.
◆ Flash coolers: they are situated behind the bar through which beer flows and is cooled immediately prior to it being dispensed.

Cellar services

Breweries and pub companies have teams of 'cellar service' staff who are on hand to attend to any problems with the dispensing or cooling of beer. They also have a team of experts on hand to attend to any problems with the beer itself. Faults are normally reported by telephoning a helpline number and call-outs are made within an agreed timescale depending on the nature of the problem. It is a good idea to keep these telephone numbers to hand and also ensure that your staff are aware of them, in case of any difficulties.

GLASSWARE FOR BEER

Styles of glassware

A customer's 'drinking experience' is made up of more than just the taste of the product. The smell and appearance of the drink are vital to their enjoyment too. Good glassware plays a large part in the proper presentation of beer, thereby enhancing its visual impact. Several different styles of beer glasses have become popular to use with different styles of beer.

Ask the advice of your local licensed trade supplier for the most suitable styles of glassware for your drinks.

Branded glassware

Glassware is often used to display drinks brands; this is known as 'branded glassware'. It is an excellent way of promoting drinks and enhances the overall presentation of the product. Train your staff to make sure that they serve drinks in correctly branded glassware.

Branded glassware is often supplied free of charge from drinks suppliers or it can be offered to you at a reduced price. Speak to your brewery or pub company to obtain stocks of these. Unfortunately, branded glassware does tend to attract souvenir-hunters, and you will need to ensure that you have sufficient supplies of these to take account of stolen glassware, as well as the usual breakages.

Legal requirements of serving draught beer and cider

Draught beer and cider must be sold in quantities of $1/3$ pint, $1/2$ pint or multiples of $1/2$ pints. (Serving beer in $1/3$ pint measures is no longer popular today.) Draught beer and cider must be correctly measured using either Government (Crown) stamped beer meters or Government (Crown) stamped glasses. There are 3 main categories of beer glass that should be used in specific circumstances. It is important not to mix these up if using freeflow and handpull and metered forms of dispense:

◆ Unstamped 'oversized glass'.
◆ Government stamped 'lined glass'.
◆ Government stamped 'brim glass'.

These are explained here:

Unstamped 'oversized glass'

These glasses are not Government stamped and are legal only when using a Government stamped meter to dispense beer or lager. These glasses are oversized, ie the beer will not come to the brim of the glass, but will have been correctly measured by your metered dispense unit (subject to the unit being correctly calibrated).

Government stamped 'lined glass'

These glasses display the official 'Crown stamp' and are marked with a line which denotes the level that the *liquid* part of the beer or cider should reach. These glasses are oversized to allow the beer to be served with a reasonable head. When beer is dispensed into these glasses, sufficient beer (*liquid and head*) must be dispensed to ensure that if the head totally collapses, the liquid in the glass will be level with the line defining the measure. These glasses are to be used with handpulls and freeflow forms of dispense.

Government stamped 'brim glass'

Government stamped 'brim glasses' will hold at least ½ pint or a pint when filled to the brim. However, when allowing for the head on certain beers, the glass may not contain 100% liquid (ie liquid and head are measured to the brim). Under the Code of Practice agreed between the brewing industry and the Government, a maximum of 5% head is allowed on a pint or ½ pint of beer; and customers should be given a top-up if it is requested.

If using brim measure glasses, display a notice reminding your customers of their right to request a top-up.

Glasswashers

Nothing ruins the appearance of a pint (or any other type of drink) like scratched or dirty glasses. Grease, lipstick marks and strong odours, as well as being visually off-putting, will also make certain beers go 'flat'. It is essential to present your drinks in well-cleaned, scratch-free glasses and always provide your customers with a clean glass for each drink. (Though some customers like to keep the same glass, this practice is unhygienic and should be avoided on health grounds.)

Modern day glasswasher units are a good investment and make the task of cleaning glasses a simple operation. Glasswashers must be kept clean and the correct settings and doses of cleaning agent must be used to ensure the best performance. Poorly cleaned and maintained glasswashers are responsible for many customer complaints about poor quality beers. (They can contaminate the glassware, which then affects the beer.) Always follow the manufacturer's instructions.

Glasses can be renovated by adding strong chlorinated powder products to your glasswasher. These deep clean both your glasses and glasswasher.

 Do not use inferior glassware; replace glasses when they cannot be cleaned thoroughly or have become scratched.

How clean are your beer glasses?

Check your beer glasses regularly by doing the following:

◆ Holding your glasses up to the down-lighters above the bar canopy illuminates the glass and shows any imperfections.
◆ Wiping the inside of a clean glass with a moist white serviette will show up any protein build up as a brown deposit.
◆ Turning a pint or half pint glass upside down and looking at the outer ring of the base, will magnify any deposits as a brown ring.

◆ Checking for films of bubbles on the inside of a filled glass as these are a sign that the glass is not properly clean. (Bubbles only adhere to an impurity.)

CELLAR MANAGEMENT

Though this part of the business is hidden away from most people, the best licensees take great pride in their cellars and their cellar management. Often this involves a good deal of work at the start, bringing your cellar up to standard, but this process pays dividends in the long run by keeping the products in good condition, reducing wastage, improving stock control and making the movement and handling of stock easier.

Cellar training

No one should start running a pub without some form of cellar training. This is especially important where cask beers are to be sold. These products must be looked after carefully and kept in a clean environment to prevent them from becoming tainted. All breweries and most pub companies run recommended cellar training courses. Attending one of these courses should be a priority for you.

Cask Marque is an organisation funded by brewers and retailers that promotes excellence in the service of cask ale. They offer cellar training courses and training videos as well as awarding their Cask Marque plaque to licensees who meet their quality standards.

See: www.cask-marque.co.uk or telephone: 01206 752212.

Cleanliness

It is important to keep your cellar clean. As well as contaminating drinks products, dirty cellars and equipment attract rodents and cockroaches. Develop daily and weekly cleaning routines to ensure your cellar remains dirt-free. You should never smoke in or allow pets to use the cellar. Check the following areas:

- Floors: keep them clean by regular scrubbing and hosing down. Use diluted line cleaner to prevent infection.
- Walls and ceilings: remove any flaking paint or whitewash carefully and repaint (low odour) or whitewash on a regular basis. Special treatments may be needed to tackle any mouldy or damp areas.
- Drainage: ensure any sump pumps are maintained and free of any blockages. Keep drains and channels clean and clear.
- Equipment: keep all cellar equipment well maintained and clean.

Tidiness

Cellars should be kept tidy and well organised. Make use of storage and shelving units to keep items like beer taps, pegs, keystones and hop filters clean, dry, and easy to locate.

Ventilation

Good ventilation is important to prevent mould growth and keep the air fresh and well circulated. Good ventilation also reduces the danger of harmful levels of CO_2 building up if there is a leak in the CO_2 system.

Temperature

Cellar temperatures should be carefully maintained at between 11.5°C and 13.5°C (53°F and 56°F) in order to keep products at their optimum condition. Failure to maintain products within their prescribed temperature range can result in customer complaints and stock wastage. Thermostatically controlled cellar cooling units can be set to maintain the temperature of the cellar within these bounds. Even so, you should have a reliable cellar thermometer positioned just above the height of your beer casks to check the cellar temperature. Any problems with your cellar-cooling unit should be reported to your cellar service representative as soon as possible, to prevent further difficulties.

Line cleaning

Plastic piping or 'beer lines' carry draught beer and cider from the cellar to the bar. These build up with yeast deposits if not regularly cleaned causing beer quality and dispense problems. To keep them in good order, lines should be cleaned at least weekly, using a recommended line cleaning solution.

Unfortunately, some licensees have an undisciplined approach to line cleaning and beer lines can become heavily soiled. As a new licensee, you should ask your cellar service representative to check the beer lines that you have inherited. Badly soiled lines can be specially cleaned but in some cases, the only solution is to ask for new lines to be installed. Your cellar service representative will advise you.

 Ask your cellar services representative to show you the correct way to clean beer lines. They are usually happy to spend time with you teaching you this.

Health and Safety

Cellars can be dangerous environments. Steep cellar steps, slippery conditions, pressurised gas systems, heavy beer kegs and stacks of bottled beer cases have the potential to cause accidents. Help keep you and your staff safe by following some simple precautions:

◆ Keep your cellar well illuminated.
◆ Keep the cellar floors free from trip hazards.
◆ Keep gas bottles chained to the wall when in use (and carefully laid flat in a suitable location, when not).
◆ Ensure that cellar steps and 'cellar drops' (where the beer is lowered into the cellar) are well maintained.
◆ Keep water away from electricity supplies, do not overload sockets and check that your plugs and equipment are properly fused.
◆ Follow the supplier's instructions for using their gas systems.
◆ Do not tamper with pressurised kegs.
◆ Do not store chemicals in the cellar.
◆ Do not leave cellar drop doors or cellar flaps open unsupervised or without a suitable barrier.

Stock control

A substantial amount of money is tied up in stock, which needs to be managed in order to ensure that products are offered for sale in excellent condition, and that waste and theft is minimised.

Stock control is balancing your stocks so that you are not over-stocked (thereby tying up more of your cash) and yet have sufficient stocks to meet customer demands. Stock needs to be rotated to ensure that the oldest stock is used first (providing that the product is within its optimum shelf life).

Stock control is more of an art than a science, which will become easier as you become more experienced. Keeping good ordering records enables you to look back at your order history, helping you anticipate future demands. Nevertheless, despite experience and good forecasting, there will be times when you run out of certain products because of an unusually high demand for them. In these cases, you may have to encourage customers to try alternative products until you are re-stocked.

The shelf life of cask beer is very limited and needs careful stock control. When ordering cask beer, you should:

◆ Order in cask sizes which allow you to empty the cask within 3 days of putting it on service. (Beer quality quickly deteriorates after this time.)
◆ Calculate your cask beer orders to allow you to have 3 days stock of each cask beer remaining from the previous delivery, when you receive your new delivery (giving sufficient time for your new beer to come into condition).

Keg beers and bottled products have a longer shelf life than cask beers and are ready for sale when you receive them. However, these products need some time in your cellar or bottle fridges to reach their required serving temperatures.

MAXIMISING SALES OF BEER AND CIDER

Here are ways to maximise your beer and cider sales:

Draught beer and cider

- ◆ Serve at the correct temperature and in perfect condition.
- ◆ Use immaculate glassware.
- ◆ Use branded glassware.
- ◆ Train your staff to serve the perfect pint and to be knowledgeable about your products.
- ◆ Make sure your beer founts and handpulls are situated on your bar where they can be seen by customers.
- ◆ Make sure your founts and handpulls (and pump clips) are sparklingly clean.
- ◆ Use gleaming brass (or similar style) drip trays which enhance the presentation of draught products to customers.
- ◆ Use chalkboards to advertise in advance forthcoming cask ales or other new products that you are introducing.
- ◆ Offer customers the chance to try small samples before buying.
- ◆ Use chalkboards and professional looking 'beer menus' to describe the style, taste and strength of each of your draught beers and ciders.
- ◆ If you offer cask beers join the Cask Marque scheme and aim to be accredited to display their plaque.
- ◆ If you offer a range of cask ales contact your local Campaign for Real Ale (CAMRA) branch and aim to get into their Good Beer Guide (see their website: www.camra.org.uk).

Bottled beers and cider

Bottled beer and cider is served in different ways depending on the product, the customers' expectations, the type of pub and the occasion. For example, in YPVs it is normal practice to serve bottled products without a glass. In other types of pub, customers will expect to be served bottled products with a glass. There is also growth in demand for certain bottled ciders to be served over ice.

Here are ways to maximise your bottled beers and ciders:

◆ Stock the biggest selling brands.
◆ Serve at the correct temperature (see the section, 'Bottle Fridges' below).
◆ Display products effectively in your bottle fridges (see section, 'Bottle Fridges' below).
◆ Use back of the bar displays to promote products.
◆ Serve in a branded glass (where applicable).
◆ Ask your brewery, pub company or other supplier for any promotion kits or point of sale material (POS) that may be available.
◆ Make enticing displays of bottles stacked in ice.
◆ Run a bottled beer of the month promotion.

'READY TO DRINK' PRODUCTS (RTDs)

'Ready to drink' products are known by a variety of names such as:

◆ Alcopops.
◆ FABs – Flavoured Alcoholic Beverages.
◆ PPSs – Premium Packaged Spirits.

These drinks are spirit-based and are typically in the 4–5% alcohol by volume (ABV) range. They are packaged mainly in 275ml sized bottles. They are aimed at the 18–24 year olds and a great deal of money goes into promoting them through trendy advertising and label design.

The RTD sector is dominated by 5 or 6 big brands that account for over 90% of the RTD market. The lifecycles of many RTD brands tend to be short ones, being fashionable for a short time then declining as other RTDs become popular.

Overall, the RTD market has declined recently, with the following contributing to its downturn:

◆ Media backlash, linking RTDs to 'binge drinking'.
◆ Duty increases in excise duty on these products.
◆ Resurgence of cider.

- Popularity of high-energy drinks and vodka combinations.
- Improved promotion of spirit and mixer (over ice) drinks.
- Growth in popularity of wine.
- Introduction of extra cold draught products.

MAXIMISING SALES OF RTDs

- Keep up to date with the RTD market.
- Focus on the big brands.
- Serve at the correct temperature (see section, 'Bottle Fridges' below).
- Display prominently in bottle fridges (see section, 'Bottle Fridges' below).
- Ask your brewery, pub company or other supplier to provide you with any POS and promotion kits that may be available.
- Ensure promotions appeal to the 18–24 age group.
- Link promotions to young adult fashion/culture (avoid any types of promotion which may be seen as encouraging binge drinking).
- Use SMS text to promote these products to your young adult customers, using their mobile phones.

BOTTLE FRIDGES

Essential equipment

Bottle fridges (bottle chillers) are essential pieces of equipment for today's public houses. They chill bottled products and display them enticingly to your customers. Today's customers prefer many of their drinks to be served colder than in the past. They expect to have their bottled products nicely chilled and will not be satisfied with drinks served incorrectly. Whichever way your bar is laid out you should find ways of installing sufficient numbers of bottle fridges to chill and display your bottled products.

Bottle fridges come in a variety of shapes and styles from single and double door units that fit under your back-bar counter, to taller, upright units that require more vertical space in which to position them. There is also a range of specialist units which can be built into the bar back-fitting.

Temperature

Bottle fridges should chill products to their optimum serving temperature of 4°C. It is important to remember that it takes a bottle from room temperature 8 hours to cool to 4°C. Therefore, fridges must be restocked well in advance of opening for sale. 'Bottle-up' (ie restock your bottle fridges with bottled products), last thing at night to ensure that your bottles reach their optimum temperature before you open up.

Encouraging impulse purchases

Research shows that many people are undecided about the type of drink they want when they reach the bar. Correctly positioned and displayed bottle fridges provide you with an excellent opportunity to influence these customers to buy your more profitable products. Here are ways to make the best use of your bottle fridges:

◆ Make sure they correctly chill bottles to 4°C.

◆ Keep them clean and well illuminated.

◆ Have your fridges positioned where your customers standing at the bar can see them.

◆ Display your best selling products on the top shelf of your fridges.

◆ Display your bottles in banks of 2 to 5 'facings' (ie positioning the same brands next to each other on the shelf horizontally). Allocate more facings to your biggest selling and most profitable products.

◆ Display similar types of drinks (lagers, RTDs, soft drinks) together in vertical columns in the fridge (eg display your biggest selling lager brand on the top shelf with your second lager brand on the shelf immediately below, followed by your third and fourth biggest lager brands on the bottom shelf).

◆ Keep your bottle fridges well stocked.

WINE

Overview of the market

UK wine consumption has doubled in the last 10 years and further growth is anticipated despite the sector's first volume and value decrease for many years in 2008. Mintel predicts that Rosé is the one wine category that is forcast to grow over the next five years, and is a particularly accessible way to attract younger drinkers into the category. Wine consumption among 25–34 year olds is required to grow for the market to expand.

Consumption of 'New World' wines has increased dramatically and Australia is now the biggest producer of wine consumed in the UK with 24% of the market, and boasting 6 of the top 10 wine brands sold in the UK (2004). Wine consumed from the USA and South Africa has also grown substantially over the last 5 years, while French wines (which still account for 19% of the UK market) have seen a decline in popularity.

Wine drinking in pubs

Despite the huge increase in the consumption of wine in the UK, sales of wine in public houses have massively lagged behind this trend. While 8 out of 10 people enjoy a glass of wine, only 2 out of 10 will drink it in a pub, and research suggests that customers are not confident that pubs serve wine professionally or of the right quality, and that staff and licensees generally lack knowledge of wine. Wine is frequently stored incorrectly and is often poorly displayed. Wine choice is also generally very limited with the average pub stocking only 4 types of wine.

Be 'wine enlightened'

The growing demand for wine does provide licensees who are willing to take wine seriously with an excellent opportunity to build their businesses. With many pubs lagging behind the market, 'wine-enlightened' licensees can gain competitive advantage over their rivals. See the section below, 'Maximising Wines Sales', for ways to do this.

The Wine and Spirit Education Trust runs a range of wine courses. For more information see their website : www.wset.co.uk

Grape varieties

Wine is typically categorised by its grape variety (or combination of grape varieties). Here are the more popular grape varieties with details of their main flavour and aroma characteristics:

White grape varieties:

Grape variety	Typical flavours and aromas
Chardonnay	Ranging from citrus to ripe tropical fruit, buttery, toasty (from oak).
Chenin Blanc	Pears, green apples, wet wool, honey (with age).
Muscat	Orange blossom, elderflower, scented.
Muscadet	Hints of apple and gooseberry.
Riesling	Lemon, lime, peach, scented, petrol (with age).
Sauvignon Blanc	Green pea, grassy, nettles, gooseberry, passionfruit.
Sémillon	Grapefruit, grassy, honey and nuts (with age).

Red grape varieties:

Grape variety	Typical flavours and aromas
Cabernet Sauvignon	Blackcurrant, black cherry, green pepper, mint, cedar and cigarbox (from oak).
Gamay	Cherry, candy, raspberry hints.
Grenache	Fruity, black fruits, black olives, spices, leather.
Malbec	Juicy, fruity, plummy.
Merlot	Plums, damsons, chocolate, black cherry, spices.
Nebbiolo	Perfumed, tar, roses, woodsmoke.
Pinot Noir	Strawberries, cherries, earthy, gamey.
Pinotage	Pepper, spices, plums, bananas.
Shiraz/Syrah	Pepper, black cherry, black olives, leather.
Sangiovese	Cherry, plum.
Tempranillo	Scented, strawberries, leather, spice, tobacco, vanilla (from oak).
Zinfandel	Rich, spices, raisiny, black fruit.

Wine producers of the world

Wine is often described as coming from 'new world' or 'old world' producers.

New world wine producers include:

◆ Australia;
◆ USA;
◆ South Africa;
◆ Chile;
◆ New Zealand.

Old world producers include:

◆ France;
◆ Italy;
◆ Spain;
◆ Germany.

 For a useful source of information on the world's wine regions visit: www.wine-regions-of-the-world.com

Wine regions

Many wine-producing countries have distinct regions that specialise in the production of different types of wines with different qualities and flavours. Some of the major producers together with their important wine producing regions are described below:

New world producers

Australia:

◆ New South Wales.

USA:

◆ California (Napa Valley).
◆ Pacific Northwest.

South Africa:

◆ Distributed throughout the country.

Chile:

◆ Maipo Valley.

New Zealand:

◆ 10 main regions located mainly along the coast.

Old world producers

France:

◆ Burgundy;
◆ Bordeaux;
◆ Beaujolais;
◆ Rhone;
◆ Loire;
◆ Alsace;
◆ Champagne.

Italy:

◆ Piedmont;
◆ Valle D'Aosta;
◆ Alto Adige;
◆ Veneto;
◆ Tuscany.

Spain:

◆ Rioja;
◆ Catalonia;
◆ Jerez.

Germany:

◆ Mosel;
◆ Rheingau.

Wine terminology

French

Brut – dry (Champagne)
Cru – wine from a high quality vineyard
Sec – dry
Demi-sec – off dry (fairly sweet for Champagne)
Doux – sweet

Italian

Secco – dry
Semisecco – medium dry
Dolce – sweet

Spanish

Seco – dry
Semi-seco – medium dry

German

Trocken – dry
Halbtrocken – off dry
(If not stated, German wines tend to be slightly sweet.)

Many UK supermarkets use simple guidelines to help describe their wines to customers. White wines are numbered 1 to 9 to describe the dryness to sweetness range, with 1 being the driest and 9 being the sweetest. Red wines are displayed with the letters A to E, representing light-bodied through to full-bodied wines.

Wine classifications

Old world producers use well-established wine classifications to denote the quality of their wines. The table below shows the main wine classifications for each of the main producers:

	Special quality wine	**Quality wine**	**Regional wine**	**Basic wine**
France	None specific	AC/AOC	Vin de pays	Vin de table
Italy	DOCG	DOC	IGT	Vino da tavola
Spain	DOC	DO	Vino de Tierra or Vino comarcal	Vino de mesa
Germany	QmP	QbA or VDQS	Landwein	Tafelwein

The USA classification system, American Viticultural Area (AVA), guarantees the geographical region of the wine but not the quality, and similar systems have been adopted by other new world producers.

 For comprehensive information about wine, visit the Wine Doctor's website: www.thewinedoctor.com

MAXIMISING WINE SALES

The demand for wine is growing and provides you with an excellent opportunity to build your business. Every pub can sell wine and the majority of pubs can sell a lot more by following the simple but effective techniques explained here:

Learn about wine

Take time to learn a little about wine. The websites mentioned earlier provide you with lots of useful information about wine; there are many other websites and books that can help improve your understanding of the subject. Learning about wine builds your knowledge and confidence and is also fun. Don't just learn the theory; make sure that you know what each of the wines you stock tastes like too!

Train your staff

It is just as important for your staff to have knowledge of the wine and the wines you stock. They should be able to describe to customers the types of wine you have available and their characteristics. Neither you, nor your staff, need to be experts, but a basic understanding, which enables you to explain your wine range to customers and perhaps make recommendations, is important.

Ask your wine supplier to teach you and your staff something about wine by running a short wine tasting as part of your staff training sessions. Make sure new staff are trained to understand wine and are able to serve it correctly and confidently to customers.

Match your knowledge to your clientele

Your public house may require you to have more than just a basic knowledge of wine. For example, food pubs and pubs with a high demand for better quality wines. In these situations, you will have to develop your wine knowledge in order to fully exploit the opportunity to sell wine. You can increase your understanding of wine through research, reading, supplier tuition and by gaining qualifications or attending courses. (The Wines and Spirit Education Trust mentioned earlier in this chapter offers courses and qualifications.)

Have a 'wine champion'

The role of 'wine champion' is to make wine a priority in your pub with the aim of maximising the sales of wine. This person could be you, or someone else you have appointed with an interest in wine. They will oversee all aspects of promoting wine to customers and ensure that all staff are adequately trained.

Match your wine range to your clientele

Your range of wines should meet the needs of your customers. Waverley TSB, a subsidiary of Scottish and Newcastle, uses an interesting way of segmenting the wine market: *Six Faces of the Wine Drinker*. These describe the 6 types of wine drinker and their main characteristics:

1 The 'Classic Connoisseur'

◆ Older.
◆ Knowledgeable.
◆ Identified with Old World wines.
◆ Traditional styles and tastes.

2 The 'Enthusiast'

◆ Buys into traditional image of wine.
◆ Lacks knowledge.
◆ Relates price to quality.
◆ Prefers Old World.

3 The 'Entertainer'

◆ Drinks wine at family occasions, with or without food.
◆ Adventurous, likes New World wines.
◆ Price-conscious.
◆ Trades up when entertaining friends.

4 The 'Easily Pleased'

◆ Older, usually female.
◆ Unpretentious.
◆ Drinks cheaper, sweeter wines.
◆ Does not experiment.

5 The 'Adventurer'

◆ Self confident.
◆ Enjoys experimenting.

◆ Doesn't have detailed wine knowledge.

◆ Tends towards New World wines.

6 The 'Chardonnay Girl'

◆ Younger female.

◆ Prefers white wine for social drinking.

◆ Open to experiment.

◆ Wide drinks repertoire.

A 7th Category of wine drinker 'The Rosé Girl' can now be added to this list of wine drinkers. Sales of Rosé wine have grown dramatically over the last few years and is now a 'must stock' drink for pubs.

You can use the above types to help clarify what sort of wine drinkers use your pub or who you are aiming to attract. This can then be used as a basis for deciding which types of wines to stock.

You should also consider the kind of occasions when your customers will want to drink wine in your pub. For example:

◆ Drinking wine by the glass in a 'round'.

◆ Having a meal.

◆ Ordering wine by the bottle to share.

◆ Celebrating a special occasion with 'bubbly'.

If you provide food, the type of menu you offer will influence your wine range. An extensive menu and high quality food offering will require a comprehensive wine range that complements your menu. You will need a good knowledge of wine yourself, or assistance from your wine supplier or chef in order to put together a good wine list in this case.

If yours is a pub where wine sales have been historically low or your clientele appear to have a very limited knowledge of wine, offer a smaller range of wines, focusing on the more popular brands and grape varieties. This allows your customers to recognise these wines and gives them the confidence to order them from you.

Make wine visible!

The largest barrier to wine sales in pubs is lack of visibility, so making your customers aware that you sell wine will automatically increase sales. Make your wines visible to your customers by having:

◆ Wine displayed in your back-bar area.
◆ Wine racks and glass fronted wine coolers.
◆ Chalkboards.
◆ Table-top 'tent cards'.
◆ A professional–looking wine list.

 Most good wine suppliers will help you produce your wine list and many will have them printed for you free of charge. They will also provide you with glassware and promotional material.

For traditional pubs offering a simplified wine range, offering wine by the glass, you could have:

◆ Wine cabinets (display units which can be obtained from certain wine suppliers).
◆ Draught wine with well-positioned dispense units (normally arranged via your brewery or pub company).

Glassware

Wine appreciation involves all the senses, and the glassware you use will influence the aroma, sight and taste of wine. Here are some basic requirements, when choosing glassware for wine:

◆ Use only plain and clear glassware.
◆ Ensure it has a stem.
◆ Use glassware that tapers towards the top.

Two or three types of glassware are normally sufficient for the majority of pubs:

◆ Champagne/sparkling wine – a 'flute' or similar.
◆ Red wine – glass with a large bowl.
◆ White wine – glass with a smaller bowl.

Glass size:

Trading Standards legislation dictates that still wine, if sold by the glass, must be served in quantities of 125ml or 175ml or multiples of these. (Bottles or carafes of wine must be sold in quantities of 25cl, 50cl, 75cl, 1 litre, or multiples of these.) Wine served by the glass must be measured using a Government stamped 'thimble' measure, or dispensed using a Government stamped glass.

An excellent way of improving your wines sales is to use 2 sizes of wine glass

◆ 175ml – as your normal or standard size,

and

◆ 250ml – as your large or premium size.

The 125ml wine glass is now regarded as outdated and is perceived as not offering value for money by customers. Making your standard wine glass 175ml means that you sell an extra 40% of wine each time someone makes a standard purchase, compared with a 125ml glass. At the time of updating this edition, there are calls from the Government to make offering 125ml and 25ml measures available in all public houses as part of a new Code of Practice for Alcohol Retailers.

Serve wine at the right temperature

Serving wine at the right temperature is crucial as this affects its taste. The general principle of serving red wine at room temperature and serving white wines chilled should be followed. You can purchase digital thermometer 'bottle collars' to check the temperature of your wine.

Red wine served too cold makes it taste too tannic (a dry, mouth-puckering sensation) or acidic; and served too warm can make it taste flat and lifeless. White wine served too warm will taste alcoholic and flabby (lacking acidity), while white wines served too cold will be refreshing but nearly tasteless. Here are some guidelines for serving wine at the correct temperature:

Wine type:	Ideal serving temperature °C	Ideal serving temperature °F
Most red wines	16° to 18°C	62° to 65°F
Light fruity reds (eg Beaujolais)	14° to 15.5°C	58° to 60°F
Fine dry white wines	14° to 16.5°C	58° to 62°F
Quaffing white wines	10° to 12.8°C	50° to 55°F
Champagne and sparkling wines	7°C	45°F

Pricing wine

Most pub customers are not willing to pay excessive prices for their wine on a normal drinking occasion. Today's wine drinkers are aware of the supermarket prices of wines and can gauge your prices against these. The majority of pub wine drinkers want good value, good quality wine that can be quaffed with partners or friends. (Even though at other times, such as special occasions or during a high quality meal, they may be willing to pay more for their wine.) Pricing pub wine too highly forces customers to choose the cheapest wine available, switch to other types of drinks or encourages them to seek out other pubs offering wine at more reasonable prices.

When pricing your wine, the cash margin approach is a useful alternative to the percentage margin method (which can result in high selling prices). The cash margin approach works by adding a set cash amount to the cost price you pay for your wines in order to calculate your selling price. The two pricing approaches are compared in the tables below:

(£) Cash margin approach		
Cost price per bottle (ex VAT)	Cash margin applied	Selling price per bottle (ex VAT)
£3.00	£3.00	£6.00
£5.00	£3.00	£8.00
£7.00	£3.00	£10.00

Note: Champagne and other top quality wines will have a higher cash margin applied in order to set your selling price of these products.

(%) Percentage margin approach		
Cost price per bottle (ex VAT)	% margin applied	Selling price per bottle (ex VAT)
£3.00	70%	£5.10
£5.00	70%	£8.50
£7.00	70%	£11.90

Applying the cash margin approach has the effect of reducing the selling prices of your higher priced wines that encourages customers to trade up and purchase them. They perceive this as being given more choice and offered better value for money.

The aim of the cash margin approach is to increase your *cash* profits by encouraging customers to make more wine purchases that will compensate for the loss in your wine *percentage* profit margin. The adage 'You bank pound notes; you don't bank percentage margins' applies here.

More ways to promote wine

There are many other ways to promote wine in your pub. Here are some more ideas:

◆ Run wine tastings.
◆ Set up a wine club.
◆ Offer a 'wine of the month'.
◆ Run special offers (eg buy 2 glasses and get the rest of the bottle free).
◆ Link wine with your menu (food pubs).
◆ Promote seasonal wines (eg refreshing white wines for summer and full-bodied reds as 'winter warmers').
◆ Promote wine during special events (eg Champagne and strawberries during Wimbledon).
◆ Promote particular wines by linking them to 'fun nights' (eg 'French nights' promoting French wines, or 'Beach parties' promoting Californian wines, etc).

SPIRITS

Industry overview

The UK spirits market is one of the largest in Europe. Spirits consumption rose over the five years from 2002 to 2007, reaching 336 million bottles. By 2012, consumption is forecast to grow to more thatn 356 million bottles.

Over the last 10 years consumer preferences have shifted from dark to white spirits as consumers have come to regard dark spirits as old-fashioned and un-trendy. Consumption of Scotch whisky has declined over recent years and this pattern is predicted to continue. Vodka is now the most popular spirit, fuelled by the demand from young adults.

With the exception of gin, which is predicted to show a small decline in overall consumption between 1999 and 2008, most major spirits are expected to have seen growth during this period.

Sales of spirits typically account for 5% of the total wet sales of a public house (this excludes RTDs).

UK Spirits Market by Volume	
Vodka (including flavoured)	30%
Scotch Whisky	26%
Gin	10%
Brandy	8%
Rum	7%
Imported Whisky	4%
Liqueurs and specialities	15%

[Source: The Gin and Vodka Association]

Vodka

It is commonly thought that the term 'vodka' originates from the Slavic word 'voda' for water. Vodka is usually distilled from fermented grain or potato. The 4 main ingredients used today are potato, rye, barley and wheat (but molasses, grapes and soya beans are also used); and these give each vodka its unique flavour.

Vodka sales rose by one third from 2003 to 2007 to reach more than 96 million bottles. Consumption of vodka is forecast to grow at a faster rate then any other spirit. Premiumsation has boosted sales in recent years with sales of premium vodka growing by 40%. Vodka, being a very mixable spirit, is used as the base spirit in many RTDs; and its combination with 'energy drinks' in the late 1990s increased its popularity with the young adult market. The 18–24 year-old age group accounts for 40% of the vodka drinking market and the 35–45 age group makes up a further 25%.

The UK vodka market is dominated by one big brand, which enjoys almost 70% market share; other brands fight it out in a very competitive market place. Vodka is now offered in a variety of styles, flavours and strengths, from Russia, Scandinavia, Poland and even New Zealand!

Gin

Gin is made from the distillation of white grain spirit and juniper berries, which provide its distinctive flavour. (The name 'gin' is derived from its Dutch origins – the Dutch word for juniper being 'genever'.) In addition to juniper, it is usually made with a small amount of citrus 'botanicals' like lemon and orange peel. Other botanicals that may be used include anise, angelica root, orris root, cinnamon, coriander, and cassia bark.

Gin remains the fourth most popular spirit category behind vodka, whisky and liqueurs. Gin drinkers are typically older, female and middle class. Despite recent moves to make gin 'trendier' it has not been successful at appealing to the young adult market.

Scotch whisky

Scotch whisky accounted for almost 30% of the total UK consumption of spirits in 2003 (from 34% in 1999) and has fallen to around 26% in 2010. Despite its fall in popularity, Scotch whisky still outsells all other spirits with the exception of vodka.

There are two main types of Scotch whisky: malt and grain whisky. The malt whiskies can be divided into 4 groups, according to the location of their distillery:

- ◆ Lowland Malt Whiskies: made south of an imaginary line drawn from Dundee in the east to Greenock in the west.
- ◆ Highland Malt Whiskies: made north of that line.
- ◆ Speyside Malt Whiskies: from the valley of the River Spey.
- ◆ Islay Malt Whiskies: from the island of Islay.

Each distillery produces malt whiskies with distinct flavours and aromas. A single malt whisky is made from malts produced by the same distillery. Once produced, malts may be aged in barrels for 10, 12, 15 years or more.

Grain whisky is normally made from 10–20% malted barley together with other unmalted cereals such as maize or wheat. The distilled spirit is lighter in character and aroma than most malt whiskies and requires less time to mature. The production of grain whisky is not so influenced by geographical factors and it may be distilled anywhere in Scotland. The bulk of matured grain whisky is used for blending.

The majority of Scotch whisky sold in the on-trade is blended whisky, known as 'scotch' in the UK. Blended whisky is a combination of up to 15 or 20 malt and grain whiskies. Blending is an 'art form' carried out by experienced blenders using secret recipes.

Here are some other interesting facts about blended whisky:

◆ Whisky can only be described as 'Scotch whisky' if it has been wholly distilled and matured in Scotland for a minimum of 3 years.
◆ The law requires that when the age is declared on a label, it must refer to the youngest whisky in the blend.
◆ De luxe blended Scotch whisky is a blend which contains a higher proportion of carefully selected older, more expensive whiskies.

For more information about Scotch whisky visit the Scotch Whisky Association website: www.scotch-whisky.org.uk

Rum

Rum is made from sugar cane by-products such as molasses and sugar cane juice by a process of fermentation and distillation. The clear liquid is then usually aged in oak and other casks. The most popular rums can be divided into 3 main types:

◆ White rums, also referred to as 'light' rums are sometimes filtered after ageing to remove any colour. They are typically light flavoured and sweet.

- Gold rums, also called amber rums, are medium-bodied rums which are generally aged. The rum can be flavoured through the addition of spices or caramel. (A variation is often sold as 'Spiced Rum'.) Its darker colour comes from its ageing in wooden casks.
- Dark rum, also known as 'black rum', is darker than gold rum. It is generally aged longer in heavily charred barrels, and has a much stronger flavour than either white or gold rum. Spice flavours can be detected along with strong molasses or caramel overtones.

White rum substantially outsells dark rum in the UK and is responsible for the overall growth of the rum category. White rum has been succesfully promoted to the young adult market, whilst dark rum has suffered the same 'dark spirit' decline as whisky. The UK rum sector is dominated by one brand which has grown through strong marketing and its ownership of its popular white rum and white rum-based RTD products. Rum is ranked as the fifth most consumed spirit in the UK.

Brandy

Grape brandy is produced by the distillation of fermented grape juice. The two most popular types of grape brandy are:

Cognac

Cognac is a traditional French brandy that is named after a town in the Charente region of western France. Cognac is considered to be one of the finest types of brandy. Cognac is categorised using various initials to denote quality:

- VS (Very Special) or Three Stars: is at least 2 years old.
- VSOP (Very Special Old Pale) or Five Star: has been matured for at least 4 years.
- XO (Extra Old): matured for at least 6 years.

Armagnac

Armagnac is the oldest type of brandy in France, with documented references to distillation dating back to the early 15th century. The

Armagnac region is located in the southwest corner of France. Armagnac uses similar categories as Cognac to denote quality. Other, lesser-known, grape brandies are produced by Spain, Mexico, South Africa and America. Other types of brandy include:

◆ Pomace brandy: produced from fermented grape pulp, seeds, and stems that remain after the grapes are pressed. (Examples include Italian grappa.)
◆ Fruit brandies: distilled from fruits other than grapes. Apple, plum, peach, cherry, raspberry, blackberry, and apricot are the most commonly used fruit. (Examples include Calvados and kirsch.)

UK Consumption of brandy including Cognac and Armagnac has grown steadily since 1999. Many brand owners are now trying to broaden the appeal of brandy by promoting VS quality brandies for use with mixers or in cocktails, while better quality VSOP brandies continue to be offered as a premium drink for customers to trade up to.

MAXIMISING SALES OF SPIRITS

Growing overall consumption of spirits offers you a chance to develop this part of your business and enjoy the high profit margins that come from selling spirits. There is a number of practical things you can do to increase your spirit sales. Many of these are based on research which suggests that over 40% of customers do not know what they are going to buy when they enter your pub; this provides you with an excellent opportunity to influence their decision.

Here are some ways that you can increase the sales of your spirits:

◆ Stock big brands.
◆ De-clutter your back bar so that your spirits can be easily seen.
◆ Display your optics in banks of no more than 6.
◆ Group similar products together.
◆ Separate your light and dark spirits.

- Double face key products like vodka, whisky, gin and white rum.
- Display popular spirits at either side of your till(s) – a hot-spot that virtually all customers will look at.
- Remove slow moving spirits from display.
- Replace 25ml optics with 35ml ones. (Research shows that most customers feel that the 25ml measure is poor value for money.)
- Price your spirits competitively.
- Display fresh fruit and ice to be served with your spirits.
- Use point of sale material to promote key brands.
- Run fun nights and tastings.
- Stock important premium brands along with your standard spirits.

SOFT DRINKS

The on-trade soft drinks market is worth over £2 billion and has grown in value over recent years. Soft drinks are now the fourth largest drinks category in the on-trade, behind beers, spirits and wines. Demand has grown for the following reasons:

- They are seen as a healthy alternative to alcohol.
- Pubs have become more female-friendly.
- The numbers of family pubs have increased.
- Pub food has grown.
- Customers have switched preferences from RTDs to spirit and mixer drinks and cocktails.
- Ongoing enforcement of drink-drive laws.
- Employers' restrictions on drinking alcohol at lunchtime.
- Eight in ten people prefer to drink soft drinks rather than alcohol at lunchtime.

The table below shows the value of each sub-category of soft drinks in the on-trade for 2008.

Total on-trade soft drink performance 2008		
Type of soft drink	Total value £ millions	Percentage share of total (£ value) on-trade soft drinks
Cola	£946m	41%
Lemonade	£422m	18%
Juice drinks	£245m	11%
Squash	£170m	7%
Mixers	£158m	7%
Fruit juice	£139m	6%
Energy	£109m	5%
Bottled water	£71m	3%
Flavoured carbonates	£52m	2%
Total:	**£2311m**	

Source: Nielsen On-Premises Audit, MAT 2008

MAXIMISING SOFT DRINKS SALES

Improving your soft drink sales will have a beneficial effect on your profits because of the high profit margins you earn on them. Recognising the importance of soft drinks to your business is the first step in selling more of them. Think about your target customers and how soft drinks can satisfy their needs, and then offer a range of quality soft drinks that will achieve this.

Here are some ways that you can sell more soft drinks:

◆ Stock good quality, big brands.
◆ Keep them correctly chilled.
◆ Display your premium-packaged soft drinks in bottle fridges and on your back-bar.
◆ Serve in highball glasses with plenty of ice and sliced fruit.
◆ Make 16oz (glass size) servings your standard.
◆ Offer jugs of soft drinks to share.
◆ Offer a range of summer no-alcohol cocktails.

◆ Train staff to sell soft drinks alongside food.

◆ Sell bottles of mineral water with wine orders.

◆ Have a kids' soft drinks menu.

◆ Have 'drivers' shelf offers' (special deals for drivers).

◆ Use branded glassware and promotional material.

◆ Offer a cut-price soft drink with lunchtime meals.

◆ Stock 'diet' versions.

COFFEE

The UK's coffee-bar culture has developed significantly over the last decade. A recent investigation into the coffee chain market by leading market researchers, Allegra Strategies (2009) found the following:

◆ By 2012, the UK branded coffee market will reach an estimated £2 billion in consumer spend.

◆ Total branded coffee outlets were estimated at 4000 in 2009 and the top three operators account for 50% of the branded coffee shop market.

◆ The branded coffee shop market has grown consecutively over the last 15 years.

◆ Coffee is regarded as an 'affordable treat', even during periods of recession.

◆ There is a growing trend towards more authentic individual coffee shops serving hand-crafted quality coffee.

◆ Cappuccinos and lattes are the most popular coffee beverage and there is a growing demand for trendy beverage called a 'flat white'.

With the increasing popularity of coffee, options for earlier opening (through changes in the Licensing Act) and the increased demand for food, many UK publicans will benefit by making coffee available to their customers.

Offering good quality coffee can help:

◆ Attract new types of customers.

◆ Encourage customers to use your pub at different times of day.

◆ Extract more money from diners wanting a coffee to round off their meal.

For more information about coffee visit the British Coffee Association website:
www.britishcoffeeassociation.org/bca_home.aspx

MAKING MONEY FROM COFFEE

The first step in deciding whether to introduce or expand your 'coffee offer' is to try to assess the likely level of demand for coffee, then decide how much you are willing (or able) to invest in coffee-making equipment in order to make it profitable for you.

Different types of coffee-making equipment are available to cater for different budgets and levels of demand. Commercial coffee-making machines range from top models at £7,000 to more modest units in the £300–£500 region. You can also lease or hire many types of coffee-making machines too.

Here are ways to make money from coffee:

◆ Before investing, learn about coffee-making equipment and the different types of coffee beans and roasts available. (Talk to several suppliers and check the internet.)
◆ Choose equipment that is appropriate to the level of demand.
◆ Use good quality beans from a reputable supplier.
◆ Make sure that you and your staff are properly trained to prepare coffee.
◆ Introduce a coffee menu.
◆ Introduce a 'coffee of the week'.
◆ Promote coffee with 'A' boards, chalkboards and other POS material.
◆ Incentivise staff to sell coffee with meals.
◆ Offer flavoured and liqueur coffees.
◆ Run a coffee 'collector card' – eg 'buy six coffees and get your seventh free'.
◆ Offer 'decaf' and low fat options.

17

PUB FOOD

EATING OUT

The size of the market

The eating out market in the UK was valued at £31.1 billion in 2008 and the average UK consumer spends £10 per week on eating outside the home, according to Mintel. Their research in 2009 showed that more than half of all adults had eaten a meal in a pub or bar over the previous three months and meals served in pubs and bars was the largest market within the eating out sector with sales of £7.6 billion. Around 24 million consumers eat out for a special occasion, 19 million do so just because they feel like it and 15 million eat out as a regular treat. The rise of discounting in recent months has helped eating out to remain accessible to consumers during the recession, especially families.

Food sales were estimated to account for 25% of pub turnover in 2009 compared with 12% in 1987, showing the increased importance of food in pubs.

The demand

The demand for eating out has been fuelled by a number of factors:

- Increases in disposable income: since 1982, household disposable income per head has seen year-on-year growth (*National Statistics Social Trends Report 2004*).
- More women out at work: since 1984, the number of women in employment has increased by 30% – (*Labour Market Survey – Office of National Statistics*).
- Increasingly active retired people: the ageing population and the increased spending power of the 'grey market' means increased demand.
- Increases in single-person households: Nearly seven million people lived alone in 2006, four times more than in 1960, and numbers are predicted to keep rising (Joseph Rowntree Foundation Report).
- Personal time is at a premium: increasingly busy lives are making personal time precious.

The opportunity

The rising demand for eating out provides the licensee with an opportunity to increase pub turnover and profits. Typical gross profit percentages for food are as follows:

- Low-priced/quality food   30–40%
- Mid-priced/quality food   40–55%
- Higher priced/quality food   60–70%

Your food turnover will be driven by the following:

- Your location.
- The volume of local demand for food.
- Specific customer needs.
- The extent and quality of competition.
- How well your competitors meet the demand for food.
- How well you meet the demand for food.
- Your prices.
- Your facilities.
- The quality of your food.
- The quality of your customer service.

◆ How well you communicate with customers and potential customers.
◆ Your past reputation for food (if applicable).

WHAT TYPE OF FOOD SHOULD YOU OFFER?

You should offer the type of food that will meet the needs of your customers and potential customers. To ascertain this, it is useful to step into the shoes of your target customers, think about their lifestyle and visualise:

◆ When may they want to eat?
— Traditional meal times or at other times of the day?

◆ Who will they be with?
— Partners, family, friends, colleagues or alone?

◆ How much time do they have?
— No limits or a quick lunch break?

◆ What are their eating occasions?
— Special event, big night out, sociable get-together, meeting or a quiet visit?

◆ What is their budget?
— High spending, medium spending, low spending?

◆ What are their tastes and preferences?
— Traditional, ethnic, vegetarian, low fat, children's?

Answering these questions for each of your target customer-types helps you put together a menu which focuses on satisfying their needs, instead of writing a menu on a whim and hoping for the best.

Look for a gap in the market that is not being filled by any of your competitors.

Limiting factors

Unfortunately, you may not fully exploit the local demand for food because your 'offer' may be limited by your lack of expertise, availability of experienced staff, kitchen facilities, and equipment or limited capital. If this is the case and you wish to improve your food offer, you will need to overcome your limiting factors. For example:

Limiting factor	Possible solution
Lack of expertise:	Obtain additional training and experience.
Lack of experienced staff:	Train existing staff. Utilise local catering colleges.
Poor kitchen facilities:	Develop new kitchen.
Limited equipment:	Purchase, lease or rent new equipment.
Limited capital:	Business loan. Brewery or pub company development (lease or tenanted).

You will need to weigh the cost of each solution against the benefit of improved food sales, being careful to make an objective, well-considered assessment. For large-scale investment or additional borrowing, you should seek professional advice from your accountant before going ahead. (Use three scenarios – optimistic, realistic and pessimistic to forecast your anticipated food sales and consider the implications of each.)

Catering suppliers sometimes have reconditioned equipment available, which is much cheaper than purchasing new items.

TYPES OF PUB FOOD OPERATIONS

Here are some examples of pub food operations ranging from cold back-bar catering (which requires little or no experience and a small amount of equipment to set up) to restaurant-quality premium dining (requiring high levels of expertise, kitchen facilities and equipment).

Style of food operation	Food offered	Essential equipment/ facilities
Cold back-bar catering:	Cold sandwiches.	Chilled bar display; fridge/freezer.
Hot back-bar catering:	Pies, ready prepared– burgers, wraps and hot sandwiches.	Pie warmer or halogen oven or microwave; fridge/freezer.
Simple catering:	Hot sandwiches, wraps, burgers, chips, soup, tapas.	Kitchen area; cooker/grill; microwave; fridge/freezer; deep fat fryers.
'Pub grub':	Traditional, value-for-money meals.	As per 'Simple catering' plus bain marie; soup kettle; grill; contact grill; dishwasher; also extraction units and grease traps.
Family dining:	Value-for-money menu attracting families.	Well-planned, well–equipped kitchen.
Premium dining:	Upmarket restaurant quality food.	Well-planned, well-equipped kitchen.

STARTING CATERING

If your pub does not currently provide catering but you would like to introduce it on a small scale, with limited investment, there is a number of options open to you.

No kitchen facilities:

Introduce cold back-bar catering, for example:

◆ sandwiches;
◆ breakfast bagels, or croissants and coffee;
◆ cheese platters;
◆ cold pie and chutney selection.

Introduce hot back-bar catering, for example:

◆ hot pies from a bar-top pie warmer;
◆ hot snacks from a bar-top halogen oven;
◆ hot snacks from a microwave;
◆ hot soup from a soup kettle;
◆ hot panninis and toasties.

Other ideas:

◆ summer BBQs;
◆ hog roasts.

Limited Kitchen facilities

Introduce quick, easy to prepare food:

◆ tapas;
◆ pizzas;
◆ nachos;
◆ wraps 'n chips;
◆ burgers 'n chips;
◆ panninis;
◆ salads.

Basic kitchen facilities

Focus on one day (keeps costs down and helps assess demand):

♦ Sunday lunches (typically the most popular day for eating out);
♦ Saturday shoppers' menu;
♦ Saturday football fans' menu.

Designing your food operation

Every pub, whatever its character or situation, has an opportunity to sell food, even if it is on a small-scale basis. The aim of selling food should be to contribute to your profits; ideally directly or indirectly by helping to increase your wet turnover (attracting new customers, staying longer etc).

Decisions about the type and extent of your food operation should be ultimately based on whether it will contribute to your pub's profitability. Your level of investment should be appropriate for the level of demand and profit you anticipate. Investing heavily in catering where there is limited demand is a waste of your resources. Alternatively, offering a limited catering facility to customers in an area of high demand fails to exploit opportunities for making more profit.

Ultimately, making a 'commercial decision', based on sound research, careful forecasting of demand and accurate costing will maximise your chance of success.

YOUR MENU

Creating your menu

The purpose of your menu is to make your food sound so appealing that your customers cannot resist ordering! It should be put together based on customer needs (as discussed earlier) to ensure that you are offering customers what they want, when they want it, at a price they are willing to pay. Your menu should be professional looking and clean with mouth-watering descriptions of your meals.

Remember your menu is your most powerful food-merchandising tool, often described as your top food salesperson!

Small-scale catering operations will benefit from having a menu. For example: professional looking sandwich or pie menus are simple and effective at increasing sales. Larger-scale catering operations will require menus that are more extensive, with meals made up from the main meat categories of beef, chicken, lamb and pork. Vegetarians also need to be accommodated; research estimates that 5–7% of the adult population are vegetarian (*Key Note Research 2004, National Diet & Nutrition Survey 2001*); and, as almost 2 in 5 women and 1 in 6 of men are dieting most of the time (*Mintel report 2004*), 'healthy option meals' also need to be incorporated in your menu.

Separate menus

Separate menus can be used to target different customer needs for example: breakfast menus, quick bites, light meals, and children's menus. These can be displayed at different times of the day or week when you are targeting different types of customers.

Menus for special occasions such as Valentine's Day, Mother's Day, Easter and Christmas also need to be planned and promoted well in advance.

The new major food trends – 'grazing' and 'food sharing'

There are two new food trends that are growing in popularity –'grazing' and 'food sharing':

◆ **Grazing**: this is where people choose to eat several smaller meals outside the traditional meal times. (To benefit from the grazing trend offer light bites and snacks all day and evening.)
◆ **Food sharing**: this is where groups of friends order food that can be shared. (Provide finger food such as nachos, combos, tapas etc.)

Both trends require simple, easy to prepare food, ideally suited to a pub food menu. Ensure that your food operation takes advantage of these new trends!

 'British Tapas' is a brilliant idea! – offer 'baby-sized' fish and chips, breakfasts, ploughman's, pork pies, or black pudding.

Beer and food matching

Beer and food matching is a relatively new innovation which aims to promote beers that complement different dishes (much in the same way as wine is sometimes sold).

In practice, this requires you to suggest complementary beers with each dish on your food menu or have a separate 'beer list' describing the draught and bottled beers you stock, together with a description of their qualities and the types of food they complement.

 For ideas on food matching visit
http://www.craftbeer.com/pages/beer-and-food/pairing-tips/pairing-chart

The general principle is to balance the intensities of food and beer, for example:

◆ Delicate beers with delicate foods.
◆ Strongly flavoured beer with strongly flavoured foods.
◆ Sharp tasting beers with sharp tasting foods.
◆ Sweet tasting beers with sweet foods.

However, there are occasions when beers and foods with contrasting flavours work well too.

Here are some basic suggestions for matching beer and food:

Food	Beer style
Aperitifs	Hoppy, dry, cold lagers
Shellfish	Dry porters and stouts
Fish	Wheat beers
Chicken	Malty lagers
Red meat	Full bodied ales
Spicy foods	Hoppy pilsners
Cheese	Strong, hoppy ales
Desserts	Speciality honey, fruit or chocolate beers or wheat beers

Bottled beers are an excellent way of offering an extensive beer range to complement your food without the cost or commitment of having draught products installed.

Signature dishes

A signature dish is a dish that the public associates with you and your pub. As well as tasting superb, it is unique and interesting and gets people talking about it (and you). Be creative and develop a menu with a signature dish of your own. It should be in keeping with the type of pub that you run and your target customers. It could be a simple dish with your own special twist such as mussels cooked in wheat beer, or a more unique offering like kangaroo steaks.

Signature dishes need not be limited to menus in pubs that offer premium dining; even sandwich menus can include a 'signature sandwich', and pie menus can include an extra special pie that's out of the ordinary. All that is needed is a bit of creativity!

Individual touches

There are lots of little touches that will help to set you apart from your competitors, such as offering a range of homemade breads, chutneys or salad dressings, providing a selection of real teas, including a quality chocolate with every coffee, a choice of relishes with every pie order, or several types of mash potatoes. Try to think of little touches that you can incorporate into your food offering. No matter how limited your menu, there are simple things you can do to make the meal more memorable for the customer and set yourself apart from the competition. They also add value that the customer may be willing to pay a little more for.

Avoid 'menu fatigue'

However good your menu, regular customers can quickly become bored of the same dishes. They may then look elsewhere for new food experiences. Specials boards are a simple low cost way of keeping your menu varied (as well as using up surplus ingredients). Specials boards can also be used to display seasonal menus and special occasion menus.

The alternative is to change your menu periodically. Many of the large pub food operators change their menus every six months in an effort to keep their customers interested in what they have to offer. This can be a costly process, with menu reprints and advertising. It also carries the risk of alienating some customers whose favourite dishes are removed from the menu. However, the major pub food operators believe that the benefits outweigh the costs and risks associated with the change.

Be aware of 'menu fatigue' and monitor the popularity of different dishes and overall food sales. Consider making changes to your menu 'at least' on an annual basis, keeping the popular dishes and replacing slow-selling dishes with new ones. Allocate time, and budget for the cost of reprinting

Use a specials board to trial new dishes before adding them to your printed menu.

menus and monitor the impact of your new menu after it has been introduced.

Menu layout

The average customer only takes 3 to 4 minutes to look at a menu, so first impressions and a clear layout are vitally important. Rather than simply listing all your dishes, break up your menu into distinct food categories, containing no more than 6 items per category. Use the top right-hand portion of each section or page to place your high-profit dishes as this is where customers' eyes will be automatically drawn to when reading a menu.

PRICING YOUR MENU

Deciding what price to charge for each dish is often quite difficult, especially when starting a new food operation. Charging too little results in a lost opportunity to make more profit, while charging too much keeps customers away. You have to strike a tricky balance between maximising your profits and keeping customers happy. However, there are some ways to make the task easier, and these are explained below.

Recipe costs

Every dish you sell should be costed so that you know the total ingredient costs of each. You should include the price of *all* ingredients including spices, garnish and sauces etc. You will need to set standard weights/ volumes for each ingredient and use these for all future dishes (see the section, 'Portion Control', below). The easiest way to do this is to use a simple spreadsheet that you can update easily to take into account price changes. It is useful to update these records at least on a quarterly basis to keep up to date.

Required GP%	Multiply dish cost by:
30%	1.679
35%	1.808
40%	1.958
45%	2.136
50%	2.350
55%	2.611
60%	2.938
65%	3.357
70%	3.917
75%	4.700
80%	5.875

Once you have established your dish cost you can use industry standard gross profit percentages (GP%) quoted earlier in this chapter as a guide to setting your price. You can use a multiplier to find your VAT inclusive selling price for different gross profit percentages. These are shown in the table below, together with an example.

For example: If your dish costs £2.50 to make and you wish to achieve a gross profit percentage of 60%, multiply £2.50 by 2.938 to give a VAT inclusive★ selling price of £7.35.

You can verify this with the following calculation:

Selling price (inc. VAT)	£7.35
Selling price (exc. VAT)	£6.25 (100%)
Less: Cost of goods sold	£2.50 (40%)
Equals: Gross Profit	£3.75 (60%)

(ie gross profit divided by selling price (exc. VAT) x 100 = 60%)

*Note: VAT-registered businesses selling food that is ready to eat should charge VAT at the standard rate. But you are not normally required to charge VAT on cold take-away food.

Know the market you operate in

Although the above cost-based approach to setting prices is relatively straightforward, it is your customers that will ultimately determine what you will be able to charge. Bear in mind that your customers are not concerned with your gross profit calculations; their decisions whether to pay a certain price are based on their perceived value of the dish and any added value they obtain by eating in your pub.

You need to understand your target customers in terms of their levels of disposable income, the eating establishments they frequent, and the prices they are used to paying. You also need to know what your competitors are charging and what they offer. Look at their food operation and compare it with your own:

- location (prime site or back street?);
- food quality;
- portion sizes;
- service;
- décor;
- atmosphere;
- access;
- reputation.

Use your competitors' prices as benchmarks but be prepared to adjust the price of your own dishes in line with the above. Customers will be willing to spend more for your dishes if your food quality, service and facilities are superior to your competitors. Conversely, if they are inferior, don't expect customers to pay the same price as they would in your competitors' establishments.

Examine your sales

Studying your food sales provides you with useful information. It is good practice to keep a record of sales for each dish you sell. If you are selling a large percentage of higher-priced items, this can indicate that your customers are not so 'price sensitive' (influenced by price) and that their buying decisions are influenced by other factors.

Other ways to establish prices

Your staff often have a very good understanding of your customers through the large amount of interaction they have with them. They are present when customers order their meals and can see their reactions to the menu. This is useful feedback for you. Regular comments about the expense of certain dishes may indicate that customers consider them to be overpriced. Alternatively, comments like 'great value' may mean that these dishes are perceived as being underpriced.

Specials boards can also be used to test the water of dishes prior to adding them to your main menu. They provide an opportunity to test levels of demand for dishes at different prices. For example, what is the effect on demand if the price is increased or decreased by 50p or £1? (It is much easier to change the price of a dish on a specials board than on a printed menu.)

MENU ENGINEERING

Menu engineering is a way of analysing your menu and making changes in order to maximise the profitability of your food operation. It examines the sales history of each dish and the gross profit it contributes. It then relates the profit margin to the popularity of the dish to see which items are both popular and profitable.

Though it is usually undertaken by the larger food operators, some menu engineering techniques are useful to the pub food operator.

A fictional example is given on page 270 for a range of pizza dishes:

Explanation of the table

35% of all pizzas sold are cheese pizzas and they contribute £3.76 gross profit per pizza. 5% of pizzas sold are 'Jumbo specials' and they contribute £4.10 per pizza. The average sales percentage is 14.3% (ie 100% divided by the number of dishes – 7 types of pizza), and the average gross profit is £3.16 (ie total gross profit of each pizza divided by the number of dishes.) These figures are then used as a benchmark to assess the profitability and popularity of each pizza dish.

'The Barking Dog' – pub pizza sales % and gross profit		
Pizza type	Sales percentage (sales as a percentage of total pizza sales)	Gross profit (£) per pizza
Cheese	35.0%	£3.76
Seafood special	14.2%	£2.50
Spicy chicken	9.2%	£2.74
Jumbo special	5.0%	£4.10
Tuna	10.6%	£2.89
Beef	15.0%	£2.25
Super deluxe	11.0%	£3.86
Average:	**14.3%**	**£3.16**

Dishes are placed into four categories according to their profitability and popularity. Using a useful US menu engineering model, these categories are given memorable names.

STARS	Stars are high in both popularity and profit margin. These are the Signature Items.
These dishes should have prime place on your menu and be promoted by staff to further improve your overall profitability. Other than finding ways to reduce the recipe cost of these items (increasing dish gross profit further), they should be left alone.	
Examples (using fictional data from previous table): Cheese pizza	

PLOUGH HORSES	Plough horses are high in popularity but low in profit margin. Price-sensitive.
These dishes are typically very price-sensitive and sometimes used as 'loss leaders'. They can be pushed into the 'star' category by improving profit margins by reducing recipe cost.	
Examples: Beef pizza	

PUZZLES	Puzzles are low in popularity but high in profit margin. Higher in profit per sale but hard to sell.
Typically the more expensive dishes on a menu. May act as 'image makers' but too many of these dishes should be avoided. Price reductions may be a way of improving popularity but must be carefully assessed. Otherwise candidates for repackaging, replacing or elimination.	
Examples: Jumbo and Super deluxe pizzas.	

DOGS	Dogs are low in popularity and low in profit margin. Unpopular and little profit.
Possible candidates for elimination, repackaging, repricing or replacing. However, these dishes may serve a particular market segment such as kids' menus and need to remain in place to be competitive.	
Examples: Spicy chicken.	

CONTROL YOUR COSTS

Poor management of your food operation will drain cash from your business and damage your profitability. Food operations are particularly vulnerable to the following problems:

◆ food spoilage;
◆ wastage;
◆ over-portioning;
◆ improper stock rotation;
◆ theft and unauthorized consumption;
◆ cooking errors;
◆ stock breakage;
◆ unrecorded sales.

Good controls need to be in place to ensure that your food operation is correctly managed and costs are minimised. Some of the key areas for controlling costs are discussed below:

Portion control

Careful control of the amount of ingredients you use in each dish is vital if you are to stick to your profit margins. The objective here is to ensure that the same dish is produced for the same cost each time it is prepared. Once you have established your dish cost (including spices, garnish, vegetables, rice etc), you need to be able to replicate the dish using the same ingredient quantities. The easiest way to do this is to use standard sized measuring scoops and ladles to serve up each dish.

Regularly over-portioning dishes, even by a seemingly small amount, can cost you many hundreds of pounds annually.

The following types of food supplies are more costly to buy but have the advantage of cutting down on preparation costs, making portion control simpler and cutting wastage:

- pre-portioned items such as butter and sauces;
- pre-prepared foods such as peeled vegetables;
- pre-cut meat and fish;
- convenience meals.

It is also to be remembered that better quality fresh food usually means a better yield than more inferior food. For example, low quality meat will require more trimming to remove excess fat than better quality meat.

Portion control maintains dish consistency in the eyes of your customers, at the same time as helping you keep a firm control over dish costs.

Stock control

The perishable nature of food makes good stock control even more important. This makes sense from a financial point of view as well as from a food hygiene stance. Here are some important things to remember when dealing with food stocks:

- Stock is no more than a cost until it is sold. Excessive food stocks tie up your cash flow and increase the chances of wastage, spoilage and theft.
- Manage stock in line with food laws (see the section, 'Food Safety Management – HACCP', below).
- Make sure your monthly stocktake includes food stock (check that your stocktaker has the skills to undertake food stocktaking).
- Set clear rules about staff consumption of food and make sure that you and your family abide by them too.
- Ensure all staff are correctly trained to prevent wastage, cooking errors and breakage.

 Handle your frozen chips with care! Research by food manufacturers McCain show that dropping a case of frozen chips can result in 18% fewer portions.

Staffing costs

Staff should be appropriately skilled for the job they are required to do and you need sufficient staff to maintain the levels of service and standards you have set for your business.

The biggest staffing cost in a food operation tends to be the kitchen staff. They need to be of a standard appropriate for the type of food served and style of operation. Qualified chefs are often very expensive and may not be required for many smaller catering operations. Many pub food operations benefit from less expensive, good quality cooks who can competently handle duties in a pub kitchen. Kitchen staffing costs can also sometimes be reduced by using catering college staff or other students whose wages may be subsidised by the government in exchange for the work experience you provide them with. Contact your local colleges to find out if they run such a scheme.

SERVICE

Ego needs

Satisfying customer needs is not solely about providing them with the food they want; you must also consider their other expectations. Customers have 'ego' needs that will, when satisfied, greatly increase their experience with you. Examples of ego needs are:

◆ being recognised;
◆ feeling wanted;
◆ being respected;
◆ being appreciated;
◆ being listened to;
◆ wanting some control over a situation;
◆ wanting people to empathise with them.

Customer service takes 'ego needs' into account and aims to satisfy them by adopting the following principles:

Attentiveness	Eye contact and undivided attention.
Courtesy	Calling the customer by name and displaying tact.
Friendliness	Smiling, positive attitude, open body language and friendly tone.
Helpfulness	Anticipating and responding to needs, helpful suggestions and resolving problems.
Efficiency	Speedy, hassle-free transactions.
Competency	Thorough, mistake-free transactions.
Value	Thanking the customer.

Customer service is something that should be at the heart of your business if you want to be successful. Both you and every member of your staff must be aware of the importance of providing a first-class service to your customers.

 Make sure that customer service training is given to all new members of staff.

Being excellent

Research shows that excellent service builds your reputation and your profits. ('*Service Excellence=Reputation=Profit*', *Professor Robert Johnston, 2001.*) In this report, excellent and poor providers of service were distinguished like this:

The excellent	The poor
Deliver the promise.	Don't do what they said.
Make it personal.	Are so impersonal.
Go the extra mile.	Don't make any effort.
Deal well with problems and queries.	Don't deal with problems.

The report also showed that organisations providing excellent service were more productive (average profit per employee was 72% higher) and more profitable (average profit was 74% higher) than ones providing poor service.

Offering excellent service satisfies customer needs and provides tangible benefits to your business; it is also an effective way of gaining competitive advantage over your rivals.

The 'magic minute'

The 'magic minute' is a useful term that explains the importance of greeting your customers within 60 seconds of them being seated for a meal. It primarily applies to food operations where orders are taken from customers at their tables, though the principle could equally apply to people coming to the bar to order food.

Waiting for longer than a minute to be acknowledged can cause irritation and frustration; a first impression that can sour a customer's whole experience. Though a one-minute wait doesn't seem very long, a person's perception of time is often very different from reality, and one minute waiting to be acknowledged is often perceived as much longer.

Adhering to the 'magic minute' rule helps keep your customers happy.

Handling complaints

No matter how professional and customer-focused your food operation, customer complaints are inevitable at some point (justified or otherwise). Over the last decade the UK public, who were traditionally reluctant to complain, are now more likely to voice their concerns if they are unhappy. This should be regarded as a positive situation; it is better to have problems brought to your attention, giving you the opportunity of resolving them, than for people to leave dissatisfied and spread negative comments about your business.

On a positive note, research shows that nearly all customers who have had complaints resolved efficiently are later happy to recommend the business to their friends. Resolving a complaint has also been shown to strengthen the relationship between a business and its customer, with customer loyalty being greater than before the complaint occurred.

Here are the golden rules of complaints handling (from The Institute of Customer Services – see www.instituteofcustomerservice.com):

◆ Thank the customer for bringing the matter to your attention.

- Say you are sorry the problem has happened. (Not an admission of guilt, just good manners.)
- Look at the issue from the customer's perspective.
- Start with the point of view that the customer may well have a valid point.
- Gather the facts.
- Don't leap straight to the free gift route without solving the fundamental problem.
- Fix the problem.
- Learn from the complaint and change something.
- Minimise reasons for complaints through regular reviews.

 Train your staff to handle complaints correctly and confidently.

SUPPLIERS

Having the right suppliers can make running your business easier and more profitable; poor suppliers can cause disruption and add cost to your business. Choosing the right suppliers is an important task which should be carefully considered. Here are some pointers to help you find the right suppliers.

Be clear about your needs

Good suppliers offer products or services which match (or exceed) your business needs. Being clear about your business needs is the first step in assessing different suppliers. For example, is next-day delivery more important to you than price? Is quality more important than next-day delivery?

Finding potential suppliers

Potential suppliers can be found through the following:

- trade press;
- directories;

- internet searches;
- trade associations;
- recommendations;
- exhibitions and trade shows.

Criteria for choice

Availability

- Do they provide the types of goods you require?

Service

- How good are their service standards?
- Do they deliver goods when you need them?
- Do they go the extra mile?

Reliability

- How reliable are they? (If they let you down, you let your customers down.)

Quality

- Are their products good quality?
- Is their quality consistent?

Value for money

- Are you looking for the lowest price or are you willing to pay a little more for good service, reliability and quality?

Communication

- Do they keep in regular contact with you and show interest in your business?

Financial security

- Are they financially secure?

Food safety

◆ Is food delivered in a hygienic way and in line with HAACP requirements?

Trading terms

◆ Do they offer credit facilities?

Value added services

◆ Do they offer advice on putting together a menu/pricing dishes etc?
◆ Do they provide printed menus for you?
◆ Will they keep you up to date with catering trends and market research?

How many suppliers?

The simple answer is don't buy from too many suppliers and don't just have a single supplier. Using a small number of suppliers has the advantage of making supplier management easier – fewer phone calls, less paperwork and simpler payment arrangements. Regularly using a small number of suppliers also helps build relationships and ensures that you remain important in the eyes of your suppliers. (The more money you spend with a supplier, the more important you are regarded.)

Using a single supplier makes your business too reliant on them – if they have problems, you may not be able to find alternative supplies at short notice, which can significantly affect your business.

Be clear about your expectations

Before you start trading with a supplier, ensure that they are clear about what you expect from them. The larger food suppliers will have their own documentation stating the trading arrangement with you; take time to read and understand this, and make sure that you are happy with the arrangements before agreeing to go ahead. For smaller suppliers who may not have written trading terms, confirm your requirements to them in writing so that there is no room for misunderstanding.

Monitor and review

Monitor your suppliers on an ongoing basis to check that they are providing the levels of quality, service, standards and value for money in line with the needs of your business. If not, make them aware of the issue as soon as possible to give them the opportunity to make changes. Beware of suppliers who have become complacent about doing business with you. If you continue to be unhappy, then find alternative suppliers who will take more of a 'partnership approach' – working with you for mutual benefit. Remember, the more successful your food operation becomes, the more you will be ordering from your suppliers. It's in their interest to help you develop your food operation and make it a success.

BUYING EQUIPMENT

Buying as part of the pub inventory

If the pub you take on already has some catering facilities you are likely to be buying catering equipment as part of the inventory. Unfortunately, these items are sometimes in poor condition and may not work properly. It is wise to check these items thoroughly before taking on the pub (and again on ingoing day) to check whether they are fully operational. Items that are not functioning properly or are in poor condition may not be valued as part of the inventory but you will need to budget for, and organise, the replacement of items that you need for your catering operation. It is better to know of such issues in advance, rather than at the last minute, or when cash has been spent on other things.

Acquiring new items

Catering equipment can be acquired in a variety of ways – purchasing them or by rental, lease or HP. As well as new equipment, reconditioned items are available from catering suppliers at auction or by private sale.

Buying reconditioned equipment from reputable suppliers reduces the risk of problems.

When thinking of buying equipment, there is a number of things to consider:

- **Price**: what payment methods and terms are available?
- **Footprint**: will it fit?
- **Functionality**: will it do multiple tasks?
- **Manageability**: is it easy to use and clean, and is training available?
- **Quality**: is it durable enough to meet the demands of your kitchen?
- **Safety**: has it a safe design?
- **After-sales service**: what service is available if the item becomes faulty?

FOOD LEGISLATION AND SAFETY

New legislation

New EU (European Union legislation was applied in the UK from January 2006) which sets out more clearly the duty of food business operators to produce food safely. General hygiene requirements for all food businesses were laid down in EU Regulation 852/2004 and these are now enforced by new Food Hygiene Regulations 2005/2006 in England, Scotland, Wales and Northern Ireland.

A summary of the requirements of the new legislation is given below. However, you should contact your local authority for more definitive guidance on how the legislation affects your business.

 If you are considering setting up a food operation, ask your local environmental health officer for advice.

Registering your food operation

New food operations must be registered with their local authority 28 days prior to commencing trading. Once registered, food business operators must notify their authority of any changes to the business such as a change to the food business operator or major changes to the food operations. If you are taking over a pub food operation, you should notify your local authority as soon as possible and in any event no later than 28 days after the change.

Food safety management – HACCP

Food businesses are required to put in place procedures which manage food safety within their establishment based on HACCP principles. HACCP stands for 'Hazard Analysis and Critical Control Point', and is a structured approach which enables food operations to:

◆ Analyse potential hazards.
◆ Identify the points in the operation where hazards may occur.
◆ Decide which are critical to consumer safety.

These are critical control points (CCPs), which are monitored and remedial action (specified in advance) is taken if conditions are not within safe limits.

A hazard is anything that can harm the consumer, and can be physical, chemical or microbiological.

The HACCP process involves:

1 Appointing people responsible for the HACCP process.
2 Drawing up a flow chart of all aspects of food handling and preparation, from raw materials through processing and storage to consumption.
3 Identifying hazards and working out CCPs.
4 Recommending monitoring and control measures.
5 Implementing controls at the CCPs.
6 Reviewing.

Guidance on setting up HACCP procedures

Though the HACCP procedures, and food legislation as a whole, sound a little daunting, there are some excellent sources of guidance freely available, which make the task much more straightforward.

An excellent free guide called *CookSafe* is available on-line at: www.food.gov.uk/foodindustry/hygiene/cooksafe/ The complete guide can be downloaded as a large pdf document (1.17MB) or you can simply view sections on-line and print off the parts that you require.

Another good free guide called *Safer Food, Better Business*, developed by the Food Standards Agency, is available on line at: www.food.gov.uk/foodindustry/hygiene/sfbb/ or you can order a hard copy by telephoning 020 7276 8829.

Training requirements

Anyone handling food must receive appropriate supervision and be instructed and/or trained in food hygiene in order to handle food safely. Those responsible for your HACCP procedures must also receive adequate training. There is no legal requirement to attend a formal training course or get a qualification, but you may prefer that you and your staff do so.

Use different colour-coded chopping boards and knives to prepare raw and ready-to-eat foods to prevent cross-contamination.

Rules about premises

Food premises must:

◆ Meet the regulations.
◆ Be suitable for the purpose of your business.
◆ Allow you to prepare food safely.

Premises must be designed and built in a way that enables you to keep them clean and hygienic, and keep out pests like rats and flies.

Specific rules apply to any areas where food is prepared:

- Floors must be in a sound condition, easy to clean and, where necessary, to disinfect. In practice, this means that they should be made of materials that are impervious, non-absorbent, washable and non-toxic.
- Walls must be in a sound condition, easy to clean and, where necessary, to disinfect. In practice, this means a smooth surface, which is impervious, non-absorbent, washable and non-toxic.
- Ceilings should be constructed in a way which prevents the build-up of condensation, dirt and moulds, and be free from flaking particles.
- Surfaces (including surfaces of equipment), and in particular those in contact with food, are to be maintained in a sound condition, and be easy to clean and, where necessary, to disinfect. This requires the use of smooth, washable, corrosion-resistant, and non-toxic materials.
- Windows which can be opened to the outside must be fitted with insect-proof screens that can be easily be removed for cleaning.
- There must be adequate facilities for cleaning equipment and disinfecting other utensils, and they must be supplied with hot and cold water.
- There must be separate facilities for washing food, if unwrapped food is handled during your food operation (not the same as those used for cleaning equipment and utensils), and they must be supplied with hot and/or cold water of drinking quality.

Other considerations:

- Your premises must have washbasins for staff to wash their hands (separate from sinks used to wash food or equipment and utensils). These should be supplied with hot and cold running water, and soap and materials for drying hands hygienically such as disposable towels.
- Lavatories are to be available for staff use and these should not open directly into areas where food is prepared.
- Changing facilities should be provided for staff to change their clothes where necessary.
- The premises must have adequate lighting, ventilation and drainage.
- Cleaning agents and disinfectants are not to be stored in areas where food is handled.

Put signs above washbasins in food areas indicating what they can be used for – washing hands, washing food etc.

Personal hygiene

Legislation states that 'every person working in a food-handling area is required to maintain a high degree of personal cleanliness and is to wear suitable clean and where necessary, protective clothing'. Good practice includes the following:

Personal cleanliness

♦ Hands should be washed thoroughly:
  — before starting work;
  — before handling food;
  — after using the toilet;
  — after handling raw foods or waste;
  — after every break;
  — after eating and drinking;
  — after cleaning;
  — after blowing your nose.

♦ Hair should be tied back and preferably covered.

♦ Food handlers should not sneeze or cough over food.

♦ Food handlers should not smoke in a food preparation area.

♦ Cuts and sores should be covered with a waterproof (preferably highly visible) dressing.

♦ Jewellery should be kept to a minimum when preparing and handling food (a plain wedding ring and sleeper earrings are acceptable).

Clothing

♦ All staff working in the food preparation area should wear suitable, clean clothing.

◆ Clothing should be kept clean and should be changed and laundered regularly in order to protect the food being prepared.

Illness

Legislation also prohibits anyone suffering from, or carrying a disease likely to be transmitted through food, or anyone with infected wounds, skin infections, sores, or diarrhoea, from handling or entering any food-handling area if there is any likelihood of contamination.

There is a requirement to report illness that may present a hazard to food safety, and to exclude people from food handling duties where there is any likelihood of causing contamination of food.

It is good practice to encourage staff to report if anyone in their household is suffering from diarrhoea, stomach upset or vomiting.

Food handlers suffering from any of the complaints listed above must be excluded from food handling until they have fully recovered. The law puts the responsibility on employers to satisfy themselves that no food handler poses a risk to food safety.

Food temperature requirements

Keeping food at an incorrect temperature is one of the major causes of food poisoning. This is because harmful bacteria are present in many types of food and these tend to multiply rapidly at room temperature. Safe practices must be adopted in order to minimise the risk they pose. The key actions are:

1 To destroy or reduce the numbers of harmful bacteria, by cooking or re-heating.
2 To control their growth by keeping food hot or cold.

Your kitchen equipment should include good quality (and regularly tested) food probes that you can use to test the core temperature of your food. These can be purchased from most catering equipment suppliers.

Remember to test the temperature of your food at the thickest part/or centre – not at the surface.

In catering operations, the following practices are recommended to keep food safe:

Refrigeration	It is recommended practice to operate refrigerators at 5°C or below. A food temperature of 8°C is effective at controlling the multiplication of most bacteria in perishable foods.
Freezing	Freezing food at temperatures of -18°C prevents bacteria multiplying.
Cooking	Temperatures of 75°C are effective in destroying almost all types of bacteria.
Hot holding	Temperatures of 63°C will control the multiplication of bacteria in hot food.
Cooling	Food should be cooled as quickly as possible and then refrigerated.
Reheating	Reheating food to 82°C is regarded as a safe temperature.

Scores on the Doors

Consumers in certain areas can see how well a food business complies with food hygiene regulations through Scores on the Doors schemes run by their local authority.

Visit www.scoresonthedoors.org.uk/ for more information.

OTHER LEGAL REQUIREMENTS

Disposal of cooking oil

You are required to store your waste cooking oil safely to prevent spillage, and arrange for it to be collected by an authorised collector who will take your oil to an authorised site for recovery or disposal. Authorised collectors need to be registered with the Environment Agency and you are advised to check their registration documents before allowing them to dispose of your waste oil.

Oil waste must not be poured down drains or sewers as this can lead to blockages, attract vermin, and may pollute watercourses, which may result in prosecution.

Food descriptions

Trading Standards law dictates that food descriptions on menus, adverts, chalkboards or given verbally must not be false or misleading. A description can become false or misleading due to something being left out of a name or phrase, for example:

♦ The most common description, which is left out of a menu making it misleading, is the wording 'formed' or 'reformed'. A reformed product has been chopped, processed, and formed into a particular shape, usually to resemble a slice of meat or piece of seafood.

The most frequent examples of these products are reformed ham, chicken, and scampi; and to properly describe these products the word 'reformed' must be included on any descriptions of these.

Other important descriptions are:

♦ **Homemade**: which should be used only for food made on the premises.
♦ **Fresh**: which must not have been frozen or canned.
♦ **Suitable for vegetarians**: which must not contain any animal products.
♦ **Onion rings**: which must be made from rings cut from an onion and not describe products made from chopped onion and potato.
♦ **Smoked**: which must be traditionally-smoked food, not food that has chemicals added to give a smoke flavour.
♦ **Steak and burger weights**: which must be stated as the approximate uncooked weight.

GM (genetically modified) foods

At the time of writing, there is no GM fresh produce available in the UK. However, 3 genetically modified foods and ingredients are currently available in the UK, these being:

◆ GM soya;

◆ GM maize;

◆ GM tomatoes sold only as tomato puree.

If you sell GM food or your food contains GM ingredients, you are legally required to let your customers know this. You are required to do this by putting a statement next to the menu item or clearly stating that some of your food may contain GM ingredients and that further information can be obtained from your staff. You must ensure that you have a procedure for providing information to your staff that indicates which menu items contain GM ingredients.

Food allergy information

Every year, about 10 people die in the UK as a result of an allergic reaction to food, and many more are hospitalised (Food Standards Agency website). Severe allergic reactions are most commonly caused by the following foods, known as the 'big 8':

1 peanuts (also known as groundnuts);
2 nuts such as almonds, hazelnuts, walnuts, Brazil nuts, pecans, pistachios and macadamia nuts;
3 fish;
4 shellfish;
5 sesame seeds;
6 eggs;
7 milk;
8 soya.

Some people avoid certain types of foods because of food intolerance. About 1 person in 100 has an intolerance to gluten, a protein found in wheat, rye and barley (sometimes oats), because they have coeliac disease. Other people need to avoid lactose, found in milk.

It is important for you and your staff to be able to inform customers of the ingredients used in a meal, if asked. European Law (*General Food Law Regulation 178/2002*) prohibits 'unsafe' food being put onto the market. In deciding whether a food is 'unsafe', the information which a business provides to its customers in the form of staff comments and menu descriptions is taken into account. Some foods may be regarded as 'unsafe' to people with food allergies. This means that businesses must give people with food allergies accurate information about the ingredients in their food.

Here is some useful advice from Allergy UK's *'Caterer's Guide to Severe Food Allergies'* (available via their website: www.allergyuk.org):

◆ Ensure there is always a nominated person on duty who knows, or can find out, the ingredients of all dishes.

◆ Ask suppliers to provide accurate written details about all ingredients, including any planned changes.

◆ Try to avoid the indiscriminate use of nuts, eg powdered nuts as a garnish, unless this is an essential part of the recipe.

◆ If a dish is meant to contain nuts, make sure this is reflected in the name: eg Nut & Carrot Salad.

◆ Remember that salad oil may be derived from nut oil.

◆ If possible, keep certain preparation areas designated as nut-free areas.

◆ Put up a prominent sign encouraging people with allergies to question staff.

◆ Include a prominent statement on the menu encouraging customers with severe allergies to question staff.

For example, this could state: 'Some of our dishes contain nuts. If you are allergic to nuts, please, ask staff to suggest a nut-free meal'.

◆ Try to ensure that where a dish contains potent allergens – particularly nuts – this is indicated in some way on the menu. Some restaurants adopt a circled 'N'.

◆ Organise a training session on allergies for your staff. Make sure that all new staff members are aware of the serious allergies.

18

AMUSEMENT MACHINES

MACHINE INCOME

Typical earnings

Amusement machines can provide you with a steady source of income, with the average tenanted and leased pub taking an estimated £70 per week from their amusement machines, and the highest earners taking in the region of £400 per week. (Based on sharing net income on a 50/50 basis with their brewery or pub company.) The majority of your machine income comes from AWP (Amusement with prizes) machines, also known as fruit machines or gaming machines. Added to this, is income you earn from equipment such as video machines, pool tables, jukeboxes and any other types of machine, such as arcade games.

The actual amount of income you make from your machines is determined by the type of customers you attract, the kind of pub you run, how net income is split, and how well you manage your machines. Before taking on your pub, get written confirmation of how much amusement machine income is currently being earned.

Arrangements for sharing machine income

If you are a tenant or lessee, you will probably be required to use machine suppliers recommended by your brewery or pub company, and there may also be an arrangement to share the net income from your machines with your brewery or pub company. These share arrangements vary; some require you to share only the AWP income (possibly on a 50/50 or 60/40 basis), while others require a share of income from all machines and equipment such as video machines, pool table and jukeboxes. A small number of tenancy and lease agreements allow you to keep all machine income for yourself, ie you retain 100% of the machine income.

Arrangements for sharing machine income vary between different types of tenancy and lease agreements. Make sure you understand them prior to signing so that you can correctly forecast anticipated machine income.

Freehold

If you own the freehold of the pub, you will not be tied by an agreement to use particular machine suppliers, or have to share income with a brewery or pub company. You will however, have to monitor machine performance and manage suppliers yourself.

How your machine income is calculated

The machine supplier collects their rent from the gross income in their machines when they come to empty the cash on a fortnightly basis (or weekly for high-earning machines). Out of the remaining balance, they deduct an apportioned amount to cover Amusement Machine Licence Duty (AMLD) payable to HM Revenue and Customs, and leave you with your share of the net income. VAT is payable by you on the 'taxable take' of amusement machines, that is, the amount put into the machine less the amount returned as winnings to players.

There may be circumstances where a poorly-performing machine does not take enough money to cover the rental and licence duty deductions. This is known as being in 'shortfall', and you will owe your supplier money to cover this loss. In this situation, urgent action needs to be taken to prevent its reccurrence. (See section below, on 'Maximising your AWP and SWP income'.)

MACHINE RENTAL

Machine suppliers range from small local operators to national concerns. Each supplier has a portfolio of machines that is available on rental to the pub trade. In a tenanted or leased pub, the rents for each machine will have been previously set through negotiation between the supplier and brewery or pub company. The general principle is that new models have high rents while older style machines have lower rents. If you operate a freehold pub, you must negotiate machine rents directly with your supplier.

Highly-rented machines need to take more money to cover their costs than lower-rented ones. Typically, the newer AWPs are very appealing to machine players ('gamers'), but must earn enough to cover their high rents. Your pub may not be the appropriate place for this type of machine; a mid-range machine, at a lower rental, may be more appropriate for the level of machine-playing demand in your pub. The aim should be to install machines that appeal to your customers at a rent that allows you to make money. Speak to your machine supplier or Machine Controller for advice on choosing the right type of machine for your pub.

BUYING AN AWP

Ex-rental AWPs are available to buy from suppliers, though this may not be allowed as part of your tenancy or lease agreement. They are also a poor investment as players quickly become bored of playing the same machine. As a guide, AWPs should be changed approximately every 12 weeks (or less) to ensure that playing demand remains high. The benefit of renting machines is that you can replace them with other models when their popularity begins to wane. Monitor the performance of your machines and ensure that your supplier changes your machines regularly.

MACHINE CONTROLLERS

Where your brewery or pub company takes a share of income, they have a vested interest in ensuring your machines are managed to maximise their income. The more successful your machines are, the more money both you and your brewery or pub company make out of them.

The brewery or pub company will have a small team, headed by a Machine Controller or Machine Manager, whose responsibility it is to maximise machine income. Their role is to monitor machine performance, manage machine suppliers and offer advice to licensees.

If you run a freehold pub, you will not have the benefit of a Machine Controller who is monitoring your machines and making changes behind the scenes in order to maximise your machine income. You will have to be your own Machine Controller and develop a close working relationship with your supplier in order to get the best out of your machines.

 As a tenant or lessee, if you are unhappy with the level of service from your machine supplier, contact your Machine Controller who will help resolve the problem for you.

AWP MACHINE PLAYERS

A recent survey by Mintel (*Gaming Machines – UK, 2004*), shows that AWP machine players, also referred to as 'gamers', are a relatively small part of the population. Their research showed that gamers account for only 14% of the population, and are typically 25- to 44 year-old males in the 'D' and 'E' social grade categories. (D – working class semi- and unskilled manual workers, and E – those at the lowest level of subsistence including casual or lowest grade workers.)

In trying to establish the market opportunity for gaming machines, Mintel researched people's attitude towards gaming machines, and concluded that the UK market was split as follows:

◆ Gamers (14% of the sample or 6.8 million adults).
◆ The Unconvinced (20% of the sample or 9.8 million adults).
◆ The Uninterested (44% of the sample or 21.5 million adults).
◆ Anti-Gamers (22% of the sample or 10.7 million adults).

Other research shows that hardcore gamers (regular players) account for less than 7% of all pub-goers, and these people play your machines most regularly and provide you with the majority of your machine income.

YOUR PUB IMAGE

Despite the opportunities to earn income from machines, some licensees decide not to have AWPs installed in their pubs, as they do not fit the image they are trying to portray. Noisy, flashing machines may be an annoyance to their customers, and therefore they choose not to install them in their pubs. Better quality food pubs are not usually an appropriate place to install AWPs because of this.

For the more typical pub operation, it is worth remembering that machine noise levels can be turned down and less flashy equipment can be used that may be more appropriate for your style of operation. It is worth discussing with your machine supplier or Machine Controller, what machine options you have that best suit the style of your operation and clientele.

PERMITS

Gaming machines in your pub

Pubs and other alcohol licensed premises are automatically entitled to two category C or D gaming machines upon notification to the licensing authority of their intention to make gaming machines available for use. Licensing authorities can issue gaming machine permits which allow additional category C or D gaming machines to be provided.

Machine Categories

Sections 282 and 283 of the Gambling Act 2005 provide for two types of gaming machines which can be located in alcohol licensed premises. These are:

- Category C: Maximum state = 50p/Maximum prize = £35.
- Category D: Maximum stake = 10p or 30p non-monetary/Maximum prize = £5 cash or £8 non-monetary.

Gaming Permit

The permit's duration is indefinite as it is linked to the Licensing Act 2003 Premises Licence. There is a first annual fee payable:

(i) where a permit comes into effect on the issue date, the first annual fee for the permit shall be paid within 30 days after that date.

(ii) where a permit specifies that it is to come into effect on a date after the issue date, the first annual fee for the permit shall be paid within (a) the relevant period, or (b) 12 months after the issue date, whichever is sooner, and an annual fee payable after that before each anniversary of the date of issue of the permit. Failure to pay the annual fee may result in the cancellation of the permit. The annual fee is £50.

GAMBLING ACT 2005

The Gambling Act 2005 replaced most of the previous gambling law. It applies to the whole of Great Britain, but not generally to Northern Ireland. It put in place more comprehensive regulations and created a new independent regulatory body, the Gambling Commission.

Code of Conduct

Operators who provide gaming machines are required to protect the interests of children and vulnerable people, under new codes of conduct.

Codes were introduced alongside an increase in game machines' stakes and prizes, following an agreement by the Department for Culture Media and Sport and industry trade bodies.

The codes are backed by the Gambling Commission and GamCare, and ensure that:

◆ all gaming machines display the GamCare helpline number;
◆ all machines have clear signage forbidding play by under 18s; and
◆ all machines are supervised to ensure that there's no underage play.

GamCare provides support, information and advice to anyone suffering through a gambling problem. Tel: 0845 6000 133. Website: www.gamcare.org.uk

ISSUES AFFECTING MACHINE INCOME

Over the last few years, income from pub AWP machines has been under pressure from the growing popularity of other forms of gambling. Many hardcore gamers have switched from pub AWPs to other ways of gambling which offer higher payouts. The result has been an overall decline in the amount of money gambled in pub AWP machines and a consequent reduction in machine income for many licensees. Though there are calls to increase payouts of pub AWP machines to make them more attractive to gamers, the attraction of other forms of gambling remains very strong. Some of these other forms of gambling are discussed below.

FOBTs

Fixed Odds Betting Terminals (FOBTs) are a recent phenomenon which have been installed in betting shops, and have become very popular. FOBTs have 'touch-screen' terminals and look similar to quiz machines found in pubs and clubs. They offer a number of games, with roulette being the most popular, and maximum prizes of £500, which far exceed that of traditional AWP machines. Many bookmakers claim that revenue generated from FOBTs now exceeds traditional over-the-counter gambling. Pubs located close to betting shops are likely to feel the impact more than those located further away.

On-line gambling

There has been a huge expansion of internet-based gambling over recent years with an estimated 1,800 websites devoted to on-line gambling. Although on-line gambling still tends to attract a small percentage of overall gamblers, there is evidence that it is becoming more mainstream, and may well be luring some traditional pub AWP gamers. The Gambling

Act 2005 allows internet casinos (previously outlawed) to be based in Great Britain for the first time.

Expansion of casino facilities

The Gambling Act 2005 allows for an increase in the number of UK casinos. (There were 140 casinos operating in 2006.) New legislation allows for the introduction of regional casinos, which could be up to 10 times the size of many existing casinos, along with a further 8 large and 8 small casinos.

Although figures for 2004 show that casino gambling is undertaken by a small percentage of the population (3% of men and 1% of women had played table games in a casino over the last 12 months: *Gambling Commission website*), changes in legislation in 2005, allowing casinos to operate without membership restrictions and increases in machine payouts, have caused an upsurge in casino attendance. The full impact on pub gaming machine income is yet to be predicted.

AMUSEMENT MACHINE LICENCE DUTY (AMLD)

Requirement for licences

All amusement machines, including gaming, video, pinball and quiz machines, provided for play on any premises in the UK need a licence, unless they fall within the list of exempt machines. Licences are issued by HM Revenue and Customs and you are legally required to display your licence prominently in the premises where your machines are located. If you are renting your machines, your supplier will normally make the application for your licence.

Payment of Amusement Machine Licence Duty

Amusement Machine Licence Duty (AMLD) is payable to HM Revenue and Customs for certain types of machines. Your machine supplier normally collects a proportion of AMLD each time they empty their machines and pays this to HM Revenue and Customs. They normally deduct this from the machine takings, together with their rental, before paying you your machine income. If you own a machine which is liable for AMLD, you are responsible for making these payments to HM Revenue and Customs yourself.

 Double check that your machine supplier has made all necessary applications for machine licences and is collecting AMLD. (You will be committing an offence if your machines are not properly licensed.)

Machines generally not needing a licence

The following machines do not generally need a licence and are not liable to duty:

◆ crane grab machines;
◆ children's rides;
◆ table football games;
◆ snooker and pool tables;
◆ bar billiards;
◆ vending machines and jukeboxes;
◆ laser games usually played in a labyrinth with a portable 'gun'.

Scope of AMLD

From 1 August 2006 an amusement machine that was not a gaming machine (e.g. video or pinball machine) was removed from the scope of AMLD. The scope of exempted machines was also revised:

◆ The 2-penny machines remain exempt.
◆ Machines with a maximum stake of 10p and maximum cash prize of £5 are exempt.
◆ Machines with a maximum stake of 30p and maximum prize of £8, where the cash element of the prize does not exceed £5, are exempt.

 Further information on machine exemptions and AMLD can be obtained from HM Revenue and Customs, Greenock Accounting Centre (GAC) by telephoning: 01475 881431.

NEW TECHNOLOGY

Most machine suppliers now offer several high-tech machines based on the latest digital technology. Many of these new 'entertainment terminals' not only offer prize video games, but also provide facilities for tournament playing and downloading ringtones and games onto mobile phones. Touch screen AWPs are also being introduced which aim to replicate the traditional 'reel spinning' fruit machines in a video format.

Both these types of machines have their content changed regularly via a telephone link, preventing the need to physically remove and replace the equipment when customers get tired of the games.

As machine technology advances, you can expect more games and services available from pub machines, which aim to broaden their appeal from the traditional hardcore gamer to a wider audience.

MAXIMISING YOUR AWP AND SWP INCOME

Machines need to be managed if you wish to maximise the income you earn from them. Here are some simple but effective ways you can do this:

- Position your machines where they can be seen and in areas of good 'traffic flow'.
- Make sure your machines are switched on, otherwise they cannot be played.
- Keep them clean and well presented.
- Report any faults to your supplier as soon as possible.
- Monitor the performance of your machines and ask your supplier to replace machines that are not popular, or have declined in popularity.
- Listen to feedback from your core machine players and communicate their views to your supplier.
- Seek advice from your machine supplier or Machine Controller on which types of machines would suit your pub and clientele.

19

COMPLYING WITH OTHER REGULATIONS

REGULATIONS

Public houses, like other small businesses, are subject to a range of regulations that must be complied with. Many of these have been discussed in other parts of this book, but a number of other regulations apply to you and your business, and these are discussed in this chapter. Though this is not an exhaustive list, it does explain many of the key areas that you need to be familiar with.

 The Business Link website provides useful information on regulations applying to businesses (they also have a facility that emails updates to you, to keep you up to date with any changes). Their website address is: www.businesslink.gov.uk

As a publican, you must take particular note of the following areas and requirements.

PERFORMING RIGHT SOCIETY

Background

The Performing Right Society (PRS) is a non-profit making membership organisation of composers, songwriters, authors and publishers of music. Its essential function is to collect and distribute music royalties on behalf of its members.

PRS Licence and fees

PRS collects royalties by issuing a licence to the music user, which is usually charged on an annual basis. If music is played to the public in your pub, then you are regarded as a 'music user', and are therefore required to obtain a licence from PRS and pay a fee to them. The amount depends on several factors:

◆ The type of equipment you use to play your music, eg TV, CD, radio.
◆ The size of your venue.
◆ The frequency of the performances.

Standard charges for pubs and bars up to 120 sq m are given below (effective 1st October, 2009). Where the music user has applied for and obtained *PRS for Music's* licence before musical performances commence, the **standard** royalty rate will be charged and payable for the first year of the licence. Where the music user *has not* applied for and obtained *PRS for*

Category	Annual charge	Standard royalty
Television in bar area (up to 120 sq m) CD player in bar area (up to 120 sq m) Audio jukebox in bar area (up to 120 sq m)	£105.17 £262.95 £308.81	£70.11 £175.30 £205.87
Live music per session (for the first 100 persons capacity)	£12.00	**Price per session:** £8.00
Karaoke per session	£12.00	£8.00

Music's licence before musical performance commence, the **higher** (standard plus 50%) royalty rate will be charged and payable for the first year of the licence.

Where to get a PRS licence

You can telephone PRS on 0800 068 48 28 (Monday–Friday, 9am–5pm) to obtain a quotation for your premises or make out a licensing agreement. You can also apply for your licence on-line.

For more information visit the PRS website at: www.prsformusic.co.uk

What happens if you do not take out a PRS licence?

If you use copyright music and do not apply for the relevant PRS licence, the PRS in most cases will take all reasonable steps to ensure that you are fully aware of your legal obligations and allow you time to obtain a licence before considering legal action, but this will depend on the circumstances. If, however, you still refuse to comply, the PRS will apply for an injunction to prevent you from using any copyright music until you take out a licence.

PHONOGRAPHIC PERFORMANCE LIMITED

Background

Phonographic Performance Limited (PPL) is a music industry organisation collecting and distributing airplay and public performance royalties in the UK on behalf of over 3,000 record companies and 30,000 performers. It was set up in 1934 by the recording industry to grant licences for the playing or broadcasting of sound recordings such as CDs, tapes and records in public.

Important note!

PPL and PRS are not the same. Whenever you play a sound recording in public there are two separate licences that have to be paid:

♦ **PRS**: which distributes payments to composers and publishers.
♦ **PPL**: which distributes payments to record companies and performers.

PPL Licence and fees

Getting the right licence is a legal requirement. If you play recorded music or music videos in public, or broadcast them (or copy them in order to do so) in the UK, you will be infringing copyright unless you are appropriately licensed by PPL.

A public performance occurs whenever sound recordings are played outside the domestic or family circle. Whenever a sound recording is played in a commercial environment, even if only one person can hear it, it becomes a public performance and a fee is payable to PPL.

TV, radio and CDs

Your TV licence only covers domestic use of your television equipment. Any use of your television within your business premises constitutes a licensable performance of copyright sound recordings. Radio stations, including news and talk radio, use copyright sound recordings (such as theme tunes and background music during programmes) so any radio broadcasts within your business premises constitute a licensable public performance of copyright sound recordings. When you buy a CD it only gives you the right to use it for private use such as playing at home or in your car. If you wish to use it in a commercial environment, such as background music in a shop, you require a licence from the rights owner which in this case is PPL.

Music systems

If you hire a background music system, the fee you previously paid to your supplier also included the PPL public performance fee. However, this is no longer the case and you will need to secure a licence direct from PPL. If you hire a Jukebox, the pubic performance fee is still included in the fees you pay to your supplier.

Music videos (DVD)

If you are playing music videos you will also legally require a licence from VPL (obtainable via PPL). The VPL licence fees are assessed according to the number and size of the screens upon which music videos are played.

Tariffs

PPL fees are based on tariffs for different activities. Example tariffs are given below (valid to 31st December, 2010).

Tariff PPLPP001: Specially featured entertainment	
This tariff applies whenever sound recordings are played as a main or special attraction, rather than for background music. Eg discos and DJ presentations.	
Fee is calculated according to the average attendance and duration of the event	For example a 5-hour event with up to 75 persons attending: £8.72 (exclusive of VAT)

Tariff PPLPP003: Pop/music quizzes	
This tariff applies when sound recordings are played at premises providing pop/music quizzes or any general quiz involving some musical content.	
Flat rate fee per quiz	£3.15 per quiz (exclusive of VAT)

Tariff PPLPP010: Jukeboxes with background music

This tariff is used for premises when a jukebox with a background music facility has been installed (ie a jukebox with a freeplay facility).

Single rates	£132.27 per annum (exclusive of VAT)
Multiple rates (for machines owned or supplied by multiple operators)	£99.20 (exclusive of VAT)

Tariff PPLPP011: Jukeboxes

This tariff is used for premises when a jukebox without a background music facility has been installed (ie a jukebox without a freeplay facility).

Single rates	£99.24 per annum (exclusive of VAT)
Multiple rates (for machines owned or supplied by multiple operators)	£66.16

Tariff PPLPP210: Background music – public houses/bars/restaurants and cafes

This tariff applies to the public performance of sound recordings as background music.

Size of premises (audible area) in metres squared (m²)	Fee per annum
1–400	£108.21
401–450	£121.74
451–500	£135.27
501–550	£148.80

Where to get a PPL licence

You can telephone PPL on 020 7534 1070 (during normal working hours), for further advice and to apply for a licence. You can also apply for your licence on-line.

 For more information visit the PPL website at www.ppluk.com/

What happens if you do not take out a PPL licence?

If you publicly perform sound recordings without a PPL licence, you are infringing copyright. If you obtain your PPL licence after you have already started to publicly perform sound recordings, you will also need to pay for a licence that retrospectively covers the period since your public performance began. Surcharges of up to 50% may also be applicable for failing to obtain a PPL licence.

FIRE SAFETY LAW

New fire safety law

The Regulatory Reform (Fire Safety) Order 2005 was approved by Parliament in June 2005 with the aim of reducing death, injury and damage caused by fire. The new law will:

◆ Emphasise preventing fires and reducing risk.

◆ Make it your responsibility to ensure the safety of everyone using your premises.

◆ Do away with the need for fire certificates.

The new legislation came into force in October 2006 and applies to England and Wales (Scotland and Ireland will have their own laws), and consolidates most of the existing fire safety legislation.

A summary of some of the main provisions is explained below.

◆ Responsibility for complying with the Fire Safety Order rests with the 'responsible person' – the owner, employer or other person who has control of the premises.

◆ The 'responsible person' is required to carry out a fire risk assessment, which must focus on the safety in case of fire, of all relevant persons.

◆ The risk assessment should identify risks that can be removed or reduced and help you decide the nature and extent of general fire precautions you need to take to protect people against the risk of fire.

◆ If you employ five or more people, you must record the significant findings of the assessment.

◆ Fire certificates will be no longer valid under the new legislation.

Carrying out a fire risk assessment

A fire risk assessment should cover the following 5 steps:

1. Identifying the fire hazards

For fire to occur there must be a source of ignition, fuel and oxygen. If all 3 are present, and in close proximity, then there is an increased fire risk. Your fire risk assessment should list all the potential sources of ignition and fuels present in your premises.

◆ Potential sources of ignition include: naked flames, smokers' materials, matches, pilot flames, heaters and arson.

◆ Potential sources of fuel include: textiles, wood, paper, card, plastics, packaging, rubber, fixtures and fittings, waste materials, petrol, white spirit, paraffin, paints and varnish.

2. Identifying the people at risk

If there is a fire, the greatest danger is the spread of fire, heat and smoke through the premises. Your fire risk assessment should consider:

◆ The likely speed of growth and spread of any fire, and associated heat and smoke. (Some fuels burn faster than others.)

◆ The numbers of persons in the premises, including customers, employees and visitors.

◆ How they will become aware of any fire that occurs (will there be some form of fire detection and alarm system?).

◆ How they will make their escape (can they make their way out quickly, easily and safely?).

3. Evaluating the risks and making changes

Once the hazards and the persons at risk have been identified, you must assess the effect of a particular hazard on the occupants of the premises, taking into account any control measures that are already in place. You then need to decide what other measures are required to reduce the risk to an acceptable level. These measures may include:

◆ Removing possible ignition sources.

◆ Moving the hazard to another area.

◆ Providing an improved fire detection and alarm system.

◆ Training staff to reduce the possibility of fire.

◆ Providing appropriate fire fighting equipment.

4. Recording your findings

If you employ 5 or more employees, you must record the significant findings of your risk assessment and the measures you have taken to reduce risk and improve fire safety.

You can find more information about conducting risk assessments by visiting www.hse.gov.uk/risk/index.htm

5. Reviewing and revising the risk assessment

Fire risk assessment is a continuous process, and should be reviewed on a regular basis. Similarly, any changes to your premises, equipment, staff numbers, work practices, or the materials you use should prompt you to revise your fire risk assessment.

Other fire safety requirements

- All items of portable electrical equipment should be inspected regularly and fitted with the correct fuses.
- All new upholstered furniture for non-domestic use must comply with the requirements of British Standards.
- Fire exits must always be unlocked when your premises are in use or be capable of being opened without the use of a key.
- Fire escape routes must be clearly signed with the 'running man' pictogram.
- Fire escape routes should be adequately lit with artificial lighting and emergency lighting if required.
- Staff should be trained in general fire safety, including the use of fire fighting equipment, and the location of fire exits and assembly points.
- Ensure your fire alarm system is in good working order and is tested on a weekly basis.
- Ensure that an adequate number of suitable fire extinguishers is available, and that they are serviced annually.

Getting more information on fire safety

You can find more information on the new fire regulations by visiting the website of the Department for Communities and Local Government – www.communities.gov.uk/fire/firesafety

A number of guides is available that tell you what you have to do to comply with fire safety law, help you to carry out a fire risk assessment, and identify the general fire precautions you need to have in place. These can be found by visiting www.communities.gov.uk/fire/firesafety/firesafetylaw

HEALTH AND SAFETY LAW

General requirements

Under Health and Safety Law, businesses have a duty to protect their employees and customers. In general, you must:

- Make your premises safe and without risks to health.

◆ Ensure equipment is safe and safe work practices are set and followed.
◆ Ensure articles and substances are moved, stored and used safely.
◆ Give staff information, training and the supervision necessary for their health and safety.

Causes of accidents

Health and Safety Executive reports for 2004/5 show the following accident statistics:

Fatal accidents 2004/5	
Type of accident	**As a percentage of all fatal accidents**
Falling from height	24.1%
Struck by moving vehicle	15.9%
Struck by moving or falling object	20.9%

Non-fatal major injuries	
Type of accident	**As a percentage of all non-fatal major accidents**
Slipping and tripping	35.7%
Handling, lifting, carrying	16.1%
Falling from height	12.4%
Struck by moving or falling object	12.8%

Over-3-day injuries*	
Type of accident	**As a percentage of all over-3-day accidents**
Handling, lifting, carrying	41.6%
Slipping and tripping	22.7%
Struck by moving or falling object	11.7%

*Note:** an over-3-day injury is one which result in the injured person being away from work or unable to do their full range of normal duties for more than 3 days.

Assessing risks

You must undertake a health and safety risk assessment following the 5-step process:

1 Look for the hazards.
2 Decide who might be harmed and how.
3 Evaluate the risks and decide whether the existing precautions are adequate or whether more should be done.
4 Record your findings.
5 Review your findings when necessary.

 Visit the Health and Safety Executive website for comprehensive information on Health and Safety Law: www.hse.gov.uk/index.htm
or telephone their helpline number: 0845 345 00 55.

Other obligations

You must also:

♦ Provide adequate first-aid facilities.
♦ Avoid hazardous manual handling operations; or where they cannot be avoided, reduce the risk of injury.
♦ Ensure safety signs are provided and maintained.
♦ Display the 'Health and Safety Law Poster' if you employ anyone. Alternatively, provide your employees with individual copies of the same information in a leaflet called *Your Health and Safety – a guide for workers*. (The poster and leaflet are available from the Health and Safety Executive, HSE Books.)
♦ Prevent or adequately control exposure to hazardous substances.
♦ Take precautions against danger from flammable or explosive hazards.
♦ Make sure that the workplace satisfies health, safety and welfare requirments, eg noise, ventilation, temperature, lighting, sanitary and washing facilities.

◆ If you have 5 or more employees, you must draw up a health and safety policy statement, and bring it to the attention of your employees.

Your employees also have legal duties. These include:

◆ Taking reasonable care for their own health and safety and that of others.
◆ Cooperating with you on health and safety issues.
◆ Correctly using work items provided by you, including any personal protective equipment, in accordance with training and instruction.
◆ Not interfering with, or misusing, anything provided for their health, safety and welfare.

 You can order a range of useful publications from HSE books via their website www.hsebooks.com or by telephoning: 01787 88 11 65.

COSHH REGULATIONS

Background

Using chemicals or other hazardous substances at work can put people's health at risk, so the law requires employers to control exposure to hazardous substances to prevent ill health or injury. COSHH (Control of Substances Hazardous to Health) regulations 2002 place duties on employers to protect employees and others from such hazards.

Hazardous substances

Hazardous substances include:

◆ Substances used directly in work activities, such as cleaning agents, adhesives and paints.
◆ Substances generated during work activities, such as fumes.
◆ Naturally occurring substances, such as dust.
◆ Biological agents, such as bacteria and other micro-organisms.

Effects of hazardous substances

The effects of hazardous substances include:

◆ Being overcome by toxic fumes.
◆ Skin irritation or dermatitis, as a result of skin contact.
◆ Asthma, as a result of developing an allergy.
◆ Cancer, after long-term exposure to certain chemicals.
◆ Infection, from bacteria and other micro-organisms.

The implications for your business can be considerable, with lost productivity, possible prosecution and civil claims.

Complying with COSHH

To comply with COSHH you must follow an 8-step process:

Step 1	Assess the risks:	Assess the risks to health from hazardous substances used in, or created by your workplace activities.
Step 2	Decide what precautions are needed:	You must not carry out work which could expose your employees to hazardous substances without first considering the risks and the necessary precautions, and what else you must do to comply with COSHH.
Step 3	Prevent or adequately control exposure:	You must prevent your employees being exposed to hazardous substances. Where this is not reasonably practicable, then you must adequately control the exposure.
Step 4	Ensure that control measures are used and maintained:	Ensure that control measures are used and maintained properly and that safety procedures are followed.
Step 5	Monitor the exposure:	Monitor the exposure of employees to hazardous substances, if necessary.

Step 6	Carry out appropriate health surveillance:	Carry out appropriate health surveillance where your assessment has shown this is necessary, or where COSHH sets specific requirements.
Step 7	Prepare plans and procedures to deal with accidents, incidents and emergencies:	Prepare plans and procedures to deal with accidents, incidents and emergencies involving hazardous substances, where necessary.
Step 8	Ensure employees are properly trained, informed and supervised:	You should provide your employees with suitable and sufficient training, information and instruction.

 Download a free guide from HSE – *Working with substances hazardous to health – What you need to know about COSHH* here: www.hse.gov.uk/pubns/indg136/pdf

RIDDOR

Background

RIDDOR stands for the Reporting of Injuries, Diseases and Dangerous Occurrences Regulations 1995, which came into force on 1st April 1996. As an employer, you have duties under RIDDOR, which require you to report some work-related accidents, diseases and dangerous occurrences. The information is used by the Health and Safety Executive (HSE) and local authorities to identify where and how risks arise, and to investigate serious accidents.

What you need to report

- ◆ Death or a major injury.
- ◆ Over-three-day injury.

- Disease.
- Dangerous occurrence.

Death or major injury

These include accidents connected with work, where an employee, or self-employed person working on your premises, is killed or suffers a major injury, or where a member of the public is killed or taken to hospital.

Examples of major injuries include:

- Fractures other than to fingers, thumbs or toes.
- Amputation.
- Dislocation of shoulder, hip, knee or spine.
- Loss of sight (temporary or permanent).
- Injury resulting from an electric shock or burn leading to unconsciousness or requiring resuscitation.
- Acute illness requiring medical treatment, or loss of consciousness arising from absorption of any substance by inhalation, ingestion or through the skin.

Over-3-day injury

If there is an accident or incident at your premises and you, an employee, or a self-employed person working at your premises, suffer an over-3-day injury, you must report this within 10 days.

An over-3-day injury is one which is not major but results in the person being away from work or unable to do their full range of duties for more than three days, (not counting the day of the injury itself).

Reportable disease

Work-related diseases, classed as 'reportable' by a doctor must be reported using a 'disease report form' (F2508A). Examples of reportable diseases include:

- Certain poisonings.

- Some skin diseases such as occupational dermatitis and skin cancer.
- Lung disease including occupational asthma and asbestosis.
- Infections such as leptospirosis, hepatitis, tuberculosis and tetanus.

Reportable dangerous occurrence

If something happens which does not result in a reportable injury, but which clearly could have done, it may be a dangerous occurrence which must be reported immediately.

Examples include:

- Electrical short circuit or overloading causing fire or explosion.
- Explosion or fire causing suspension of normal work for over 24 hours.
- Unintended collapse of: any building or structure under construction, alteration or demolition where over five tonnes of material falls; a wall or floor in a place of work.

Who to report to

You should report the accident, incident or disease to the RIDDOR 'Incident Control Centre'. You can complete reports (F2508/F2508A) on-line at the RIDDOR website: www.hse.gov.uk/riddor or you can telephone them on 0845 300 9923 (8.30am–5.00pm).

Keeping records

You should keep a record of any reportable injury, disease or dangerous occurrence for 3 years after the date on which it happened. You should include:

- The date and method of reporting.
- The date, time and place of the event.
- Personal details of those involved.
- A description of the nature of the event or disease.

All accidents should be recorded in an accident book, which should be kept on the premises.

Further information about RIDDOR

You can download a free guide (pdf) to RIDDOR called *Incident at Work* here: www.hse.gov.uk/pubns/misc769.pdf. A free HSE guide: *RIDDOR explained: Reporting of Injuries, Diseases and Dangerous Occurrences Regulations* is also available via HSE books website: www.hsebooks.co.uk or by telephoning 01787 88 11 65.

DISABILITY DISCRIMINATION ACT 1995

Background

The Disability Discrimination Act (DDA) was passed in 1995 with the aim of protecting disabled people in the following areas:

- employment;
- access to goods, facilities and services;
- the management, buying or renting of land or property;
- education.

The law took effect for employers in December 1996 and other provisions were introduced over a period of time. The following requirements were introduced for 'service providers' (eg businesses and organisations, providing a service to the public):

- From December 1996, it has been unlawful to treat disabled people less favourably than others for a reason related to their disability.
- From October 1999, reasonable adjustments have had to be made for disabled people, such as providing extra help or making changes to the way services are provided.
- From October 2004, reasonable adjustments have had to be made to the physical features of premises to overcome physical barriers to access.
- In April 2005, a new Disability Act was passed which amends or extends the existing provisions of the DDA 1995.

Discrimination

Discrimination under the Act occurs:

◆ By treating a disabled person less favourably than other customers because of their disability

or

◆ By not making reasonable adjustments to the way you deliver your service, which allow disabled persons to use them.

Treating a disabled person 'less favourably' than other customers includes:

◆ Refusing to serve them.
◆ Providing them with a lower standard of service.
◆ Providing them with a service on worse terms.

Discrimination claims

Any disabled person who feels that they have been discriminated against has the right to take civil proceedings against the service provider in the County Court. This is a civil action, not a criminal one, and there is no possibility of a criminal conviction. However, if successful, compensation may be awarded to the applicant and an injunction, preventing the service provider from repeating the discriminatory act, may be imposed.

Defining disability

The Disability Discrimination Act defines a disabled person as someone who has a physical or mental impairment that has a substantial and long-term effect on his or her ability to carry out normal day-to-day activities. Disabilities include:

◆ physical impairments;
◆ sensory impairments;
◆ mental illness;
◆ severe disfigurement;
◆ recurrent and progressive conditions.

According to The Disability Rights Commission, around 1 in 5 people of working age are considered to be 'disabled' and are likely to have rights under the Disability Discrimination Act (DDA).

Making reasonable adjustments

As of October 2004, service providers must have made reasonable adjustments to any physical features of the premises, in order to overcome any physical barriers to access by disabled people. Failure to do so, without justification, can leave the service provider open to claims of discrimination from disabled people.

In deciding what changes are reasonable the following factors will be taken into account:

◆ The size and resources of the service provider.
◆ The costs of making the adjustments.
◆ The extent and impact of any disruption caused by the adjustment.

Examples of reasonable physical adjustments may include:

◆ Ensuring premises are well lit, where appropriate.
◆ Providing well-defined signs.
◆ Installing a ramp and a handrail at the entrance where there are steps.
◆ Reserving disabled car parking spaces near the entrance to your premises.
◆ Clearly marking the edges of steps in a contrasting colour.
◆ Providing handrails in at least one toilet cubical, if no disabled WC is available.
◆ Adjusting the width of at least one entrance to allow access by wheelchair-bound persons.
◆ Ensuring that the approach to your pub is free of trip hazards.
◆ Ensuring the layout of tables and chairs allows easy access for disabled people.

Other reasonable changes

◆ Providing large-print menus and price lists.
◆ Offering to read menus to people with visual impairment.
◆ Installing an induction loop for people with hearing impairment.
◆ Providing table service.

◆ Providing a pencil and paper for people with verbal and hearing impairment.

 As a new licensee, you may be inheriting a pub where the previous occupant has not made reasonable changes to the premises in line with DDA requirements. These will become your responsibility when you take on the pub.

Further information about DDA

More information about DDA and a downloadable (pdf) guide *Making Access to Goods and Services Easier for Disabled Customers – A Practical Guide for Small Businesses and Other Small Service Providers* can be found under the Disabled People/Access to Everyday Services section of the www.direct.gov.uk website.

SMOKING LEGISLATION

Background

In April 2004, the Irish Government implemented a ban forbidding smoking in places of work in Ireland under the Public Health (Tobacco) Act 2002, which included pubs and bars. Scotland introduced a ban forbidding smoking in public places in March 2006 under the Smoking, Health and Social Care (Scotland) Act 2005, and the UK Parliament implemented a similar ban in summer 2007. Northern Ireland and Wales introduced comparable legislation in 2007.

Obtaining more information

You can obtain more information on smoking legislation by visiting the following websites: www.smokefreeengland.co.uk (England), www.clearingtheairscotland.com (Scotland), www.smokingbanwales.co.uk (Wales), www.spacetobreathe.org.uk (Northern Ireland), www.otc.ie (Ireland).

The aim of the legislation is to protect workers and the general public from the harmful effects of passive smoking.

Offences under the Acts

Offences under the Acts include:

◆ Smoking in no-smoking premises.
◆ Permitting others to smoke in no-smoking premises.
◆ Failing to display no-smoking signs.

Fixed penalty fines and other penalties can be applied for anyone breaking the law.

Outside smoking areas

Structures located outside the premise may be designated as smoking areas as long as not more than 50% of the structure's perimeter is covered by a wall or window. (New structures may require you to obtain planning permission before you can erect them.)

Obtaining more information

You can obtain more information on UK smoking legislation by visiting the website of the Office of Public Sector Information: www.opsi.gov.uk/

DOOR SECURITY LEGISLATION

Background

All door supervisors in England and Wales (and Scotland from the end of 2007) must hold an SIA (Security Industry Authority) licence. Working without a licence is a criminal offence, punishable on conviction by a fine of up to £5,000 or 6 months imprisonment or both.

Two types of licence

There are two types of licence:

◆ **Front-line licence**: – for door supervisors (including publicans who supervise doors).
◆ **Non front-line licence**: for some publicans, managers, supervisors and directors or partners of security companies.

Important note: If you act as a door supervisor yourself, you must hold a 'front-line' licence. If you employ door supervisors and pay their wages, you must hold a 'non front-line' licence.

If you use contracted-in door supervisors provided by an agency, and do not work as a door supervisor yourself, you do not need a licence.

SIA qualifications

To get the SIA qualification, door supervisors need to attend a 2-part training course and take and pass two exams. The course is usually delivered over 4 days, during weekends and/or evenings. The total training time is 30 hours, and includes two hours of exams.

Training is delivered in two parts as follows:

◆ **Part 1**: Role and responsibilities of a door supervisor (14 hours).
◆ **Part 2**: Communication skills and conflict management (14 hours).

Where someone has already completed a training course and holds a qualification in door supervision, they may be exempt from all or part of the training required for an SIA licence.

Obtaining more information

You can obtain more information via the Security Industry Authority (SIA) website at: www.the-sia.org.uk

APPENDICES

APPENDIX (I) – USEFUL WEBSITES

Alcohol concern
www.alcoholconcern.org.uk
www.drinkaware.co.uk

Alcohol studies
www.ias.org.uk

Amusement machines
www.gamblingcommission.gov.uk
www.rigt.org.uk
www.bacta.org.uk

Accountants
www.icaew.co.uk   (England and Wales)
www.icas.org.uk   (Scotland)
www.icai.ie   (Ireland)
www.accaglobal.com   (England, Wales, Scotland and Ireland)
www.aat.co.uk.

Banks
www.bba.org.uk
www.chipandpin.co.uk

Beer
www.beer-pages.com/notes.php
www.beeracademy.co.uk
www.cask-marque.co.uk
www.camra.org.uk
www.cellardoctor.co.uk
www.craftbeer.com/pages/style-finder
www.cyclopsbeer.co.uk

Book-keepers
www.bookkeepers.org.uk

Business advice
www.businesslink.gov.uk
www.fsb.org.uk/

Business rates
www.businesslink.gov.uk
www.voa.gov.uk

Coffee
www.britishcoffeeassociation.org
www.scae.com

Customer service
www.instituteofcustomerservice.com

Catering supplies
www.caterer-directory.com

Chartered surveyors
www.rics.org

COSHH regulations
www.coshh-essentials.org.uk

Companies House
www.companieshouse.gov.uk

Criminal records check
www.disclosurescotland.co.uk
www.crb.homeoffice.gov.uk

Daltons
www.daltonsbusiness.com

Disability
www.direct.gov.uk/en/DisabledPeople/index.htm

Debt
www.nationaldebtline.co.uk

Door security
www.sia.homeoffice.gov.uk

Environmental health
www.cieh.org

Finance
www.moneymadeclear.fsa.gov.uk
www.moneysupermarket.com

Fire safety information
www.hse.gov.uk/risk/index.htm
www.communities.gov.uk/fire/firesafety

Food safety
www.food.gov.uk/foodindustry/regulation/hydleg/
www.scoresonthedoors.org.uk
www.allergyuk.org

Food legislation
www.food.gov.uk
www.scoresonthedoors.org.uk

Food and drink information
www.foodanddrinkeurope.com
www.fdf.org.uk
www.foodintoleranceawareness.org

Gambling
www.gamblingcommission.gov.uk/
www.gamcare.org.uk

Gin and vodka
www.ginvodka.org

Health and safety
www.hse.gov.uk

Insurance
www.abi.org.uk
www.biba.org.uk
www.fsa.gov.uk/pages/register/

Legislation
www.businesslink.gov.uk
www.opsi.gov.uk

Licensing law
www.culture.gov.uk

Licensed trade news
www.morningadvertiser.co.uk
www.thepublican.com
www.thedrinksbusiness.com

Licensed trade organisations
www.bii.org/
www.flva.co.uk
www.beerandpub.com

Licensed trade qualifications
www.bii.org/
www.goalonline.co.uk

Marketing
www.cim.co.uk
www.bbc.co.uk/onthisday/
www.twitter.com
www.facebook.com
www.blogger.com
www.youtube.com

Market research companies
www.mintel.com
www.acnielsen.com

Neighbourhood research
http://neighbourhood.statistics.gov.uk/dissemination/
www.upmystreet.com
www.multimap.com

On-line ordering
www.barbox.com

Pensions
www.thepensionservice.gov.uk/employer/home.asp

Performing right society
www.prsformusic.com

Phonographic performance limited
www.ppluk.com

Responsible retailing
www.responsibledrinksretailing.co.uk
www.portman-group.org.uk
www.drinkaware.co.uk

RIDDOR
www.riddor.gov.uk

Scotch whisky
www.scotch-whisky.org.uk/

Smoking
www.ash.org.uk
www.clearingtheairscotland.com
www.spacetobreathe.org.uk
www.otc.ie

Soft drinks
www.britishsoftdrinks.com

Solicitors
www.lawsociety.org.uk   (Law Society, England and Wales)
www.lawscot.org.uk   (Law Society for Scotland)
www.lawsoc-ni.org   (Law Society of Northern Ireland)

Staff
www.bis.gov/uk/
www.acas.co.uk
www.ukba.homeoffice.gov.uk
www.employmenttribunals.gov.uk
www.acas.org.uk
www.cipd.co.uk

Stamp duty
www.hmrc.gov.uk/so/new-sdlt-calculators.htm

Stocktakers

www.iltsa.co.uk

Trading standards

www.tradingstandards.gov.uk

Valuers of licensed property

www.avlp.com.

VAT & tax

www.hmrc.gov.uk

www.tax.org.uk

www.businesslink.gov.uk

Waste

www.envirowise.gov.uk

Website marketing

https://adwords.google.com

http://advertising.yahoo.com/smallbusiness

Wine

www.wset.co.uk/

www.wine-regions-of-the-world.com/

www.thewinedoctor.com

APPENDIX (II) – USEFUL CALCULATIONS

Gross profit margin (GP £)

Gross profit margin is calculated as follows:

Sales revenue *less* the cost of sales = gross profit margin.

Calculating gross profit margin on specific products:

Example 1:

Sales revenue (ex VAT)	£2.00
Less: Cost of sales (ex VAT)	£1.10
Equals: **Gross profit margin**	**£0.90**

Calculating gross profit margin on turnover:

Example 2:

Turnover (ex VAT)	£200,000
Less: Cost of sales (ex VAT)	£110,000
Equals: **Gross profit margin**	**£90,000**

Gross profit percentage (GP %)

Gross profit % is calculated as follows:

GP£ *divided by* Sales revenue *multiplied by* 100 = GP%

Calculating gross profit % on specific products:

Example 3 (using the figures from example 1):

£0.90 (GP£) *divided by* £2.00 (Sales revenue) *multiplied by* 100 = **45%**

Shown as fully worked example:

Sales revenue (ex VAT)	£2.00	(100%)
Less: Cost of sales (ex VAT)	£1.10	(55%)
Equals: **Gross Profit**	**£0.90**	**(45%)**

Calculating gross profit % on turnover:

Example 4 (using the figures from example 2):

£90,000 (GP£) *divided by* £200,000 (Turnover) *multiplied by* 100, = **45%**

Shown as fully worked example:

Turnover (ex VAT)	£200,000	(100%)
Less: Cost of sales (ex VAT)	£110,000	(55%)
Equals: **Gross Profit**	**£90,000**	**(45%)**

Calculating weekly break-even sales (£)

To calculate weekly sales required to break even:

Weekly running costs *divided by* GP(%) *multiplied by* 100 = weekly break-even sales (ex VAT). Then *multiply by* 1.175 (to add VAT) to give weekly sales including VAT required to break even.

Example:

£1,000 (weekly running costs) *divided by* 45 (GP%) *multiplied by* 100 = £2,222 (weekly sales (excluding VAT) required to break even)

Then, *multiply* £2,222 *by* 1.175

= **£2,611** (weekly sales [including VAT] required to break even)

. . . *continued*

APPENDIX (III) – EXAMPLE PROFIT AND LOSS FORECAST

		£	%
	SALES		
	Drinks sales:		
	Food sales:		
	Accommodation:		
	Machine income:		
	Other income:		
	Total sales:		
less:	**COST OF GOODS SOLD**		
	Drinks purchases:		
	Food purchases:		
	Other:		
	Total purchases:		
equals:	**GROSS PROFIT**		
	Drinks:		
	Food:		
	Accommodation:		
	Machine takings:		
	Other:		
	Total Gross profit:		
less:	**OPERATING COSTS**		
	Staff costs – bar (inc NIC):		
	Staff costs – food (inc NIC):		
	Staff costs – accommodation (inc NIC):		
	Staff costs – other (inc NIC):		
	Rent:		
	Business rates:		
	Heat & light:		
	Repairs & decoration:		
	Marketing:		
	Accountant & stocktaker:		
	Insurance:		
	Licences & fees.		

	£	%
Motor expenses:		
Water rates:		
Training costs:		
Bank charges:		
Telephone:		
Equipment rental:		
Glassware & crockery:		
Cleaning materials:		
Waste & refuse:		
Uniforms:		
Entertainment:		
Sky TV:		
Loan interest:		
Depreciation:		
Other miscellaneous costs:		
Total running costs:		
equals: **NET PROFIT**		

Note: All figures must be shown exclusive of VAT, where applicable.

APPENDIX (IV) – EXAMPLE CASH FLOW FORECAST

	month 1 £	month 2 £	month 3 £	month 4 £	month 5 £	month 6 £	month 7 £	month 8 £	month 9 £	month 10 £	month 11 £	month 12 £	TOTALS £
INCOME													
Capital introduced:													
Drinks sales:													
Food sales:													
Accommodation:													
Machine income:													
Other income:													
Total income:	£	£	£	£	£	£	£	£	£	£	£	£	£
less: **EXPENDITURE**	£	£	£	£	£	£	£	£	£	£	£	£	£
Loan payments:													
VAT payments:													
Tax and National Insurance (NI):													
Deposit payment:													
F & F purchased:													
Other equipment purchased:													
Drinks purchased:													
Food purchased:													
Staff wages:													
Rent:													
Business rates:													
Heat & Light:													
Repairs & decoration:													
Marketing:													
Accountant & stocktaker:													
Insurance:													
Licences & fees.													
Motor expenses:													
Water rates:													
Training costs:													
Bank charges:													
Telephone:													
Equipment rental:													
Glassware & crockery:													
Cleaning materials:													
Waste & refuse:													
Uniforms:													
Entertainment:													
Sky TV:													
Other miscellaneous costs:													
Personal drawings:													
Total expenditure:													
equals: **INCOME LESS EXPENDITURE**													
CASH AT START OF MONTH													
CASH AT END OF MONTH													

Note: All figures must be shown inclusive of VAT, where applicable.

APPENDIX (V) – UNITS OF ALCOHOL

Government recommended limits

The alcohol content of drinks is measured in units. One UK unit contains 8 grams of pure alcohol. The UK Government advises that men drink no more than 3–4 units a day and women no more than 2–3. Consistently drinking 4 or more units for men, and 3 or more for women, carries progressive health risks. In some situations like pregnancy, they advise drinking less or not drinking at all.

Beer, lager and cider

1 pint at 4%	= 2.3 units
1 pint at 5%	= 2.8 units
330ml bottle at 4% or 5% ABV	= 1.5 units
440ml can at 4% or 5% ABV	= 2 units
440ml can at 8% or 9% ABV	= 3.5–4 units
500ml can at 8% or 9% ABV	= 4–4.5 units

Low alcohol beer and lager

440ml can at 1.2% ABV = 0.5 units

Wine

125ml glass of wine at 12% ABV	= 1.5 units
175ml glass of wine at 12% ABV	= 2.1 units
250ml glass of wine at 12% ABV	= 3 units

Spirits

25ml measure of spirit at 40% ABV	= 1 unit
35ml measure of spirit at 40% ABV	= 1.4 units

Sherry, port, Madeira and vermouth

50ml measure at 20% ABV	= 1 unit

'Alcopop'/Ready to drink (RTD)

275ml at 5% ABV	= 1.4 units

More information

Visit the 'Drinkaware' website on www.drinkaware.co.uk

APPENDIX (VI) – IDEAL PUB CHECKLIST

Ideal Pub Checklist

Capital available: Geographical area:
£

Location:	Clientele	Facilities	Catering	Other requirements
town centre	locals	catering kitchen	no food	no. of bedrooms -
suburban	young persons	car park	snacks	garage
estate	executives	beer garden	bar meals	**Local facilities**
neighbourhood	office staff	function room	restaurant	school
rural	families	games room	buffets	hospital
village	couples	live music	outside catering	transport links
main road	manual workers	big-screen sports		
	students	disco		
	gay community			
	shoppers			
	OAPs			

Other things that you require: **Other things that are important to you:**

APPENDIX (VII) – MAJOR UK PUB OPERATORS
(Tenanted and leased)

Admiral Taverns (Pub operator)	www.admiraltaverns.com
Adnams (Regional brewer)	www.adnams.co.uk
Arkells (Regional brewer)	www.arkells.com
Batemans (Regional brewer)	www.bateman.co.uk
Brains (Regional brewer)	www.sabrain.com
Caledonian (Regional brewer)	www.caldedonian-brewery.co.uk
Brakspear (Pub operator)	www.brakspear.co.uk
Charles Wells (Regional brewer)	www.charleswells.co.uk
Elgoods (Regional brewer)	www.elgoods-brewery.co.uk
County Estate (Pub operator)	www.countyestatepubs.co.uk
Enterprise Inns (National pub operator)	www.enterpriseinns.com
Everards (Regional brewer)	www.everards.co.uk
Felinfoel (Regional brewer)	www.felinfoel-brewery.co.uk
Fullers (Regional brewer)	www.fullers.co.uk
Greene King (National brewer)	www.greeneking.co.uk
Hall & Woodhouse (Regional brewer)	www.hall-woodhouse.co.uk
Harveys (Regional brewer)	www.harveys.org.uk
Heavitree (Pub operator)	www.heavitreebrewery.co.uk
Hook Norton (Regional brewer)	www.hook-norton-brewery.co.uk
Hydes (Regional brewer)	www.hydesbrewery.co.uk
JW Lees (Regional brewer)	www.jwlees.co.uk
Marstons Pub Company (Pub operator and brewer)	www.marstonspubcompany.co.uk
McMullens (Regional brewer)	www.mcmullens.co.uk
Moorhouses (Regional brewer)	www.moorhouses.co.uk
Palmers (Regional brewer)	www.palmersbrewery.com
Pubfolio (Pub owner)	www.pubfolio.co.uk
Punch (National pub operator)	www.punchpubs.co.uk
Robinsons (Regional brewer)	www.frederic-robinson.com
St Austell (Regional brewer)	www.staustellbrewery.co.uk
S & N Pub Enterprises (Pub operator)	www.s-npubcompany.co.uk
Shepherd Neame (Regional brewer)	www.shepherd-neame.co.uk
Thwaites (Regional brewer)	www.danielthwaites.com
Timothy Taylor (Regional brewer)	www.timothytaylor.co.uk
Trust Inns (Pub operator)	www.trustinns.co.uk
Wadworth (Regional brewer)	www.wadworth.co.uk

Wellington (Pub operator)   www.wellingtonpubcompany.co.uk
Youngs (Regional brewer)   www.youngs.co.uk

APPENDIX (VIII) – MAJOR UK AGENTS
(Freehold and lease assignments)

Brownill Bateman	www.bvandp.co.uk
Bettesworths	www.bettesworths.co.uk
Christie & Co	www.christie.com
Colliers Robert Barry	www.colliersrobertbarry.co.uk
Davey & Co	www.daveyco.com
Fleurets	www.fleurets.com
GA Select	www.ga-select.com
Guy Simmonds	www.guysimmonds.co.uk
Gore & Co	www.pubsales.co.uk
GVA Grimley	www.gvagrimley.co.uk
Hymberstones	www.humberstones.co.uk
Redwoods Dowling Kerr	www.redwoodsdk.com
RTA	www.rtaonline.co.uk
Sidney Phillips	www.sidneyphillips.co.uk
The Bar Agency	www.thebaragency.com

Index